IN THE EYE OF THE TYPHOON

IN THE EYE
OF THE
TYPHOON

RUTH EARNSHAW LO

KATHARINE S. KINDERMAN

INTRODUCTION BY JOHN K. FAIRBANK

 Harcourt Brace Jovanovich   New York and London

Library of Congress Cataloging in Publication Data

Lo, Ruth Earnshaw.
  In the eye of the typhoon.
  1. China—Politics and government—1949–1976.
2. Lo, Ruth Earnshaw. 3. Teachers—China—Biography.
4. Teachers—United States—Biography.
I. Kinderman, Katharine S., joint author. II. Title.
DS777.75.L6   951.05   80–7937
ISBN 0–15–144374–2

Printed in the United States of America

First edition

B C D E

CONTENTS

by John K. Fairbank

YOU CAN EASILY identify with Ruth Lo. She is a very sane and humane person to take you through the Chinese Cultural Revolution. That is what she does in this book. She was a uniquely privileged American teacher in China, privileged to have her house repeatedly ransacked and her Chinese husband "struggled with" by the Red Guards. She lived through it, and her experience told in this book is the closest you can get to having been there yourself.

A revolution is not like any other human experience. It is really an act of nature, like an earthquake, a typhoon, a flood, except that it engulfs a whole society and you cannot escape it no matter what you do.

You see your fellow human beings so overcome by fear and at the same time by idealistic fanaticism that they commit monstrous acts. One's relations with other people become suddenly irrational, mystifying, sometimes funny, sometimes horribly terrifying. A society in revolution has somehow gone off the rails. The norms of behavior have evaporated. People live by their feelings and perform the most heroic deeds as well as dastardly crimes. Friendships with others that used to cushion life's problems turn into a jungle of ambiguities and uncertainties.

Never before have so many people gone through this kind of experience. The French Revolution was a small show in comparison. The American Revolution, by this Chinese standard, was not a revolution at all.

For a time in China there was a dissolution of both state and society. In the context of Chinese history the Cultural Revolution (or "Great Proletarian Cultural Revolution" or more literally a "Great Revolution for a Propertyless Class Culture") came as a climax to more than a century of increasing disorder and rapid change.

Consider that China was the oldest continuous state and society in the world, as well as the biggest and least malleable from outside. Remember that the Chinese civilization had been the center of East Asian culture. For a time during our Middle Ages it was the highest point in human experience.

But now think back to your grandfather's day when this great land and people were humiliated by foreigners who had invaded their country, not only because the Chinese were too weak to keep them out, but also because they seemed to be incapable of changing their society to bring it into modern times. Early in this century China was a byword for warlord corruption and disorder, a laughingstock for its ineffectual efforts at modernization and democracy.

Being justly proud of their heritage, the Chinese of the early twentieth century began to pull themselves together in a series of revolutionary efforts to remake their world in order to survive among the nations.

Dr. Sun Yat-sen and his follower Generalissimo Chiang Kai-shek came out of this effort, intent on restoring Chinese sovereignty and getting rid of imperialist privileges in their country. But under Chiang the Nanking Government of the 1930s was overwhelmed by Japan's military aggression. We Americans gave support to Free China during World War II. We were largely unaware that a further and more comprehensive revolution was gaining strength under the Chinese Communist Party.

When Mao Zedong, as its leader, came to power in 1949, the Chinese revolution finally turned a corner. It entered a phase of both destroying the old and building up the new. The People's Republic began to emerge as a new power in the world at the same time that it was wracked by wild gyrations of internal politics.

We can see now that from 1949 two revolutions were under way in China. One was trying to use modern technology to industrialize and apply science to all aspects of society—a great program for development.

The other revolution was trying to bring the peasant four-fifths of the Chinese people into national political life as patriotic citizens. To do this it had to knock down the old ruling class system by which the most literate 10 percent of the Chinese people had for centuries monopolized learning, official power, and surplus wealth.

This social revolution was so hard to bring off because the old ruling class was so skillfully entrenched. For example, they had invented the Chinese examination system, based on classical studies, at a time when Europe still had neither paper nor printed books. They fixed it so that anyone of talent, if he could study hard and if he was smart enough, could join the ruling class. This meritocracy coopted the most able people, who proceeded to maintain the ruling class system.

In the old society teachers were venerated by students, women were submissive to their husbands, and age was deferred to by youth. Breaking down such a system took a long time because one had to change one's basic values and assumptions accepted in childhood. The times called for a leader of violent willpower, a man so determined to smash the bureaucratic establishment that he would stop at nothing. He had to side with the common peasant, live his hard, coarse life, and hate the bureaucratic establishment.

Mao Zedong did all this, but then he couldn't stop.

In the 1950s he got the farm villages into collective agriculture, spread literacy, organized the masses, motivated the whole Chinese people with ideals of mass equality and fear of the party inquisitors.

In the Great Leap Forward, in 1958, Mao persuaded his party colleagues to drop the Soviet model of industrialization and try to remake China by using her plentiful muscle power. A lot was accomplished, but the Great Leap ended in economic disorganization and scarcity. Mao lost face and was practically put on the shelf while his party comrades like Deng Hsiao-ping got the economy back on the rails.

Mao's excessive idealism had brought disaster. In the early 1960s his social revolution had to take a back seat to economic development.

The Cultural Revolution beginning in 1966 was Mao's comeback. He organized it very cleverly. First he started a campaign against unnamed "persons in authority who are taking the capitalist road." Since everyone was against capitalism, like original sin, the Party leaders had to go along. Soon they found out, too late, that they were themselves the "capitalist roaders." Mao had neutralized the army. He now attacked the Party (an unthinkable idea when you are brought up to believe the Party is the one great all-powerful, immortal hope for the future). He did this by recruiting the teen-age students to wear red armbands and be Red Guards, Mao's little helpers in saving China from the evils of bureaucratism and a revival of the old ruling class elitism of the few over the many.

The result was civil war of the cruelest sort—friend turning against friend, youth against age, students against teachers, and each individual against the old evils still lodged within himself. It was an unending revival meeting, full of tension, often a nightmare. Suspicion became pandemic. No one was safe. It seemed that all the sophisticated Chinese skill in the art of friendship could be used equally well for psychological torture.

Yet it all happened in broad daylight in one's hometown among colleagues, friends, and neighbors.

Ruth Lo tells us what it was like. She has been ably assisted by Katharine Kinderman, who is herself a skilled television reporter and producer. They did this book together.

February 1980

WHEN I RETURNED to America in the spring of 1978, many old friends whom I had not seen for forty years welcomed me home. Among them was Marian Cannon Schlesinger, my fellow student at Columbia in 1937 and colleague in the production of a little educational movie called *China's Gifts to the West.* It was a delight to hear from her again and to learn that, not only had she continued her interest in China, but that she had a daughter, Katharine, who was about to visit that country. Presently Katharine came to see her mother's old friend and listen to tales of life in the People's Republic of China. It was her idea to make tape recordings of my reminiscences and responses to her questions.

At first I vigorously rejected the idea of writing a book about my experiences. I was too exhausted. There were too many books about China already. I might inadvertently harm friends or family left behind—this was in early 1978, when the lingering influence of the "Gang of Four" continued to chill the air. But my health improved miraculously. I was amazed at the amount of interest friends in America felt for events in China. And the situation there changed rapidly and for the better. Step by step, Katharine led me down the garden path, until we found ourselves committed to the book at hand.

I wish here to acknowledge first of all a great debt of gratitude to the American friends who quite literally kept me alive physically by sending us food, during the years of social turmoil, when suitable nourishment for an invalid was hard to find, and whose letters and concern cheered us during some dark times.

As partners in the production of this book, Katharine and I want to thank the Colorado China Council for the grant that made possible the original tape recordings; Alice Renouf and Sherrie Wolff for extraordinary labors in transcribing the tape material; and Michael Saltz of *The MacNeil/Lehrer Report* for arranging an interview on national TV, which aroused further interest in this book.

Thanks are also due to both our families for their collaboration and patience and support in this effort, to Lo Mingteh for his sketch map of Zhong Da, to Lo Tientung, for painstaking checking of Chinese spellings, and to both for contributions of special knowledge and insight. A special word of gratitude to John K. Fairbank for encouragement and for his contribution of the Introduction.

Finally, my gratitude and love to the Chinese people, whose life I shared for so many unforgettable years.

REL/KSK

Boulder, Colorado
February 1980

IN THE EYE OF THE TYPHOON

I STOOD BY the north window of my study, watching for the first signs of the approach of a threatened typhoon. Storm warnings had been coming over the University public-address system since dawn. Canton was often sideswiped by tropical cyclones, but this time the typhoon was expected to come ashore directly over the city. The air was tense, still, electrical. The chickens scuttled about nervously under the banana trees, and the cat prowled uneasily under the chairs.

Across the abandoned grass-grown tennis courts I saw the tops of the tallest eucalyptus trees begin to sway. A gust of wind like incoming surf swept over the grass, eliminating the chickens. Then, with a roar, a wall of air hit the house. The tumult was so great that I didn't hear the crash as a tall evergreen came down, blocking the window. I retreated hastily to the other side of the house. There the bamboos that sheltered the garden were bending nearly to the ground, from east to west. The rush of wind was deafening. Suddenly the sound rose in pitch to a high, almost inaudible whistle. The trees slowly straightened themselves and all motion ceased for what seemed an immeasurable time. Then the whistling sound sank again to the all-drowning roar, and the trees bowed to the command of the wind, bending this time from west to east, as the torrent of air reversed its direction. Drenching rain blinded as the wind deafened, and the necessity of mopping up the wind-driven water coming in under the doors occupied all my attention for a while.

Now it was much quieter outside, so much quieter that I became aware of human voices above the sounds of rain and thrashing branches. I peered out. The lawn was littered with leaves and twigs and limbs of trees, and seven of our largest—cassia, pine, eucalyptus—were lying prone, some pointed east, some west. The banana plants were a mass of tattered leaf ribbon, and sheets of water flowed over the grass down the hill. In the midst of this chaos all the chil-

dren of the neighborhood were dashing madly about, shrieking with
excitement as they salvaged the precious firewood that the fallen
trees provided. Two women were arguing fiercely over the possession
of a choice branch; one practical man was sawing away at a stump.

I cautiously opened a window, a door, admitting the fresh damp
air, scented with the bruised leaves of the cassia trees. So this, I
thought, is what it is like to be in the eye of a typhoon: first,
unbearable tension, then a brain-paralyzing rush of power in one
direction, then near silence and unearthly terror, a rush in the
opposite direction, then returning calm, and the survivors scram-
bling to salvage what they could out of the wreckage. I felt shaken,
but I had survived.

This book is the story of some of the things that happened to a
Chinese-American family, caught in the upheaval of the Chinese
Cultural Revolution, that social typhoon that shook all Eastern Asia
from 1966 onward for more than a decade.

The scene of the action is Zhongshan University (familiarly referred to as Zhong Da), a national-level university located in the
suburbs of Canton in South China.

The people are Dr. Lo Chuanfang (I call him John); his wife, Xia
Luteh (that is, me, Ruth Earnshaw); our daughter, Tientung; our
son, Mingteh; and a few of the very many friends, neighbors, and
colleagues among whom we lived.

Before plunging into the story of those years, I had better explain
who we were and how it was that we found ourselves in Canton
during that chaotic period.

Dr. Lo was born in 1904, the third son of a mathematics teacher
in a Christian secondary school in Wuchang in Central China. Like
all his brothers and sisters, he was educated in Christian schools and
colleges, and eventually he went abroad to study theology in the
United States. Although he had two theology degrees behind him
and the prospect of a challenging career in the church, in 1933 he
decided to take up the study of psychology and began to work for
his Ph.D. in that field at the University of Chicago.

At that time I was living at the International House at the University, working on the *University of Chicago Magazine* and studying
Chinese on my own. I wanted to learn more about the English

language by teaching it in a foreign country, and I had selected China more or less at random. I was not a missionary. I just wanted to teach English in a foreign country. John was offering a course in Chinese. Inevitably, I became his student and, like all his students, never found another teacher to equal him.

When John completed his work and took his degree in 1935, he returned to Wuchang to teach psychology and philosophy at Huazhong University. I remained in America, determined that I would not leap without looking first. In 1936 the opportunity came for me to go to China in the course of my work, and I met John again, met his family, visited at their home in Wuchang, and, happily, we all approved of each other. Father and Mother Lo were no strangers to Western ways, and I did not disconcert them in the least. For my part, I found them much like my own parents in America; their education, their work as teachers, their general views of life were all familiar. They even belonged to the same church I had grown up in. I didn't realize, then, that they were far from being a typical Chinese family, nor that John was by no means typical of the Chinese intellectual of his day. In any event, we all met on common ground, and after one more year in America I went back to China in 1937, and John and I were married in Shanghai on the eve of the Japanese attack.

My ambition to teach English in China was now realized. John and I both served on the faculty of Huazhong from 1937 until that fine university was first amalgamated with a local Chinese college, and then downgraded into a teacher training institute. Teachers and students of the Foreign Languages Department were sent to Zhong Da, in Canton, in 1953. During the war years we were refugees in the far west of China in Yunnan Province, on the Burma Road, and shared the hardships and challenge of keeping higher education alive in spite of bombs, illness, poverty, and exile. It was during these years that we began to understand that while China needed education, its people first needed food and a place to live. By 1948 we were back again in Wuchang, where Huazhong, returned to its home quarters, was getting on its feet.

In 1949 Wuchang was "liberated" by the Communist armies.

After much deliberation, John and I decided to stay, with our two children. Perhaps it was just as well that we could not foresee all the educational experiences that the next thirty years would bring.

Sometimes people in America ask me why John and I remained in China in 1949, when we could easily have gone back to America, where we both had family and friends. We were not Communists, not even fellow travelers looking to revolution to save China, although our experience had convinced us that economic justice was one of China's greatest needs. We were not evangelical Christians looking for some church to save China, although we were both religious in our own way. We were by temperament and conviction just the kind of persons to be attracted by the slogan of the new government—the "united front."

According to the announced policies of the People's Government, all Chinese who could unite on the basis of patriotism were to be welcome in the new order. All foreign residents who were willing to obey the laws and serve the people with their work were welcome to stay on. China desperately needed the services of her intellectuals. The goals of national unity, economic reconstruction, social justice, and educational opportunity, set forth by the Party, were such as most intellectuals could approve. The whole educational system was being reorganized, renovated, and expanded. We were, by training, experience, and conviction, educators. As we and our colleagues started life under the new regime, the future looked bright.

The first national campaign in which our own students were enlisted was the wholly commendable one of mass inoculation. Who could fail to support that? Then students were more and more involved in study classes that trained them to take part in the Land Reform (1950–51). Presently the whole faculty and student body were sent to the countryside to serve as cadres for organizing the peasants to take over the landlords' fields and redistribute them. For the first time I found myself alone in our campus home with our children, as John and all our colleagues and students disappeared into rural Hubei for an indefinite tour of duty. The few left behind on the campus were to carry on the campaign against bureaucratic corruption, embezzlement, and waste—called *San Fan Wu Fan* for short in Chinese. When this movement led to the suicide of several neighbors, I began to wonder. Following these campaigns, after the Land Reform was completed and the university people returned to the campus, came the Thought Reform (1951), in which students

and progressive teachers, led by Party workers and activists, criticized the faculty members and "helped" them reform their ideology.
By the time this had run its course through the ranks of the intelligentsia, the pattern had become plain and the future no longer
looked quite so bright.

Teachers and students were now all organized into "small groups"
of fellow workers or classmates. Political study was conducted in the
small group, all new directives and policies were implemented
through it, daily work was discussed and prepared at its meetings.
One's relationship with fellow members of the small group became
the most important thing in life. For one of the duties of the
members was to observe—and report on—ideological deviation
among the other members.

Step by step, the *hukou* system was developed. Every person's
officially designated place of residence had to be registered in a
paperbound book called a *hukou.* No one could spend a night elsewhere. Police checked homes at midnight to count the sleepers. This
soon got the message across effectively.

Between the small group and *hukou,* everyone was firmly pinned
in place and under control.

From 1950 onward, life became a series of political movements
or campaigns in which everyone had to take part, either actively, if
it involved one's work, or by spending hours studying the directives
and documents. Imperceptibly, private life and leisure shrank. Life
was work. To us, this was no great alteration in life-style. We had
always gone all-out for our work, and it was only as time brought
perspective that we realized the qualitative difference.

All these changes could not be brought about on a national scale
without some pressure, and by 1956 it was evident that a lot of steam
had been generated that had to be released. The campaign for that
year had the poetic title "Let a Hundred Flowers Bloom and a
Hundred Schools of Thought Contend," and was commonly referred to as the "Hundred Flowers." The Communist Party leadership invited the intelligentsia especially to come forward and criticize shortcomings in the work of its cadres. The response was an
astonishing outcry, so great in volume that it clearly had to be
brought under control. It was checked in 1957–58 by the Anti-
Rightist Campaign, in which thousands of too outspoken intellectu-

als were criticized in mass meetings and designated as Rightists (that is, guilty of actions or words too conservative in tone, hence detrimental to the revolutionary line of the Party). They were "hatted," not always literally, as the landlords had been in the Land Reform, but figuratively, and were punished in various ways according to the seriousness of the offense. They were not shamed, like the landlords, by being forced to wear pointed paper dunce caps but some were demoted in rank and their salaries were cut; some were reassigned to lower-grade work or sent to unpleasant places; some were sent to labor camps to "reform." Their families, unless they repudiated the erring member, shared in the ostracism. Almost needless to say, John was hatted as a Rightist in 1958, and together with the majority of the teachers of the FLD spent six months doing manual labor in the countryside. I was not sent to the country, but stayed at home in Zhong Da with the children. We were made very conscious that because we had not repudiated John we would share his disgrace.

The severity of the treatment of these alleged dissidents was sufficient to ensure a long period of conformity, which lasted up to the beginning of the Cultural Revolution in 1966. By then abuses had again accumulated to such an extent that when one element of the Party leadership called on the masses to unite and overthrow those who took a different line, the response was one of overwhelming violence. More than ten years of civil disorder, ranging from social and economic paralysis to bloody battles, ensued.

The foregoing much simplified sketch of the times between 1949 and 1966 may suggest something of the common experience of the teachers at Zhong Da at the point where our story begins.

Zhong Da is in the spacious walled compound formerly occupied by the American missionary college, Lingnan, and lies across the Pearl River from Canton. When the foreign missionaries all withdrew after Liberation in 1949–50 and the Christian schools and colleges were gradually nationalized and reorganized, this beautiful campus was taken over by the Sun Yat-sen University of Canton, and its faculty and students joined with the faculty and student body remaining at Lingnan. Teachers and students from several other institutions from other parts of the country were also sent there, and the newly formed national university was known as Zhongshan University. It was the biggest national-level university in the South. Its name preserved, in Chinese, its identity with the former Sun Yat-sen University.

The old Lingnan campus is perhaps the most beautiful and picturesque of all the colleges in China. Amply funded and supported before Liberation by generous American contributors and by its overseas Chinese alumni, it was carefully planned and skillfully landscaped. The University buildings, classroom halls, and laboratories combined modern conveniences with traditional Chinese architecture very effectively. Green and blue tiled roofs with curling eaves, like those in Chinese temples, contrast with red brick walls in buildings set among gardens, flowering trees, and lawns. From the South Gate on the boulevard leading to Canton, to the North Gate on the Pearl River, there is a broad pleasance with grass and flowers and roads on each side, lined with spreading banyans and flowering orchid trees. At the river end are a swimming pool and a marina.

On the east side of this Midway the founding fathers of Lingnan built beautiful Western-style mansions to house the foreign teaching staff. On the west side, nearest the Midway, they put up less elaborate but still quite comfortable Western-style double houses to accommodate senior Chinese teachers, and in the depths of the "southwest district" were rows of modest bungalows, where the lowest orders of Chinese faculty and staff were housed. The otherwise socially invisible workers lived in row houses in the extreme edges of the campus near the south and east walls. None of the houses, even the best, had central heating, in spite of the cold, damp winters of Canton, and because of that damp climate, few had wooden floors; tiles or concrete were the only thing that could withstand Canton's termites and mildew.

The hierarchy of housing by rank was continued when the new university, Zhong Da, was formed, and when we moved in, we found that the mansions were occupied by the "high brass" and such Lingnan professors as had managed to move quickly when the changeover came; lesser teachers and newcomers were put in the southwest district, and the more junior of the lately arrived had to settle for accommodations in classrooms, one to a family, in a primary school in the city. They commuted to work on a special bus. In the following years as new housing was built to take care of the growing population, differences in rank were still maintained; the houses built for professors each had a small room for the maid whom, it was assumed, professors would hire, while the apartments for lower ranks had no such amenity.

This kind of unequal treatment was a sore point to many, and it added to the difficulties of administering what must have been a very awkward group of people. For the faculty assembled in 1953 included teachers of widely varying qualifications, experience, and motivation.

Communist Party members were a numerical minority, as indeed they are throughout China to this day. But a Party member would be present in every administrative unit, even if he did not hold the nominally leading position. This assured that Party policy would be carried out, for the Party member held the real power. If the Party members were like the nervous system of a living creature, transmitting messages and directing actions from a brain center, then "the activists" were the muscles. These were non-Party people who wanted to rise politically. Many of them no doubt acted from the purest of motives, but it was undeniable that there were advantages in being an activist. Filled with enthusiasm and not tempered by the discipline of years of revolutionary warfare and mass movements, the activists and new 1956–57 vintage Party members were sometimes responsible for excesses that later had to be rectified by veteran, principled Party cadres.

Academic life at Zhong Da was no love feast. Coming from different provinces, from institutions of differing standards, the teachers were constantly engaged in unequal competition for prestige and power. To be politically progressive was more useful in the struggle than to be expert, but to be more expert was some protection. In the Foreign Languages Department, naturally, I occupied a somewhat sheltered position, because I was the only native speaker of English, and so became the court of last appeal on all questions of pronunciation and usage. I soon learned that innocent-seeming questions about "How do you pronounce . . ." usually meant that the questioner was trying to prove that some rival had made a mistake, thus winning a point against him in the constant struggle for place. John, bilingual in Chinese and English and reading comfortably in French, German, Russian, Hebrew, and Greek, was observed constantly for mistakes but was disappointingly accurate.

Since the faculty at Zhong Da had been brought together from several different provinces, some of the teachers spoke dialects that were unintelligible to the others. (Spoken Cantonese, for instance, differs as much from Wuhan dialect as Danish from Italian, although the written language is the same all over China.) It was necessary to use Standard Chinese (the national language based on the dialect of the capital, Peking) as the medium of communication in our work. A strong effort was made to popularize it, to promote unity and to discourage provincial cliques, but it took a long time to establish it, and some of the older teachers never liked to use it. In the Foreign Languages Department it was often easier to communicate in English than in Chinese of any kind; few of those who did not speak Cantonese as natives had the time—or flexibility—to master the dialect.

Thus, linguistic differences were added to the factors dividing the faculty, already divided in so many other ways: Party and non-Party, activists and masses, provincials from different provinces, Western-educated and purely Chinese-educated, the "red" and the "expert." In the FLD, in addition, each linguistic discipline was pitted against the others—Russian, English, French, Japanese; as was each rank—instructors, lecturers, associate professors, professors—each seeing its own interests as paramount; at times even males were set against females. The atmosphere was not one in which pure scholarship had much chance.

When we arrived in 1953, we found that all that was Russian was good. A Russian textbook was used for teaching English, rather than one originating in England or America—or China. Presently this book was jettisoned, and there was a great effort to find "the" best method. The various schools of thought argued endlessly and fruitlessly; direct method vs. oral-aural, translation, grammar, linguistics, or literature. By the beginning of the Cultural Revolution, a much more reasonable scholarly atmosphere prevailed and the Department had decided to produce a textbook of its own, and John and I had been set to work with a team of teachers to write it.

Neither of our children was living at home at this time. Our daughter, Tientung, then twenty-four, was a fourth-year student in the English Speciality in the FLD. Our son, Mingteh, at twenty-one was working as an "educated youth" in a commune near Canton.

These careers were not by any means what either of them had ever chosen. They had both been in high school when John was "hatted." Properly progressive young people would have criticized their father and prospered thereafter, but they failed this test. Thus, both also failed to be admitted to college after graduating from high school. It was only after her father was "dehatted" in 1961 that Tientung's potential as an English teacher was recognized and she was pressured into becoming a student at Zhong Da.

Meanwhile Mingteh, determined not to sit at home in the city eating rice produced by his friends (who had failed the entrance exams for reasons similar to his), had left home two years earlier to join eighteen of his classmates in a commune south of Canton. There he worked in the fields by day and studied electronics and English at night.

For those of the new generation who benefited immediately from the revolution—the landless peasant, the Party cadre, the urban unemployed—family interest and political line were united, and there was not necessarily a split between the generations. But among those like us who were downgraded in the struggle, there were painful choices to be made by the children. To repudiate a backward father or mother and rise with the progressives? To cling to the family and feel like an outcast in the larger world? To take on the burden of always pretending to be something you were not?

When Mingteh was denied college entrance because of his father's political "hat," he had rallied from his disappointment and plunged into the life of his generation, going as an "educated youth" to serve the people in the country. When Tientung was forced into preparing to teach English, she made it clear from the beginning that she did not intend to make her fortune by rejecting her parents or by limiting her friends to those of her own "class" (in the political sense).

However, it was painful to know that our children would always be under the shadow of John's "hat." We hoped against hope that they would find liberation from our past by going their own way.

This was how things stood in June 1966, at Zhong Da in Canton, with the Lo family.

June 1966

ON JUNE 13, 1966, we were having a rare meeting of the younger English teachers at our house, Number 48. We glanced critically around the living-dining room, with its study alcove, to see if everything was ready. John helped me pull the large round dining table into a corner to make room for all the wicker chairs we could muster, set around the walls; the firebrick tile floor had been swept carefully after lunch by Ho Jie, our housekeeper, and I had checked personally, with the feather duster, on possible cobwebs under the seldom-used chairs. The whitewashed walls looked rather festive with newly hung red paper slogans, all displaying quotations from Chairman Mao, and the big south-facing windows, wide open to the monsoon breezes, admitted lots of light, even though it was a typically humid Canton summer day. Too much light, I decided, and lowered the bamboo splint blinds a little on the south side, all the way on the west windows.

Although this was a "foreign-style house" adapted somewhat to meet the restrictions of Cantonese building materials and climate, it had resisted my efforts to make it conform to my ideas of comfort. Window curtains, to temper the fierce light, were not only a mechanical impossibility for the casement panes, they would have looked "bourgeois," a scandalous waste of cloth, to critical neighbors. The bamboo blinds had been an inspired adaptation of the Chinese door curtain by our teen-age son, Mingteh. He painstakingly scissored them to fit the windows and adapted the pulleys and strings to the peculiar requirements of screens that opened inward, glass that swung out, and transoms that came down.

I wondered a little about the blue-green vase of African daisies on the round table. Our daughter, Tientung, had left them for me that morning before class; I knew that the flowerpots on the balcony of the Common Room of the Foreign Languages Department had been condemned as bourgeois. No, I'd keep my daisies. My home was my castle.

Or was it? There was no time to debate. The first of our guests were on the doorstep.

John went to the door to let them in. As he stood there, facing the light, I noticed with sharp anxiety how thin his face looked, and how the gray was spreading in his hair and moustache. There was a little sadness about his eyes now, but the warm smile with which he welcomed the young people had not changed since our student days.

As was to be expected in Chinese society, the first comers were the youngest, two young men who had been our students earlier on and who were now our colleagues in the English Speciality Section of the FLD.

They greeted us warmly and took seats near the door. Shortly the others followed: several more young men, a couple of young women —one thin, pretty, and defensive about her English pronunciation, the other thin, round-faced, with earnest round spectacles, and very sure about everything—then a slightly older man (a bit higher in rank than the first comers), and then a pause . . .

"Shall I go and see if Comrade Yuan is ready?" volunteered one of the youngest. Comrade Yuan was the second-in-command of the Department and, as the most senior member of the group gathered here, would naturally come last. To send for her would be a proper courtesy. We dispatched a posse to round her up, no difficult task as she lived in the next house. In a few moments she appeared, laughing and chatting volubly with her escort, and our meeting could begin.

"I was waiting for a telephone call," she remarked as she seated herself at the head of the table, explaining the slight delay. (As a senior administrative officer and Party member, she had a telephone in her home; private persons in the People's Republic of China of 1966 did not have this privilege.) I thought the comrade looked a little pale, although in her usual ebullient spirits. She was taller and a good deal huskier than the average Cantonese woman, her hair was stylishly dressed, and her uniform, of excellent material, was cut with an eye to fit that suggested the services of one of the skilled Cantonese tailors who still functioned in the back streets of the Old West End of the city. Comrade Yuan would not have looked out of place on the streets of her old home in Hong Kong, although technically she conformed to the correct style of a *gan-bu* (an official).

The meeting had been arranged at the urgent request of the young teachers to discuss our new English language textbook, which they were trying out in the beginners' classes. John was responsible for the Chinese explanations and grammar, and I had to produce suitable original dialogues and bits of narrative to illustrate the patterns and vocabulary to be learned in each lesson. Others had decided what the subject matter of the dialogues must be, and still others produced drills and exercises. This kind of collective work was now an old story to us all, and we were resigned to the time-consuming circular discussions and the curiously impersonal quality of the finished product. In John's and my opinion the greatest advantage of the method was that it was a very good way to train the young teachers. It also relieved every member of the team of personal responsibility for the ideology implicit in every sentence, as all decisions were collective. John and I had been working happily on the material all spring, grinding out a lesson a week, enjoying the pleasure of working at home together. He had time to work on his linguistic research on the side, and the more relaxed program, with no classroom lectures, was, I had hoped, improving his frail health.

However, one cannot collaborate without contact with one's collaborators, and it had proved extraordinarily difficult to get in touch with the young teachers to discuss the text and learn whether or not the material was proving suitable in the classroom. Time after time I attempted to bring them together, only to have my efforts fail. Presently I learned from Tientung that two new foreign teachers, an English couple, had joined the staff. They had been formally and warmly welcomed by the rest of the faculty and by the students, but not, alas, by us. We were left officially in ignorance of their presence. Until and unless the authorities brought us together, it would not be correct for me to obey my natural impulse to seek them out and do what I could to help them feel at home. Although the prospect of having a real modern Englishwoman to talk to filled me with joy, I had learned now that politics came first. The appointment by Peking of a couple of new foreign teachers to Zhong Da indicated something significant about national policy in higher education. Our marked segregation from the newcomers also was significant, at least on the local level.

An old familiar pattern began to become visible even to me. Even though John's work and mine were useful to the Department, we were in trouble. Why we were being singled out this time, we did not know. But such a situation was not new.

It recalled the bad time in 1958, when John had been "hatted" as a Rightist for ideological errors detected by the alert leadership of the Department. For four long years the family had lived in the shadow of his political "crimes." John and I had continued our work as teachers, but we had been kept in isolation from all normal social contact. Was it all beginning again? And if so, why?

From time to time during the spring of 1966 we had been hearing rumors of political developments of a sort that presaged trouble. There was a great political debate going on in Peking, reported at length in all the papers—something about the criticism, or the suppression of the criticism, of some Chinese opera. I was not too clear about it. The Chinese opera to me was remote. I could take it or leave it. John had a clearer appreciation of the possible political significance of such a debate, but to him, too, it seemed remote. But there was a teasing, nagging feeling of increasing tension in the air, like the atmospheric disturbance just before a typhoon. We were vaguely aware that there were more meetings going on than usual, but we were told we were "not required to attend." The present assemblage of young teachers was the largest group I had been in for months, and I hoped that somehow we might learn something helpful about other matters than the teaching of the English anomalous finites, the ostensible reason for the gathering.

The din of youthful voices arguing about this delightful subject rose higher and higher, and I had a pleasant feeling that this was almost like old times before Liberation, when our house in Wuchang was so often the scene of gatherings of enthusiastic young people happily expressing themselves about anything from past perfect infinitives to their hopes for immortality. Today it was pleasing to see their minds working and to try to answer their challenging questions. But was the sound today a little shrill? As I wondered, there was a knock at the door. "Would Comrade Yuan please come home to take a phone call?"

There was a moment of silence as Comrade Yuan made her exit upon this cue. Younger Party members present looked questions at each other. No one spoke. Then, with concentrated effort, the discussion was resumed. But not for long. A voice in the front yard called through the window, "Comrade Chang, you're wanted at the Office. Excuse please!" Comrade Chang rose and, smiling apologies, departed, taking with him certain others, all Party members.

The conversation now became difficult. Discussion in English about classroom problems and grammar faded into tense dialogues in Cantonese, which I did not understand, then died away into an uncomfortable silence. When a third messenger knocked at the screen door and called for the student representatives to come to "an urgent meeting," those who were left no longer pretended to ignore what was becoming a Situation. The Leadership had gone. The other Party members had gone. The student activists had gone. All that were left were a few "members of the masses"—people with no special political duties—and John and me. We could do no good by further communion. With one accord, all departed.

When the Department messenger came round that evening with a notice (since no one but administrative officers had phones at home, a man on a bicycle circulated information), we were not entirely surprised to be told, "All classes are to be suspended for two weeks as from June 13, to carry on activities connected with the Great Proletarian Cultural Revolution."

"Two weeks?" "The Great Proletarian Cultural Revolution?" There was no reasonable reason why the problems of the Chinese opera should involve John and me, but we had a strong premonition, based on years of experience, that in any big political movement we would probably be found to be wrong about something.

Next morning I was picking caterpillars off the rain lilies in the front yard when a neighbor hurried by, on the way, clearly, to a Meeting. I greeted her tentatively and remarked, "Is there a meeting about this new cultural movement?"

Not pausing in her rapid progress down the lane, she answered over her shoulder, "Movement? This is not just a new political movement. This is The Revolution."

Nearly one month after this, I was walking down the narrow dirt road that led directly to the entrance of the Foreign Languages Department building. It was payday, the tenth of July, 1966. The mid-July noonday sun was hot on my head, and I wished I could have carried an umbrella, but I am so lame, I can't walk without my stick, and in my other hand I had to carry a bag to bring back the pay envelopes. On either side of the way, sunlight glinted on green rice fields, the experimental plots of the biology students; now a bamboo grove, tossing restless plumes against the blue sky, gave a patch of welcome shade. I stopped a moment and stared down the road, trying to make out what was riveting the attention of a hundred or more teachers and students.

What were all those people in front of the office building looking at so silently, I wondered. Overnight a row of bulletin boards, made of bamboo matting, had been set up on either side of the wide front steps of the Department Office Building. The boards were covered with *da zi bao,* posters in big characters written with Chinese black ink and a brush on sheets of old newspaper. As I approached, a chill struck my heart. On every one I could see John's Chinese name, "Lo Chuanfang."

The thin young woman teacher, with her large round spectacles flashing on her small round face, detached herself from the silent throng and came toward me. Formerly my student, now a teacher, she was a loyal, active Party member.

"Where is Lo Chuanfang?" she asked crisply. She did not use the courtesy title of "comrade" or "teacher." A sure sign that he was in political trouble. Again.

"He is at home. Ill. I have come to collect our pay," I replied.

"He should come and read these *da zi bao*'s," she said.

"Can you give me any idea of what this is all about?" I asked. "He is really ill, you know—his heart and high blood pressure. He has not been out of the house for days. What has happened?"

"At a recent meeting it was revealed that Lo Chuanfang has been engaged in anti-Party activities for a long time," she said sternly.

"These *da zi bao*'s expose how he has secretly sabotaged Chairman Mao's Thoughts in his lectures on teaching methods."

My heart sank. At the repeated request of the younger teachers and with the somewhat reluctant consent of the Department authorities, John had given a series of lectures during the winter on the psychology of language learning. Recognizing that many in his audience would be totally ignorant about such fundamental concepts as perception, attention, recall, and so on, he had dwelt on these points, defining terms, in his first lecture. With the specialist's enthusiasm for his subject, he had given most of his time and attention to what he considered essential information, and had scanted the now more or less required introductory genuflections to Chairman Mao's Thought.

When the lecture was declared open for discussion and questions, the leading Party member present, our Departmental Number Two, had risen up and denounced him scathingly for his nonpolitical approach. John had offered to drop the project. However, after a short time we had been astonished to hear that other Party members had later rebuked his critic, and he was asked to continue his lectures. Now it appeared that the whole matter had been brought up again, and this time under the banner of the recently announced Great Proletarian Cultural Revolution. John had been selected by someone in authority to be a target for mass criticism.

"I know that Dr. Lo had no intention of attacking the Party's leadership," I said. "He only wished to help the young teachers. But I will tell him about this and he will come out to study these *da zi bao*'s as soon as he is able to walk this far."

I turned away and moved toward the foot of the steps leading up into the one-story brick building that housed the Foreign Languages Department offices. Through the double doors I could see the clerks sitting behind the table, with the pay envelopes (thriftily handmade out of old newspapers) spread out before them. But all the teachers for whom the envelopes were intended were standing outside, staring at the *da zi bao*'s.

The crowd parted to let me through. No one spoke or met my eye. Almost all my colleagues were there, some of them my students in years gone by, all the people we knew best and had worked with for a lifetime as teachers, before Liberation and since. Many of the current generation of students mingled with the crowd. They were easily distinguished by the new red armbands they wore, as members of the very recently formed Red Guards, the activists of the Cultural Revolution.

I had to negotiate more than twenty shallow steps made of cracked, irregular old red bricks, not steep, but without a handrail. It was difficult for me to climb them with my lame leg, but I could not hesitate now. I mounted steadily, hoping I would not fall on my face before this large and silent audience. I entered the office and gave the clerk our seals with which to stamp the receipt book and picked up our two pay envelopes. I went through the motions of counting the currency, as was customary, but knew that I was incapable of adding one to one. I thanked the clerk, put the envelopes into my bag, and faced the even more difficult descent. My head swam as I stood at the top of the steps, looking out over the upturned faces of my colleagues, all intent on reading about John's newest mistakes. As I started down, a man stepped out of the crowd and ran lightly up to my side. He offered his arm with the formal courtesy of a cavalier inviting a duchess to join a minuet. Gratefully I leaned on it and we silently and safely descended. I thanked him with equal formality. He disappeared into the crowd. How had he dared? No one spoke. I walked on toward home.

This man was a Party member, newly come to the University, with no special ties with either my husband or myself. I don't know what has become of him since, but I will never forget him.

Slowly I walked back home, dreading the moment when I should have to tell John the bad news—that he was again "on the wall," the subject of mass criticism. At a time when political tensions were increasing, it could mean further ostracism for us and, probably, our children, too.

July 1966

BETWEEN THE DAY in June when the meeting melted away and the day a month later when the *da zi bao*'s appeared accusing John, nothing much had seemed to go on locally. There were no classes. The two-week holiday extended itself without further notice. Meetings were constantly being announced over the *guan bo,* the public-address system, and sometimes messengers would come to the house to tell John to attend—or not to attend. From what appeared in the official newspaper (there were no others) it was evident that a great struggle was developing in Peking, but, as had happened before, there was a time lag between developments in the capital in the North and in Canton in the far South.

John and I began to think that the accusations against him were probably a kind of diversionary tactic in a struggle that involved far more than local personalities. He was being used "as a stone to throw at someone else"; that is, persons in one inner Party faction were using him to embarrass persons in another. While this was not exactly flattering, it held out the possibility of the whole thing's being straightened out in the course of time.

This point of view was soon confirmed by our daughter, Tientung. She was a student in the English Speciality of the FLD, a difficult situation for her because of her father's "political problem," and one which she occupied much against her will and against our judgment. But the powerful Number One of the Department had pulled strings and arranged matters to suit his own ideas; her bilingual abilities would be a convenience, so willy-nilly she had to prepare to teach English, and I was appointed to be her special professor. In 1966 she, like all her classmates, lived at the University dormitory not far from our house; she shared their life, except that, being so close to home, she could come to see us frequently.

John and I were finishing a supper for which neither of us had much appetite. Being "on the wall" was depressing, no matter how philosophical one tried to be.

The monsoon wind was blowing steadily from the south, banging and rattling the bamboo blinds; the single overhead light bulb swung on the end of its cord, shifting the shadows in the corners. The room felt too big for us two, and the table had been meant to seat four. Then the screen door slammed and everything began to look better as Tientung slipped in and sat down in her old place.

Her wavy black hair, most unbecomingly cut in a revolutionary childlike style, was ruffled by the night wind. Her cheeks were flushed and her brown eyes danced. The lavender print shirt, which we had labored over together, cutting and hand-sewing, was not really a very good fit, I had to admit, but the color was just right against her olive skin. Picking up a pair of chopsticks, she began poking hungrily among the bits of fish on the platter; she beamed at her father and patted my arm with her unoccupied left hand.

Ho Jie looked around the corner into the room, nodded approvingly, and went back to the kitchen to get Tientung a bowl of hot rice.

"Oh, thank you, Ho Jie, I've eaten"—she smiled—"but I can always hold a bit more." (Student meals were long on rice and short on meat.) She took up the bowl and began to eat. "I've really got some news," she said between mouthfuls. "A Task Force from the Provincial Party Committee came to the University today."

This was wonderful to hear. Apparently, then, we had not been alone in being confused by the changing directives about the Revolution.

"They say now," Tientung continued, "that the real targets are 'persons in authority taking the capitalist road.' All this business of criticizing old professors was a diversionary tactic by the 'persons in authority.' They are the ones in trouble, not you, my dear Daddy— you're anything in the world but a person in authority. So I think you can just relax—and have a little more rice perhaps, if I get it for you?"

"Well, half a bowl then." He looked less strained already. John continued, "I thought it must be something like that. You see, it wasn't necessary to worry so!"

No, I thought. But it's an old habit.

The next day Tientung came in to tell me that a representative from the Task Force wanted to see me to explain the situation. This was a surprise but, on the whole, reassuring. It implied that somewhere in the rarefied upper regions of policy my existence was known, and I was not entirely at the mercy of the local squalls.

"Who is it?" I asked naturally.

"Just a cadre," she answered. (In the PRC, "cadre" is the word in English for *gan-bu*, to indicate almost any person who draws pay from the government, whether city primary school teacher, college president, factory head, or government clerk.) I should have known better than to expect to learn her name. A "cadre" on an official mission is not an individual. "She's staying in our dormitory and, between you and me, she is a very nervous woman."

"What is she doing?"

"Well, she talks to us girls and keeps telling us to study Chairman Mao's Thoughts and be loyal."

"Can't argue with that," I commented. "Is she the only one?"

"No, there are some men who are staying at the men's dormitory. They spend all their time at meetings with the Red Guards, trying to persuade the two factions to get together."

"What two factions?"

"Well, you know how it is in our class. If X says it is raining, Z says the sun is too hot. They are just two different kinds of people. They all say they support Chairman Mao, but they can't agree on how to express it or who shall be the leader."

With a most unacademic hug and kiss for her "professor," she ran down the steps, and I watched her go briskly down the lane back to the dormitory. I turned to John beside me, who was gazing with equal fondness at her retreating form.

"She's as tall as you, dear," I doted.

"And as plump as you," he teased. (Who wouldn't love a man who thought you plump, not fat?) And he proceeded to demonstrate that he could be just as unacademic as his daughter.

Next day, toward the end of the afternoon, Tientung brought the cadre to see me. She greeted me in English, a special politeness, and I responded in my most careful Standard Chinese to reciprocate her gesture. Tientung excused herself to prepare the tea of hospitality, and we were left alone—an unusual situation: cadres, like nuns, usually operate in pairs.

She was a very nervous woman, no doubt about that. She looked around the room and twisted her handkerchief like an embarrassed schoolgirl. I wondered how old she might be. It is often hard for me to guess the age of a Chinese; usually they look younger than they are, until a certain line is passed and suddenly they look much older. Hairstyles are a clue. I guessed from my visitor's conservative perm that she might be in her early forties, possibly a veteran cadre from the Korean War; that would give her the seniority and prestige necessary to qualify her for the responsibility of being on an important Task Force. But I couldn't be sure where she came from. Although she spoke Standard Chinese, it was not quite like that of Peking. Her summer uniform of gray slacks and white blouse gave no clue to her native province. She was as nearly anonymous as one well could be.

At first she was only mannerly; she inquired exhaustively about my health and age, as was proper. I told her I was fifty-six years old, lame since childhood, but able to get about. I assured her that the local authorities had shown proper concern for my welfare and provided me with housing as close to my classes as possible. Then, without too much encouragement, I volunteered some information about the health of my husband: he suffered from chronic heart disease and high blood pressure, and after his half year of manual labor had contracted tuberculosis. However, I added, after he had been "dehatted" in 1961, he, too, had received appropriate consideration and was allowed to work on his linguistic research at home.

She nodded approvingly and nervously throughout this declaration and then expressed official appreciation of our work. She hoped that I would understand that the present Cultural Revolution was a very important and very complex event. I said something about "revolutionary movement" and she corrected me in words I had heard before: "This is not a revolutionary movement, this is The Revolution." (The full significance of this distinction was less apparent to me then than it was several years later.) Perhaps, she conceded, some mistakes had been made locally because people did not all wholly understand what the correct line was, but mistakes would always be rectified in accordance with Party policy. The important thing was to study Chairman Mao's Thought and "to learn from the masses."

"What should I do?" I asked. "There are no classes, and no one seems to know whether I should attend meetings about the Cultural Revolution or not. While I have the greatest respect for Chinese culture and try my best to study it, I am, after all, a foreigner, and cannot hope to understand it as a Chinese does. I am not in a position to have opinions of my own and might easily be misled."

This idea seemed to meet with approval. At this point Tientung came in with tea, and they talked together in rapid Cantonese. Between them they summed up their discussion: it was not considered necessary for me to take an active part in all the meetings and revolutionary activities that were going on, partly because my lameness made it "inconvenient" and partly because the situation was complex and I could not be expected to follow all the developments. My "duty" was to study the documents as they appeared in English in the *Peking Review* (which she saw on my desk), to learn from the masses and from my students (with a smile at Tientung), and to continue to serve the people.

Then, with more smiles and nervous politenesses, she departed with Tientung, and I turned to my *Peking Review*.

I had hoped to have further words with this helpful Task Force comrade, but when I asked about her a few days later, Tientung told me that the whole Task Force had been recalled. The Party authority who had sent them was now in turn under fire.

However, during the brief time that the Task Force was on campus, the students had been directed by higher authority to continue living in their dormitories. They were to draw their stipends as usual. Instead of attending classes they were to carry out what was called the "Anti–Four Olds" campaign. The Four Olds were defined as "old ideas, old superstitions, old customs, old bourgeois life-styles." This was the first gun of the Cultural Revolution. Pursuit of the victims of the *pre*–Four Olds Campaign should be dropped. Now the important targets were the "persons in authority taking the capitalist road." These were usually high Party officials or university administrators. John and others like him were now rather summarily rehabilitated by action of the mass organizations and he was told that he was welcome to join in The Revolution.

He was looking quite cheerful the morning he came back from a meeting called to impart this good news.

"Thank God," I said. "Let's just sit tight for a while."

"Oh, I think I might do well to take part," he objected, "just to make it clear that I'm not holding any grudge. I won't have to do much, just go to a few meetings."

"Tell me," I said, seething inwardly, "did anyone definitely tell you you *had* to join a mass organization?"

"No, no," he admitted. "They just made me feel I would be welcome."

"Then for heaven's sake learn from experience and stay *out of it.* The Task Force cadre said it would not be necessary for me to take part because of my health. You are a lot sicker than I am; you're in no condition to get involved in meetings morning, afternoon, and evening, with who knows what marches and demonstrations. You know how it can be. And besides, whatever you do, *someone,* you guess!, is not going to like it."

"There is something in that," he agreed ruefully. "Well, for once I'll . . ."

He could not bring himself to say "take your advice," but I was satisfied.

To make doubly sure of my position, I asked Tientung to ask representative students from the now definitely dividing factions of the Red Guard in the Department to come and talk with me about what they recommended I should do.

Next day student Red Guards from each faction came, separately, to see me. They were courteous and friendly, and each confirmed my resolution to confine my activities to study and observation. Active participation by a person like myself might be a real nuisance to some of them!

And so it came about that I experienced the Great Proletarian Cultural Revolution mainly through my husband, children, and friends. They, however, were inevitably involved in it, and through them I shared the agony of destruction and loss to the land and the people I cared for. I was in the eye of the typhoon.

July 1966

I HAD BEEN taking my habitual midday nap. The sound of voices on the ground floor aroused me and I got up reluctantly and started down. On the stairs, to my considerable surprise, I met a group of my students coming up. They looked embarrassed when they saw me.

"What is it?" I asked. "Isn't Dr. Lo in his study?"

"Oh, yes," they replied. "We have come to tell you about the Anti–Four Olds Campaign." I noticed that they were all wearing red armbands, with Chinese words written on them in yellow paint, some saying: "Mao Zedong Thought Red Guards," others, "Mao Zedong-ism."

"Well, that's very kind of you." Somehow I turned them around and headed them downstairs. They were nice boys and I liked them all—in class—but to find them wandering uninvited in my private territory! I was shocked at the primitive rage it provoked. "We'll just go down to my study and talk it over." It sounded as if people were running all over the house.

As we went downstairs, the sound of voices in John's study was getting louder. About a dozen young fellows were in the hallway crowding about the door, and someone who had squeezed inside seemed to be pounding on the desk. I pushed my way in and stood beside John. He was leaning far back in his chair, to put space between himself and the desk pounder. "What do the students want?" I asked him.

"They say everyone must get rid of his burden of old ideas, old customs, and so on," he explained, sitting upright as the pounding ceased. "In our case they are encouraging us to hand in old books with bourgeois ideas in them, and anything else that we associate with old culture."

He looked about his rather sparsely furnished study, wondering what to offer up first. Few people with any pretensions to "culture" could ever have had so little material evidence of their tastes. But our Spartan life-style was the natural result of our family's history. We had been refugees for years, particularly in the late 1930s and early forties during the Japanese invasion. All our possessions had been sifted through by war, fire, air raids, flight, until we had learned to live with a minimum of material objects. The only thing we had in any abundance was books, as all four of us were compulsive book buyers. We excused ourselves on the grounds that they were the tools of our trade, and we miraculously acquired them as fast as we lost everything else. John's study, though bare of scrolls or porcelains or little works of art, even without any comfortable chairs, was lined with shabby wicker bookcases, every shelf sagging with its burden of double-ranked volumes, magazines, bundles of papers, and boxes of file cards.

My eye lighted upon a veritable ram entangled in the bushes, a row of Russian journals on psychology, long untouched, subscribed to in the heyday of the fifties campaign, "Learn from the USSR," glanced at, and never discarded. (Just as it had been politically "correct" to acquire these when we did, it was politically "incorrect" just to throw them out. The Anti–Four Olds Campaign made it possible to get rid of them at last.)

"Oh," I said, "certainly we, among so many others, have been influenced by the revisionist science of the USSR. We'd be only too glad to get rid of these." I began piling the offenders on the desk, thrusting them into the hands of the young fellows who had been most active in the pounding. Disconcerted, they drew back, but some of the less aggressive, who had stood in the background, now expressed approval of my action, saying, "Good, good, that's the right idea."

The tide seemed turning in our favor when a couple who had been prowling the house independently pressed forward in a rather menacing way.

"We'll just confiscate this bicycle of Lo Chuanfang's," they announced.

It was John's turn to look disconcerted. It was our daughter's bicycle, not his. I rushed in, not thinking of the possible consequences. "That isn't Dr. Lo's," I cried. "It belongs to Lo Tientung, your classmate."

"What right does a student like her have to own a bicycle?" shouted the aggressive one. "She isn't a worker."

"No, of course not," I replied, smothering John's efforts to respond. "She is not. But *I* am. I've been working in China longer than you've been alive, and if I save my wages and buy my daughter a bicycle because she's lame, that's quite within my rights. You are all just students, but I'm a working woman."

Other students now joined in the argument, some supporting my stand, others sputtering, still hoping to attach the bike. But the moment had passed when they could have forced the issue, and after some grumbling they began to leave. Some took armloads of discarded journals; others added a final warning addressed more to John than to me, urging him to go over all his books and papers immediately and be ready to hand things in the next day. Then they trailed out, leaving us both feeling limp.

That evening, after dark, Tientung stopped in. We told her about the visitation and she laughed. "Some of the boys just wanted another bicycle," she said. "I'll take my bike back to the dorm with me and turn it over to our girls' small group for common use. Then they won't dare meddle with it. But you and Daddy had better get some things ready to hand in, in case they come again."

"What do they want?"

"They want to be able to show that every old professor has been educated about the Four Olds," she answered. "Some people have handed in old Chinese scrolls, some 'yellow novels' [almost any romantic tale]—I know you don't go in for them." She grinned. "Some have handed in Bibles and religious pictures, some gramophone records . . ."

"What on earth will they do with them?"

"I expect they'll have an exhibition," she replied. I had seen such exhibitions before. They had been a regular part of the propaganda machinery for educating the masses during earlier political campaigns. To supplement the effect of the spoken and written word, collections of objects would be assembled to illustrate more vividly the political point to be learned. During the Land Reform in 1951, for instance, masses of peasants (and intelligentsia serving as cadres) were marched to view former landlords' houses, so they could contrast the luxury and comforts of the rich with the poverty and misery of the landless peasants. During the Thought Reform in 1952 I saw an exhibition exposing the bourgeois life-style and imperialist connections of the older professors. The exhibition featured a pair of pretty fur-lined boots; a foreign missionary had given them to a young teacher she had befriended, and somehow the sight of those enviable boots had more impact than hours of oratory.

"It certainly ought to be interesting," Tientung continued. "The Red Guards visited Li's place last night, and they sealed up her piano."

"Sealed up her piano?" I couldn't believe my ears. Li, another of our former students, taught music in a local middle school.

"Yes, they closed the lid down over the keyboard and pasted a paper seal over it so she can't play it anymore. They said the piano was a bourgeois foreign imperialist instrument and that poor peasants never have pianos. So Li had to criticize herself for having it. They probably won't put the piano in the exhibition though; it's too much trouble to move it. They'll just have a picture of it."

"But how can a piano be a political offense?" I sputtered.

"Easily." She chuckled. "It was last night, anyway. But the best item in the show will be Professor Lao's Cupid."

"What's that?"

"He has a statue of Cupid in his back garden, you know, a life-size image of the little Greek god of love, with wings and a bow and arrows."

"Surely no one thinks that is an object of religious superstition!" Professor Lao was an extremely sophisticated scholar who had studied in France and had collected European art, music, and books.

"No, I don't imagine anyone thought Professor Lao was offering up sacrifices at midnight or going through some exotic ritual in his back garden." She smiled. "It was because the little fellow has nothing on but his quiver of arrows. They decided that it was a 'yellow work of art' [read 'porn']. So they wrapped it up carefully in a large sheet of brown paper and Scotch-Taped it securely and put a label on it, 'Do Not Unwrap.' "

We both broke down in helpless laughter.

"But it's no laughing matter," Tientung said as we recovered. "If you don't volunteer to hand in some things, who knows what someone might do? Let's go over the books and find a few for me to take back with me."

It was nine o'clock and the three of us were still going over the books, sweating, streaked with dust, pestered by mosquitoes. We were not making much progress, because we all had the tendency to stop and read bits of each book we picked up. The pile of discards was comparatively small. Happily, at this point we heard a hail from the lane behind the house and Ho Jie bustled to open the back door. It was Mingteh, unexpectedly come in from the commune in the country where he lived. We seldom knew in advance when he might appear, but since the Canton–Hong Kong railway line ran through the commune land, it was sometimes possible for him to get a pass on short notice and catch an evening train, going back on the early morning one.

We all rushed to greet him. In the kitchen Ho Jie was already heating up the frying pan and getting out the bread. She was convinced that he never got enough to eat at the Homestead, the youth hostel where he stayed with a score of his former high school classmates.

John, laboring in his study, peered over the stack of dusty volumes he was sorting with an expression comically combining anxiety and pleasure. "Son! Are you all right? How long can you stay?"

"I'm fine, Daddy. I have to go back in the morning."

Tientung paused only long enough to give a sisterly tug at his unruly hair. "*Wah,* do you ever need a haircut!" she muttered as she headed upstairs to fix him a bath and find him a change of clothes.

I just looked at him. Taller than his father, broad and sturdy, sun-browned, dressed in filthy blue cotton pants, patched and faded, sweaty, once-white T-shirt with a red Chairman Mao badge tearing a new hole in it, barefooted, holding a dilapidated dirty khaki shoulder bag by its one remaining strap. He looked like a million other young men in their early twenties, farm laborers of the new kind, educated youth from the cities, now committed to the world of peasants. But his face, a fascinating blend of his father's features and my father's expression—quizzical, reserved, but alert—was to me the most satisfying sight in the world.

"What's up?" He flung his bag on a chair and squatted down to look at the books we had piled on the floor.

"It's the Anti–Four Olds Campaign," I explained, resisting the impulse to pat him. "The students came by this afternoon to show us what we should discard. Are you hungry?"

"Naturally. Ho Jie's already frying eggs," he grinned. Tientung came in and pulled him to his feet.

"Go take a bath." She led him off, talking rapidly in the Cantonese dialect they used between themselves.

Half an hour later, a good deal cleaner and well filled with fried eggs and most of a loaf of Ho Jie's good homebaked bread, the normally silent Mingteh became quite communicative.

"Everyone's going all out for the Anti–Four Olds in Canton," he told us. "Some of the fellows from the Homestead were in town over Sunday—Zero and Pigsy and Monkey [the Homesteaders retained their high school nicknames]—and they told us when they came back how it was going here at Zhong Da. Zero said his father's house was searched and Pigsy saw someone at the station having his head shaved. There were Red Guards also—just high school kids some of them—stopping people as they got off the train and taking away their Hong Kong shoes. . . . That's why I came barefoot!"

I looked at his feet, sunburned, with lighter stripes where his sandal straps had covered them at the high instep. A mental picture of his Michigan grandfather on horseback flashed through my mind. I said nothing.

"Never mind about my feet," he muttered to me aside. "You know our slogan at the Homestead? 'Your shoes will wear out but your feet just get tougher.' " His father and I exchanged wry looks. "Anyway, nobody bothered me coming here tonight, and nobody'll bother me tomorrow morning going back. What we've got to do now is go over the whole house very carefully. . . ."

We got busy at once and under his direction soon rooted out suitable offerings from every room. Whenever I recalled the snugly bundled Cupid, no longer a menace to revolutionary morality, my feelings wavered between seething indignation, blind panic, and hysterical amusement.

In a rather foolish gesture of repudiation, I took down from my study walls the only two Chinese scrolls that had survived all our moves: a harmless but possibly bourgeois peony, and a dim, fading landscape with tiny figures climbing a Guilin mountain, undoubtedly up to no political good. John unearthed a bulky treasure in the form of the old Soviet encyclopedia; lingering regretfully over its pages, we remembered the many hilarious moments it had given us with its assurances that practically every scientific discovery in history had been made by Russians. Stoically, Mingteh went over his collection of gramophone records and pulled out a few to sacrifice. A self-taught musician, he hungered for Western music, and his records were his greatest treasure. In the commune, of course, he could hear nothing but politically correct songs.

"Mother, have we a spare Bible?" asked Tientung as we met on the stairway, where our varied offerings made an impressive pile now. "They know you must have one. They took Uncle Peter's away [it was returned in 1978] and then everyone praised him for giving it up!"

"Yes, I have." I thought fast. "You can have this one." (I never saw it again.) It was a very attractive illustrated three-volume concordance, with maps and cross-references—a scholar's delight. "They'll surely like these pictures. They won't be able to resist reading some of it!" (A less spectacular but just as useful modern translation remained comfortably on the shelf between Wordsworth and Keats.)

"Good. I'll hand this in tomorrow. Now I really have to get back to the dorm." She looked dubiously out into the darkness.

"I'll walk along with you." Mingteh bumped her bike down the steps and they disappeared together.

Upon his return Mingteh sat down with me in my study, looking serious. "This sort of thing could become a nuisance to you, Mother," he said. "I'll tell you what I'll do. I'll put up a big *da zi bao* on the outside of the front door, welcoming the revolutionary action of the Red Guards. Now, where can we find a big piece of paper, and have we any red ink in the house? This must be in red characters, of course, because it is a celebration."

We looked everywhere for paper, but that is always in short supply in China, especially big pieces of good quality. Then Mingteh made the supreme sacrifice of the day. He came downstairs trailing after him his six-foot-square map of the United States, the prized decoration of his bedroom when he lived at home. He had bought it for himself at the bookstore during the period when study was a respectable preoccupation and bookstores still sold maps, even of imperialist America.

"I'll cut a strip off this and write on the back," he said. So the Pacific coastal states were sacrificed, and on the beautiful white back, with lavish use of red ink, he declared our wholehearted welcome of the Red Guards and our resolution to follow the correct political line. Pasted securely on the front door, it was to serve as the hyssop branch of the passover for some weeks to come.

"Will all the girls in your room join the Red Guards?" I asked Tientung a day or two later when she dropped in for a clean shirt. I thought it might be as well to have an idea whom I might be welcoming.

"Mercy, no. Red Guards are very elite indeed." She set aside a new shirt in favor of a more faded and mended one. "You have to be of 'good class origin' to be a Red Guard; that is, only the children of former poor and lower-middle peasants, industrial workers, or PLA [People's Liberation Army] soldiers can belong."

"Are they mostly Party members?"

"Actually not. That's the point. There are lots of Party members who aren't of 'good class origin.' [I thought of the Department's Number One and Number Two, and said nothing.] And there aren't all that many Party members among the college students. Middle school students are mostly too young to join the Party, though there are lots of middle schoolers in the Red Guards."

"I see." I felt a little relieved to know that Tientung would not be a solitary outsider in the group of five girls with whom she roomed. "How about Sue? She's of good class origin." Sue was Tientung's most intimate friend in the little group, a tough-minded, strong soul, an ardent patriot and idealist, but with her feet firmly on the ground.

"Oh, Sue. She could join if she wanted to, but she is very cautious about new things and she is waiting. Sue's folks are peasants, you know, and are very experienced people." I pondered the word "experienced." Yes, that was just it. Sue's people came from that vast reservoir of human experience of every kind of calamity and hardship life could present and they believed in facts more than in words.

"Well, you follow Sue's advice—I know you will. She's got good principles and she won't do anything foolish." Too often, I knew, people with good principles were rash.

"Who started all this Red Guards business, anyway?" I had, of course, read the official mythology in the weekly *Peking Review,* which reported that the Red Guards were a kind of spontaneous development among the youth in response to Chairman Mao's call to carry on the Cultural Revolution. But I couldn't swallow this simple explanation. Nothing in China was ever as simple as that.

"I'd like to know myself." She, too, doubted the spontaneous combustion theory. "All the Red Guards say their purpose is to support Chairman Mao, but they have already split into two groups in the Department." In 1966 Chariman Mao was the symbol of all that was good in the Liberation. It was unthinkable to oppose him. So I could only explain the split to myself by the analogy of my Western experience of denominational factions among Christians.

The two opposing groups of Red Guards were to polarize until the two highly organized factions not only disagreed on nearly everything but fought each other to the death.

Presently, those among the "masses" not eligible to belong to the elite Red Guards were encouraged to form "voluntary" mass organizations. By the spring of 1967 nearly everyone at Zhong Da—teachers, students, staff, and workers—had become attached to one or the other group. The innumerable small groups combined and formed alliances until the "Red Flag Commune" and the "Revolutionary Rebellion Committee" emerged. There were Party members in both. But in both it was not the Party members, nor the older teachers, but Red Guards, who took the lead.

Perhaps the chief difference in the makeup of the two factions was that the Committee contained a larger proportion of Party members. They had more political professionals. The Committee appeared to function with a clear purpose of protecting the existing Party apparatus from attack by non-Party elements. When members of the Commune forcibly entered the Party offices for the purpose of seizing political papers, the Committee defended the Party. But from time to time the two factions united to struggle with and overthrow Party members in authority.

The Red Guards, who called themselves *Hung Wei Ping,* were based in the universities and schools all over the country. As the Cultural Revolution developed, similar organizations came into being among factory workers and even among peasants in the communes. There, groups were less strict about membership requirements, perhaps, but they also polarized into factions that fought each other, all in the name of upholding the inspired thought of Chairman Mao. It was confusing to everyone.

In 1966 attacking the Four Olds served to get the *Hung Wei Ping* off to a good start. In the university campuses it was comparatively easy to find suitable targets among the older teachers, those educated before Liberation. In the cities, especially in a city like Canton, there were plenty of visible reminders of that traditional culture which had not been replaced by revolutionary symbols: such superficial things as street names, shop signs, trademarks were easy targets for the youngsters to attack. With much enthusiasm, teen-agers plunged into the task pointed out to them—to destroy the old, the past. Posses of Red Guards "searched" and "inspected" premises formerly used by churches and temples, and pulled down an occasional Buddha or cross or stained glass window. No one could interfere with such acts of vandalism without risking being labeled counter-revolutionary for obstructing the campaign.

But this campaign against dragons and phoenixes, curled hair and Bibles was only the opening move in a vastly more complex and fundamental struggle between "persons in authority" who disagreed among themselves as to how to bring about the completion of China's revolution. The Red Guards, and the mass organizations which they led, became the weapons in the hands of those in conflict all over the country. Perhaps all, certainly some, of the Red Guards were aware from the start of the stakes for which they were playing; some of the mass organizations' members may have fully realized the significance of what was going on, but probably very few of the masses could foresee what would follow the drums and gongs and scarlet banners that summoned them to action in 1966.

August 1966

FOLLOWING THE ADVICE of the Task Force cadre that I learn from the masses and mind my own business, I had been staying quietly at home, and John was occupied with his favorite project, research on British-American linguistic differences. Not surprisingly, after the flurry of excitement of going "on the wall," his blood pressure was up and quiet was mandatory.

It seemed to me that it was almost too quiet in the kitchen for five o'clock in the afternoon, so I set aside my work in the study and headed for the back of the house to investigate. I met John in the hallway on the same errand.

"Where's Ho Jie?" he asked.

"She had a *Jia-shu* meeting this afternoon," I answered as we entered the small, rather dark kitchen and opened the back door to let in the hot late-afternoon sunlight. (*Jia-shu* means "family members," and is often used to refer to the residents' organization to which all nonemployed adults belong. Its activities include volunteer social work as well as political study.) Obviously Ho Jie had not had time to eat lunch—the rice pot on the back of the cement cookstove counter was half full of cold rice, and the dish of vegetables and meat she should have eaten with it had been set aside in the screen cupboard.

"Are they doing outdoor labor today?" asked John. "She'll be hungry. She hasn't eaten her lunch."

It often happened that the women of the *Jia-shu* organization would spend an afternoon doing such manual labor as raking up leaves, chopping out weeds from the college lawns, leveling ground, even working in the college brickyard. On these occasions there was a marked tendency for the nonemployed wives of professors (*tai-tai*'s) to come late, while the servants came early and did the bulk of the heavy work. Ho Jie was always in great demand at such times, because she was a strong, competent peasant woman, willing and able, in spite of her fifty-odd years, to do more than her share. The *tai-tai*'s would praise her as a "model worker" and let her do their share of the dirty work.

One of the functions of the *Jia-shu* organization was the political education of residents not employed in "productive labor." As well as women, it included men who had retired, but naturally the majority were house-workers like Ho Jie, or faculty wives.

Housekeepers and amahs (older women who are hired to take care of children), although actually privately employed, were treated as if they were members of the family for whom they worked. Thus, membership in the *Jia-shu* cut across the hierarchies of the University society, putting the *tai-tai*'s on the same level with the servants in their own houses. I was employed by the University as a professor, so I did not come into the *Jia-shu*'s scope, but Ho Jie was there as a member of our household. It was still possible in 1966 for professors' families to employ servants. In our case, because both John and I worked and both were handicapped physically, there had never been any question about Ho Jie's presence in our home.

"No, it was a big meeting this afternoon with a PLA man talking." I knew that Ho Jie had been quite excited about it and felt it was of special importance.

John emptied the ashes out of the bottom of the red clay firepot and carefully set a fresh coal cylinder at the top, pressing it down to ignite. He fanned it gently with a battered palm-leaf fan. I watched him anxiously. So many things could go wrong with that kind of stove, burning that kind of fuel. Sometimes the mixture of coal dust and clay in the cylinders was such that they couldn't possibly ignite, no matter how many balls of old newspaper you burned underneath. Or if it did ultimately catch, it would smolder sullenly, never getting hot enough to bring water to the boiling point. When you added a new cylinder, you had to match the holes precisely and if you pressed too hard you could even cause a crack and an uncontrollable draft, making it burn too fast. Then the kettle would boil over and extinguish the flame entirely. I never knew which was the better policy to follow when Ho Jie was out: to ignore the stove entirely and risk letting it go out, or to try to add the cylinder and become personally responsible for the disaster if I did something wrong. I was thankful when John was there to cope with it. Leaving it to him, I scraped the cold rice out of the pot, daringly stole a little hot water from the tea kettle to wash it, and measured out the supply of grain for the evening meal. I knew that Ho Jie would notice if I used any hot water. Hot water to her meant fuel used up, and fuel used up was money burned.

Getting coal cylinders was a major preoccupation for every family we knew, since the amount rationed to each household per month was about enough, with careful management, to last twenty-seven days. Because most months have thirty or thirty-one days, everyone inevitably ran short. This had led to an elaborate system of alliances and credit transactions among neighbors, and with the coal delivery woman, who, happily for us, was Ah Bi's mother, a distant relation of Ho Jie's. Somehow, whenever we got down to the last cylinder she would appear with a few extra to tide us over. Those who ran out of fuel totally and lacked credit—that could happen if one's public relations were bad—had no alternative but to fetch all meals from the University canteen, along with a thermos bottle of boiled water for drinking, and just give up hot baths until the next month.

"This Cultural Revolution thing is not on the same scale as the Education Revolution of 1958," John commented. Little blue runners of flame were appearing through the holes in the cylinder now. "This time the very next day after classes were suspended on June thirteenth the students were parading, all equipped with red silk banners and drums, and ready-printed slogans and posters were all over the place. There must have been a lot of preparation going on for some time."

"Yes." I finished washing the rice, poured the milky-looking wash water into the earthenware jar in which we saved swill and scraps for the coal delivery woman's pig. "Last time there was a *Jia-shu* meeting Ho Jie brought back a big bundle of slogans all printed on red paper, and that was even before June thirteenth. Those were the ones we put up in the living room before the teachers' meeting."

At this point, in came the missing Ho Jie, her pleasant round face a little flushed from excitement and hurrying, her gold tooth flashing as her usual good-natured smile greeted us. She was wearing her second-best suit of black, shiny cotton cloth, wide flapping trousers, and a tunic that buttoned up the side; her hair was slicked back from her forehead and tightly confined in a little round bun at the back of her head. A bit of white thread on this bun indicated her status as a widow.

Ignoring John, who so recently had been "on the wall," she addressed me in the modified Cantonese in which we communicated. "Oh, Lok Tai, I mean Comrade Xia, I'll fix the rice."

"Okay," I replied (literally—Cantonese permits a good deal of liberty of this sort. Neither John nor I could speak this dialect, but Ho Jie could understand our version of Standard Chinese).

"No matter." She eyed the rice pot, which in her judgment I had overfilled, and subtracted a handful, spreading it on a plate to dry.

"A PLA comrade spoke. He explained to us all about the Great Proletarian Cultural Revolution. This is the biggest revolution of all, and all of us masses are going to be really liberated at last." Her black eyes shone with excitement. "We workers aren't going to be exploited by the *tai-tai*'s anymore. Chairman Mao has learned about our troubles and he himself is leading this revolution to final victory."

John had retired to his study and I sat on a low bamboo stool in the doorway while Ho Jie, after carefully covering her tunic with a blue cotton apron, went on swiftly and efficiently washing and chopping vegetables, keeping a weather eye on the rice pot till it bubbled, and refreshing herself occasionally with a mouthful of the cold rice.

"Just look, Lok Tai, I mean Comrade Xia." She brought out her bundle of bright red slogans from behind the screen cupboard. I noticed the slight difficulty in her speech. For years she had addressed me as "Lok Tai," meaning approximately "Mrs. Lo"; now, clearly, one of the first cultural fruits of the revolution was going to be a change in language style. The old-fashioned form of address, using my husband's family name, was one of the Four Olds which were to be criticized and rejected. I gathered that Ho Jie and all the houseworkers had been told to call the *tai-tai*'s by their maiden names instead of their husbands'. My American name of Earnshaw became "Xia" in Chinese and the revolutionary title of "comrade" was to take the place of the bourgeois *"tai"* or "Mrs."

In China names and titles are very important and have political as well as social meaning. Just as in the old extended family every member would be addressed by a title indicating his/her place in the family structure (first older sister, third younger aunt on the female side, and so on), even now, in the "socialist society," titles rather than personal names are used. In our family of four we always spoke English, and I called my husband by his Christian name, John. He called me Lu, an abbreviation of my Chinese personal name, Lu-teh (the translation for Ruth). Our children took an impish delight in addressing me as Lu, too, but only in private. It would have seemed nearly indecent to them to let anyone hear them name my personal name. They somehow never called their father anything but Daddy, which is actually nearly the same word in English and in the dialect of Hubei, John's native province.

"What are these?" I asked. She was unrolling some ten or fifteen bright red posters, about a yard long and a foot wide, each displaying a slogan in big black characters.

"These are the words of Chairman Mao himself," she announced. "We have been studying them in our small group meetings and I can read them all." She was glowing with pride. From the year of Liberation (1949) onward, she had been struggling persistently to learn to read Chinese. A peasant girl-child, growing up in a country village, married off to an opium addict in her early teens, deserted and cast off, she had earned a hard living all her life and had had no chance of schooling. In her present job as our housekeeper, she was enjoying to the full the opportunity that her membership in the *Jia-shu* organization gave her to study. Our children, during their school days, had regularly shared their lessons with her in the kitchen after supper and we were all proud of her progress.

"Oh, teach me how to say them in *putong hua*, then I'll understand what the students are shouting," I asked her. I could recognize some of the characters, enough to be able to guess which quotations they were; we had the English translation of the Little Red Book, and I had used such slogans in my language classes. Written Chinese is the same all over China, of course, and the characters convey the same meaning everywhere, but speakers of Cantonese dialect will pronounce them differently from Standard Chinese speakers.

"Of course." She was obviously pleased at the idea that she, a peasant-worker, would be teaching me, the college professor. "But now you'd better go away. I'm going to fry the cabbage and it will be too smoky for you in here." So I obediently departed.

Next morning when the marketing was done and the first flurry of the day subsided, I sought out Ho Jie again and together we put up more slogans all over the house, a pair in my study, a pair in my husband's, a whole row on the wall going up the stairs; from now on, anyone entering our front door would be greeted by the injunction "Serve the People," and inspectors of our living-dining room could study the instructions of the Chairman on every wall. A picture poster of a mass meeting in the countryside was hung near the kitchen door, and over Ho Jie's bed in her tiny cubicle went a portrait of Chairman Mao. Well pleased with the effect, we then went round the room. Pointing at each character with the feather duster, Ho Jie repeated the words carefully and clearly in her Cantonese *putong hua* for me to imitate.

The next afternoon, and the next, and the next, little housework was done in our college neighborhood, as the servants (and the somewhat dismayed *tai-tai*'s) met to discuss the meaning of the Cultural Revolution. Ho Jie would rise a bit earlier to make sure that the washing got done, and while meals became a little sketchy, no essentials were neglected. She took enormous pride in her role as housekeeper, observing carefully what we liked, and even though John had recently been "on the wall" and was still temporarily untouchable, I noticed that his favorite dishes appeared more frequently than usual.

One day Ho Jie came back from her meeting with a really shocking gleam in her eye and announced somewhat belligerently: "All you *tai-tai*'s are going to have to work from now on. The PLA comrade said so. We workers aren't going to be exploited anymore by the big cadres' wives. You won't be strutting around in silk dresses while we sweat in the kitchen."

"That's great," I agreed. "I've always worked myself and I know it's much better to work than sit around idle."

Ho Jie's gleam was somewhat dimmed. She seemed to feel she had perhaps gone a little too far. "That's true, Comrade Xia, you *do* work, too."

"You help run the house so I can serve the people by teaching; isn't that how it is with us?" I asked.

"Yes, yes." She was relieved to realize that she was not being totally exploited by a bourgeois *tai-tai.* "That's so. My brother—he's a Party member [of course, I knew that well; it was the glory of Ho Jie's life]—my brother told me Norman Bethune was a foreigner [Canadian]; he was a doctor and he served the people in medicine. You serve the people, too, by teaching."

Thankful that Brother had put this idea on record, I proceeded to ask, "About those silk dresses, Ho Jie, just think a minute. Have you ever really seen me wearing one?" After years of being refugees and moving from place to place, I was about as simply outfitted as decency would permit. Silk dresses were a dim memory. In Canton I usually wore a kind of semi-American dress, a skirt and blouse; I was rather resistant to efforts by friends to persuade me to "look like a Chinese woman" because I felt I would be play-acting. Ho Jie began to tie knots in her apron string. She looked down uneasily. "You know everything I have in my trunk—you help me air my things, and you know what I have better than anyone else in the world," I pursued the point.

"That's true, Lok Tai," she interrupted. "You really *don't* have any silk dresses, not even a new cotton dress for this summer. And you *do* work. The *tai-tai's are* different."

"Now teach me about the slogans we put up on the stairway," I said, not wanting to embarrass her by pushing the matter any further. "This one is 'getting rid of objects of superstition,' isn't it?"

"Yes," she agreed, happy to reach firmer ground. "We must cleanse our house of all superstitious pictures and stop worshiping old devils and gods." This was one of the points of the Anti–Four Olds Campaign.

"Fine," said I. "What would be a superstitious picture, Ho Jie? I don't know much about Chinese culture. Have we any things of that sort?"

She considered carefully, looking about my somewhat Spartan study. "Now dragons are *not* real. The PLA comrade says so." She looked at me challengingly. I nodded. "Lots of people, in the villages especially, believe in dragons—that is superstitious." Her manner changed. "You know, Lok Tai, when I was a girl in the village, I often saw dragons, usually early in the morning when the mist would be rising from the rice fields in the spring. Dragons are in charge of the waters, you know, so it's important not to do anything to offend them. You don't see them in the city, though, not with all this self-coming water in pipes. . . ." She automatically spat on the floor, then, embarrassed, eradicated that mistake with her bare foot.

"So pictures of dragons would be objects of superstition?" I ignored the reversion to village etiquette and picked up a small lacquer box I kept on my desk to hold paper clips and rubber bands. It was beautifully decorated with an unmistakable dragon, rising with iridescent coils out of a conventionalized cloud pattern.

"There now," she brightened up, "you should get rid of that, Lok Tai."

"Okay," I said meekly. "If you advise it, it shall go."

I began removing the contents. Ho Jie looked dubious. "But you really need that box to keep your things in," she remarked, flicking imaginary dust off the corner of the desk with her apron in an abstracted way.

"Yes, I do," I answered carefully. "But I don't want anyone to think we are not carrying out the directives about superstitious objects. I say"—inspiration struck me—"would it do if I just covered up the dragon with a piece of paper?"

Ho Jie looked pleased. In no time we had securely pinned that dragon down with a respectful square of red paper. My paper clips were put back, and I must admit in all candor that we had no trouble from dragons thereafter.

We went on with the search. I was glad that I had already put away one or two surviving prints of Western paintings, a small Sistine Madonna and Saint Genevieve watching over sleeping Paris. I had had a premonition that Saint Genevieve would do better in the obscurity of a trunk, after the Red Guards' visit. Happily they had not recognized her. The picture of the Sistine Madonna had been covered over with a harmless landscape. When we looked into Ho Jie's tiny sleeping room off the kitchen, she unhesitatingly pulled out a box of incense sticks and announced a trifle defiantly, "I just burn these to get rid of mosquitoes."

"Of course," I answered. "I would use them myself except that they make me sneeze."

In the pantry I picked up a lacquer tray, also decorated with an unmistakable dragon, on which my morning coffee normally was served. Ho Jie did not hesitate for one instant. "We use that every day," she said firmly. "That doesn't matter." And, her duty done by the dragon king and The Revolution, she proceeded to prepare the vegetables for lunch.

Some days later, in the afternoon, I went to the kitchen to make fresh tea for John and was surprised to find Ho Jie sitting on her bamboo stool, busy with one of her favorite leisure-time occupations, sorting a can of peanuts, discarding any that looked doubtful, eating one now and then, and eventually spreading the survivors on a big bamboo tray to sun. "Why, Ho Jie, don't you have a *Jia-shu* meeting this afternoon?" I asked. "I saw your friend, Hing Jie, go by some time ago."

"Oh, a meeting!" she snorted. "Talk, talk, talk. Now the *Jia-shu* worker members are criticizing the people in our neighborhood." She went on sorting the peanuts.

"Well, hadn't you better go?"

"Next time, by and by, maybe. Today they are criticizing Comrade Yuan." I made no comment. But Ho Jie had to go on. "Lok Tai, can you imagine such a thing? Her amah says that when they have meat, they send one of the children to the kitchen when she dishes it up, to count the pieces and make sure she doesn't eat any." Ho Jie's eyes were opened wide in indignation. She waited for my response.

"*Ai yah,*" I said. What else could I say? "And you don't want to criticize that?"

"Of course that shows the wrong attitude toward the working class and it is bad," she answered. "But Comrade Yuan lives in the next house, and Hing Jie lives way over in the northeast district of the college."

Red Guard actions against the Four Olds would continue intermittently for some time to come, but now, in the University, there was a shift of direction. The mass organizations were burgeoning, backing up the Red Guards in united attacks against the now officially announced targets of the revolution, the "monsters" (high Party officials who were not following the Mao line).

One evening, just at twilight of a hot, rainy day, we heard the now familiar clang of cymbals and crashing of drums down the lane and looked out to see the Foreign Languages Department Red Guards leading the whole mass of FLD students out to a "big meeting." Disregarding the light rain and the rising typhoon wind that tugged at the ranks of scarlet silk banners, they marched purposefully down the road, alternately singing the song of the season, "The Helmsman," and shouting slogans. Many carried portraits of Chairman Mao, held up on bamboo poles; many had placards with quotations from the Little Red Book held aloft in the rain. I felt John stiffen to attention as he noted the words written in big characters on one as it passed by.

"That's really important," he muttered. "That's never been put forward before in public like this."

"What is it? What does it say?"

"There goes a slogan saying, 'It's right to rebel'!"

August 1966

"DID YOU HEAR a lot of yelling this morning at the end of the road?" Tientung had, as usual, slipped in to see us and bring us up to date on the situation in the campus. (I never ceased to marvel at the way the normal routine of meal-times, rest hours, and work hours continued throughout the Cultural Revolution. The students and teachers in the mass rebel organizations ate their breakfast at the canteens at the usual hours, then went off to make revolution from seven-thirty to eleven-thirty: sometimes to accusation meetings, sometimes to demonstrations in the city, sometimes to sessions of reading and discussing the Little Red Book, sometimes to writing *da zi bao*'s, sometimes to take part in street fights. At eleven-thirty, everyone knocked off for lunch and a good nap. At two they would get back to whatever they had been doing, until five-thirty, suppertime, and then quite frequently they took on an extra shift in the evening of collective work of some kind, preparing for the next day. It was almost as if they agreed, "Tomorrow at ten-fifteen we will assemble at X place to express our flaming indignation . . ." and at the appointed hour they would be on hand to flame, often very convincingly.)

"Why? Were you there?" As usual we discussed the news while she prepared to take a bath. Hot water was scarce in the dormitory and the bathroom was the least conspicuous place to talk.

"Not I, said the little Red Hen!" She smiled ruefully. "We've had quite a busy day!"

"Come on, Red Hen, tell me!"

"Well, four of us girls were studying the Little Red Book in our room this morning, each watching the others to see what they would be doing. [The five girls, who had been sharing a room together for three years, belonged to different factions but continued to share the room to which they had been assigned.] Sue had disappeared early on, so we had a hunch we would be called out, but there was no way of knowing how, when, why, so we all kept together. It's safer if someone always knows where you are when something happens. Sure enough there was a blowing of whistles, calling everyone to line up and take part in a mass 'revolutionary action,' so down we trotted. Everyone was lined up as usual outside the dorm, people of both persuasions, all set to do something, but we masses didn't know exactly what to do."

"Who does the planning?" It seemed to me only reasonable to know who was sending whom to do revolutionary deeds.

"Oh, the collective leadership of the Red Guards." The idea of individual responsibility for such actions didn't seem important to her. I thought of the anonymous cadre on the Task Force and the impersonality of the forces that moved through our lives.

"With a good deal of shouting and gong banging, we marched off to the Midway. When we got to that small red pavilion in the middle, there were a lot of people there already, milling about and shouting slogans and yelling, and in the pavilion, like on a stage for everyone to see, they had rounded up all the Department heads in the University."

"Why?"

"Because they were 'persons in authority' supposed to have taken the capitalist road."

"What a sight! Was our FLD Number One there?"

"Of course. He was always ducking behind the others, trying to keep out of sight, but he's taller than most and he was very visible, especially in his hat."

"Do you mean they all had dunce hats on, like during the Land Reform Campaign [1951], when they paraded landlords?" I couldn't believe it.

"They certainly did—big, tall, pointed paper hats. I had no idea how horrible it would be to make a man wear a paper hat."

I was thankful that so far, in spite of the various charges that the same Department Number One had been able to organize against John, so far, my husband had never had to go through this particular kind of ordeal of public shame. The Anti-Rightist Campaign in 1958, although called a "hatting," in Zhong Da had never required any parading or wearing of dunce hats. I had heard it said that there was too little mass support of the accusations at the University for such tactics to be used. Traditionally in China, public shame has been the lot of anyone accused of any kind of crime: political or criminal, whether innocent or guilty.

"What happened next?"

"They just yelled a lot at them, each Department's students calling for their own, so to speak, and then the Red Guards made them all march around and around the pavilion, like a fashion parade, and then they were sent home—under escort—still hatted. And then our students started back, arguing as usual."

"How about the Department Number Two?"

"That's what the students were arguing about. Some said she should have been there, too, and some disagreed. They wrangled and shouted while they walked over this way. Angel and I had the bright idea that this would be a handy moment to drop in at the Clinic to get some aspirin, since we were so near. So we did." She looked demure.

"So you went to the Clinic while the rest went to call on Number Two?"

"Yes, we did. Mother, I hate cruelty, and that kind of thing *is* cruel. Maybe it is justice. Goodness knows everyone who got it today had probably done harmful or even bad things—I don't just mean they didn't follow the Party line correctly, anyone can make mistakes like that when it changes so fast—but they had all done things that would be considered unjust and mean anywhere. They had some kind of punishment coming to them. But not like that. It's degrading to see a man, even such a poor excuse as some of those were, trembling with fear, and it's just as bad to see people you have to live with howling at them."

"Did anyone notice that you and Angel had left?"

"I doubt it, but I don't care. At lunch the others were talking about what they had done. They went to Comrade Yuan's door and yelled at her to come out, and when she did, they all yelled a lot more, and some of them wanted to cut her hair—she still has the tag end of a perm, very bourgeois—and others didn't agree. I don't know if they ended up doing it or not. Anyway, they concluded that she was a 'monster,' too, and I expect they'll all have a tough time from now on."

They did. Every morning I watched the FLD's "persons in authority" going down the lane past our home, "monsters on parade." First there would be a squad of Red Guards, with their red armbands safety-pinned onto their shirt sleeves, some of them carrying theatrical-looking bamboo spears with red tassels, like children playing soldiers. Then would come four of the young political instructors, cadres who were very low in the political hierarchy, but whose power over the students was enormous. Every student belonged to a small group; every small group was directed by its political instructor, who knew everything about his students and reported to the higher authorities. A secret record was kept on file for every student, and what the political instructor put into it (never seen by the students) could make or break careers in the future. Political instructors' advice had decisive weight in the assigning of jobs after graduation; it could facilitate or frustrate student love affairs and marriages. Now the political instructors were put on the "monster" list and paraded with the rest, their expressions as they walked past ranging from sheepish embarrassment to dumb bewilderment. Like the other "monsters," they were marked with a badge of shame, a wooden tag hung round their necks, proclaiming to the world their crime in being a monster. Behind them shambled the tall, thin figure of the Department Number One, walking with head bowed, eyes on the ground, hands clasped behind his back, tagged like the others. More Red Guards brought up the rear, yelling slogans about monsters, hustling the little procession along. The parade would stop at the end of our row, and Red Guards would shout for our Department Number Two to come out, and quickly, to join the other monsters in manual labor. If she was not ready and waiting on the doorstep, there would be more pounding on the house door and more shouting to hurry her up. Then they would all be marched down the lane to a nearby field and set to digging with the heavy hoes under the hot summer sun.

I wondered what century, what world, I was living in. This punishment by public ridicule and shame, the wooden tag around the criminal's neck, these were not the political actions of people in the twentieth century, these were the traditional punishments of dynasties past in the Middle Kingdom. This casting out of the wrongdoer, degrading to both those punished and those wielding the whip—what was it doing to the people involved? This was vengeance by mob action, not justice. What would come after? I felt alien and terrified and alone.

John and I stood in the upstairs window well out of sight and watched the deposed leaders trudging by for their morning of aimless digging. (Why, when manual labor was supposed to be honored, was it chosen as punishment for wrongdoers?) I wondered what was passing through John's mind. Did this seem right to him? I had myself been present at meetings during the Anti-Rightist Campaign in 1958—and since—when these same leaders had used their power to make an outcast of him. I had heard them yell and revile him. I had shared the petty humiliations measured out to break his spirit. I had read the totally false accusations in the *da zi bao*'s written under their inspiration. Now here they were passing before his eyes, gray-faced with fatigue and shock, dirty and disheveled, yelled at by their own students, mocked by passing school children. What did it mean to John?

"They really shouldn't make Comrade Yuan do that kind of heavy labor," he remarked thoughtfully, watching our neighbor, carrying a heavy hoe over her shoulder, hasten painfully to catch up with the line as the others broke into a double-quick step. "She was really seriously ill last winter. I wonder if they realize that."

I was pretty sure they knew. And didn't care. But while I still felt terrified at the possibilities for any of us in such a situation as this, and while I still felt like a hopeless alien, I no longer feared, questioned, or doubted what John's stand would always be.

Just what was meant by the term "monster"? Was it really possible for people who had been in total control of the situation to be overthrown so suddenly and with such an outburst of personal hostility?

The English word "monster" was used then as a rather rough translation for a Chinese phrase which can be more literally rendered

as "cow-headed ghosts and snake spirits." These supernatural crea-
tures from ancient Chinese mythology had a peculiar ability to
disguise themselves and appear to be human. Thus disguised, they
could do all kinds of mischief. But once they were recognized for
what they really were, their power was broken. Chairman Mao used
the expression in some writing back in the 1960s, in connection with
the Hundred Flowers Campaign and the subsequent identification
of many of the intelligentsia as Rightists. By implication, those
"hatted" were evil spirits, doing mischief, pretending to be human.
Once they were identified, they would lose their power.

In any event, a monster, in 1966, in Canton was not to be confused with the playful "cookie monster" or similar childhood thrill-
ers in contemporary America. A monster was an outcast. Since in
Chinese they were known as cow-headed ghosts, they soon were
referred to simply as "cows," the place of their forced labor or
sometime confinement was the "cowpen," and those guarding them
were "cowherds." The connotations of the word sometimes reminded me of the lettering on ancient maps in which the borders
of the absolutely uncharted and unknowable were marked by the
ominous words: "Here be monsters." With monsters in control,
what could the people not anticipate in horrors?

Up to the middle of June 1966, a certain group of administrators
had been all-powerful in our little academic world. Continuously
flattered by obsequious inferiors in rank, they had enjoyed the best
of all the available amenities: good housing, the use of the University's cars, telephones in their homes, privileges for vacation travel,
special rations, special shopping privileges, higher salaries. By the
end of July they were prisoners on a kind of chain gang, with the
special twist that their guards looked upon them as personal enemies,
and there was no court of appeal. And this sequence of events at
Zhong Da was going on all over the country, in all cultural institutions first—presently it would engulf all administration at all levels.

Ho Jie hunkered down on the kitchen doorstep and spat elo-
quently.

"Monsters!" she muttered. "I just don't know what to think."
This was rare.

"What about them?" I asked.

"Well, the students have found a lot of them all round here," she replied darkly. "You wouldn't believe the things they found out. Now, I'm not surprised about Comrade Yuan being one. I know for a fact that her family used up their amah's meat tickets and never gave her one bite of the meat. Some people are *mean.*" She spat again. "But the things those kids are doing at the middle school next door! Did you hear about Tientung's classmate?" I hadn't.

"The one they kept back to teach in the school." I knew whom she meant, a pleasant young woman, an "overseas" girl. That is, her parents lived abroad and had sent their children back to be educated (free) in the People's Republic of China. She had not been sent up to the University, but her middle school had asked her to stay on as a political instructor. She was pretty, a little more fashionably dressed than most, but by no means conspicuously so.

"A lot of those students, dressed up as Red Guards, caught her and shaved her hair off and said awful things to her. She got away from them and ran up the stairs on to the roof and threatened to jump off if they did anything more. And I think she would, too." Ho Jie's eyes were wide with horror at the idea. It was all too easy to follow her line of thought: Tientung's classmate, what about Tientung herself?

"I'll tell Tientung to be very careful," I said. "She always stays with the girls in her room. None of the Red Guards in the University have been paying special attention to the other students."

"How can you know who is really a Red Guard?" Ho Jie had a point there.

The only insigne of the Red Guards was, after all, a strip of red cloth, easily obtained, with a few Chinese characters written on it in yellow paint. Anyone who wanted to impersonate the now all-powerful elite could easily enough do so to carry out whatever private plans he might cherish. And some of these were truly appalling. Terrifying stories circulated about luckless middle school teachers being made to kneel on broken glass to confess their "oppression of the masses" of students, to drink ink, and to eat chalk. Gangs of teen-agers roamed the streets, and terrorized teachers hid at home. Even though they might feel quite sure in their own consciences that they had never done anything to deserve these outrageous punishments, long experience with revolutionary movements made potential victims cautious. There was a well-known etiquette to follow in mass movements. If a member of the masses accused someone, anyone who defended him was acting "against the masses" and could easily find himself called out as a "counter-revolutionary." This was about the worst thing that could happen, because the burden of proof of innocence was put upon the accused.

Moreover, there were rumors of counter-revolutionaries encouraging teen-agers in these excesses in order to discredit the Red Guards. The feeling of being surrounded by unidentifiable forces pushed one to the edge of paranoia. When I saw a group walking down our lane, I held my breath till they had passed. Everyone seemed to be doing things for reasons I could not guess, according to a new set of rules, which they knew, but I didn't.

Very quickly, and apparently easily, students and teachers had developed a routine for making revolution. A few days earlier, when you met a certain cadre or teacher on the road, you nodded and smiled politely; today when you met him walking with the monsters, you yelled at him and spat. The procedure was soon structured neatly; first, presumably, would come a series of secret meetings of Red Guards and activists, "investigating" the record of the potential monster, then a great outcry over the public-address system announcing what crimes had been uncovered, what plots and conspiracies exposed. Everyone would be bidden to a meeting where the accused would have to stand before the masses, head bowed, hands on his knees, like an accused criminal, while denunciations and accusations were shouted at him. Sometimes the accused would be pushed about and manhandled. The next one saw of him, he would be in the monster herd, going off to manual labor.

The public-address-system loudspeaker was hung under the eaves of a building facing our house, so it was impossible to get away from the sound of it all day and often far into the night. I couldn't help listening all the time, even though I didn't understand what was said very well. I feared that at any moment there might be some announcement that John ought to know about—a meeting he ought to attend, an accusation he ought to be aware of—if only to warn him against his incorrigible tendency to speak kindly to people in trouble. He never seemed to learn—or heed—the rules of the revolutionary game. Besides the announcements of exposure and accusations, and the blaring forth of revolutionary songs, the loudspeaker was continuously used to broadcast such routine information as where to go for a distribution of tickets to buy fish or the time of a special showing of a movie. I didn't dare not listen—what if we didn't get a fish?—and I could hardly endure the strain of trying to sort out the barrage of words. But John didn't bother at all.

"Don't worry so," he reproached me, as for the tenth time in one morning I begged him to pay attention. "If anyone wants me, they know where I am." The words flashed through my mind, "Daily I sat among you teaching, and no one raised a hand." And I stopped pestering him.

Even worse than my constant anxiety for John's safety, and for Tientung and Mingteh, was the realization of the persistent and uncontrollable cruelty that still underlay the bright surface of the socialist society we had imagined we lived in. I had perceived cruelty and suffered from it, in connection with John's experience as an outcast, but I had never before admitted to myself that it was anything but a personal characteristic of a few individuals with whom we had chanced to come in conflict.

Now, when I saw the monsters on parade, I knew what was meant by the often quoted comment of Chairman Mao to the effect that making revolution was not like strolling in a garden. But how easily people accepted the "inevitability" of other people's pain! What had transformed the courteous, pleasant, delightful people whom I had come to love into yelling personifications of hatred? Was it a transformation or a release of something pent up and hidden all the time?

October 1966

A DAPPER LITTLE man in a faded khaki jacket and army cap stepped briskly up our walk. He looked exactly as if he thought himself the hero of a movie in which the demobilized soldier leads the masses in one of the battles of peacetime. He was followed by a still shorter man, looking precisely like everyone's conception of a *gan-bu* of good class origin, devotedly following the lead of the PLA. He was a minor official from the Clock Tower, the building housing all the University administrative offices. (The Party offices were in a separate building.) The very words "clock tower" had come to mean "bureaucracy" to everyone in Zhong Da. The two men advanced upon the front entry of my neighbor's house, the other half of duplex Number 48, and rapped smartly on the wooden door.

I was sitting upstairs in the small front bedroom, which had formerly been Mingteh's and which we had recently transformed into a study/sitting room for John and me. Even with Mingteh's poster on the street door, it seemed more comfortable to be upstairs and inside. Number 48's walls were thin and I could not help hearing my neighbor's excited remarks to her husband in the corresponding room next door.

"That's the man from the Housing Bureau," she said in hushed tones.

"I told you they'd be around." Exasperation combined with despair. "They criticized me at the meeting for occupying a whole house with six rooms when there's only you and Dee-dee and me living here now."

"But when the older children come home from school ..." Her voice was rising. She was defending her lair for her young. A second knocking at their door.

"Go let them in. There's no choice."

"I'll tell them about your illness, that you *have* to have quiet. ..." She hurried down the stairs and opened the door, all polite apologies for keeping the comrades waiting. They pushed on in. The door closed. For the next hour voices rose and fell, indistinguishable, in the downstairs study next door. I could hear Mrs. Liu's polite company voice change to one of indignation, to pleading, to hysteria, while the visitors varied from correct pompousness to righteous wrath.

Would the visitors come to our house next? If they did, how should I deal with them? John and I had already given a lot of thought to the problems of University housing. It was a matter of principle with us both not to accept privileges; they inevitably entailed obligations. This was an awkward position to maintain in a society still operating, partially, on the the age-old system of "Face, Fate, and Favor"—the person in power gives favors and face to his inferiors in return for loyalty and favors. If it was your fate to be favored you would be a fool to refuse.

So we had really been embarrassed when the administration moved us into Number 48 in 1957, when "high intelligentsia" like John were being cultivated. It was more convenient in many ways. There were three rooms downstairs, a kitchen, a cubicle for a maid (in 1957, eight years after Liberation, it was still assumed that professors employed at least one domestic and that domestics needed much less room to live in than professors did), and three bedrooms and a bath with Western plumbing upstairs. Ventilation was good except in the maid's cubicle, and it was a great comfort that we each had a study. The children enjoyed the uncommon luxury of rooms of their own, and the master bedroom had a delightful little recessed balcony looking into a clump of bamboos. The only drawbacks were our awareness that nothing is ever done in China for no reason, and that there were others more needy of room and equally deserving of having it.

However, when Tientung moved into the college dormitory and Mingteh went to become a commune member, we decided that for two people to occupy so much space was not fair. When our children were small and we needed more space, we had often said that it was one of life's ironies that senior teachers with no children at home were usually given more and better housing than the young families whose lives would be so much easier if they had a bit more room.

Now we were senior, we didn't intend to do what we had disliked having done to us.

Therefore, some time before the beginning of the Cultural Revolution, we had written to the housing authority at the Clock Tower asking to be moved into smaller quarters. Frankly, this was not pure altruism as far as I was concerned. I could foresee that sooner or later the inequity of the housing was bound to cause some kind of explosion, and I knew that there would be quite justifiable criticism of people occupying more space than they really needed. A small cottage would suit the two of us very well. However, no one had answered our request. We were naïve not to realize at the time that our acting in such a way would embarrass other senior teachers who might not share our views. When the Cultural Revolution came along, we were still rattling around in our "palace." Tientung had a room at home for weekends, and Mingteh's books, maps, radio parts, records, and electronic odds and ends occupied his former quarters, although his removal to the commune had been officially registered in the *hukou* (the little brown paperback book that constituted the permit to live in a particular place).

When we heard on the public-address system that the mass organizations were going to reform the housing distribution as part of the revolutionary program, we knew that we would certainly have to move. We decided to disarm criticism by contracting, voluntarily, into the upstairs rooms, preparing for eventual removal into our dream cottage. In September the move was made . . . and so it was that we were comparatively well prepared for the visit of the new housing authorities that fine October day in 1966.

After an hour's impassioned rhetoric next door, the team moved on to our house. Ho Jie admitted them with the kind of sniff reserved for people who came to the front door who should have come to the back. They seemed to delay downstairs (presumably looking over the now nearly empty rooms), then marched up to our little common room.

"Good morning, comrades," I greeted them politely. "Please sit down."

They grunted rather than greeted, and sat down suspiciously on the wicker chairs. (People of our rank were universally presumed to loll upon nothing but "sofa chairs," overstuffed easy chairs covered Russian-style with white slipcovers and piled with cushions, incomparably uncomfortable in hot, humid Canton, but a prestige symbol few would forgo. New acquaintances seeing our home for the first time often expressed surprise at the absence of teakwood and sofas. It seemed wrong that I didn't want what was a status symbol to them.)

"You are living in a house that could accommodate far more people," began the man in khaki severely. "The masses demand that you give up this space. Many of the workers in this University are living in just one room with all their families. Why should you have all this luxury while they suffer?" He was getting up steam.

"That's just what I think, too," I broke in. "In fact we had asked to be moved to smaller quarters some time ago, when both our children left home. We would be perfectly satisfied to live in the upstairs here, except that there's no kitchen. Could we keep the use of the downstairs kitchen and Ho Jie's bedroom next to it?"

The PLA type looked questioningly at the *gan-bu* type and the latter confirmed my statement about our having already applied for smaller quarters, looking somewhat miserable as he did so. "We'll see. Be ready to have everything out of the downstairs *at once.* Someone will be moving in *immediately.*" The PLA type had come prepared to struggle, but, lacking opposition, was deflated.

"Very well." I rose in a hostess-dismissing-visitors manner, holding out my hand. "There's one big table downstairs that belongs to the college, and a big bookcase. I'll have them sent back as soon as the Clock Tower can send someone for them. We will welcome anyone who comes to share the house." At the moment I meant it. After a while I was to recall that remark with mixed emotions. With a limp handshake the two departed, and Ho Jie came to review the situation and forecast woe.

"Well, the housing people came this morning," I told John over our lunch. "Just as we feared, someone will move in downstairs, but we can keep the kitchen."

"What about the bathroom?" said practical John.

"Oh, my word, I never asked! They'll have to put in some kind of facilities under the stair, like they did in our neighbor Liu's house." I felt a cold premonition of disaster ahead.

"They'll have to," John reassured. "Who is moving in?"

"Oh, Joe Doakes or Richard Stokes, who knows?" I answered. And diverted by this bit of linguistic delicatessen, we went on to other things, but "Joe Doakes" was inevitably thereafter our private name for our future housemate.

Poor Joe Doakes. As fate would have it, he turned out to be the dapper man in pseudo-uniform himself. For weeks we lived in suspense, not knowing who was to come in. He spent these weeks trying to find something a little more advantageous, but when the time limit for moving drew near, the man in khaki decided our space was the best he could find.

At the time of assigning space, he registered his family as including himself, his wife, two children under the age of three, his crippled sister-in-law who kept house for them, his wife's aunt (who actually had housing at the primary school where she taught), his aged mother (who lived in the country and didn't want to live in town at all), and a general baby-sitting teen-ager. When I thought of eight living in one room and their happy expansion into our three rooms downstairs, I tried not to be too severe in judging them. However, I was not displeased when his aged mother returned to her village after a token appearance, and when it turned out that the aunt only came for weekends. Accustomed as I was to doing a good deal of academic work at home in my study, I couldn't see how six people could manage in the space they had now, but I was yet to learn about proletarian lifestyles.

Home for the "Doakeses" was just the place where one slept, and a private room for husband and wife was a luxury. Mrs. Doakes worked in a nearby factory and ate most of her meals there. The three-year-old girl went to the nursery and ate there. The teen-ager would disappear for hours at a time, carrying the baby who knows where. Joe Doakes himself was usually at meetings, where he was an active, very active, Committee man, struggling for the rights of the downtrodden, meaning, a lot of the time, the rights of Joe Doakes.

Yet, wasn't that what everyone else was doing? Trying desperately to seize the chance to improve the standard of living for his family and himself?

Born and raised as a peasant in a poor village outside Canton, having served briefly in the PLA, Joe Doakes had been transferred to work at the University in the Physical Education Department, teaching motorcycling, a skill he had learned in the army. "Good class origin," political zeal, and a technical skill had made possible a dizzy ascent from the rice fields, and now only in his early thirties, he had risen to the position of a member of the teaching faculty of a major university. He was deeply convinced that he and his family and all his "class brothers" had been badly treated in the past, and he was out to get back a bit of his own. He was easily persuaded by political education to believe that anyone who had something he wanted had taken it from him and was a personal enemy. The more his life improved, the more bitter he became.

Late in the evening of the last day when moving was permitted, there was a pounding on the front door. I heard Ho Jie let someone in, and then a good deal of loud excited talk. I recognized Joe Doakes's voice of authority and heard Ho Jie shifting gears from frigid politeness to rage. John was already in bed. I hastened down. In the doorway to my erstwhile living room stood Joe Doakes, armed with a large new broom, and behind him a pretty little woman, his wife, clutching a feather duster in one hand and a mop in the other. Ho Jie, arms folded over a bosom heaving with wrath, said over her shoulder to me, "They say they are moving in tomorrow and they think they have to clean the rooms tonight."

The next day, when they moved in, Joe Doakes immediately established belligerency as the mode of life among us. He announced sharply and loudly to his assembled family that the upstairs rooms were occupied by a convicted Rightist and a foreign woman and the duty of every one of the masses was to supervise them continuously and keep them from doing any more bad things. My heart sank as I heard his fiery harangue. I had done all I could and had urged a reluctant Ho Jie to do all she could to help them move in. She had boiled drinking water for them and helped to move boxes to clear the way for the promised WC in the stairwell. No matter what we might do, it was impossible to make friends. We were just the wrong kind of people.

Confronting John at the front door one day, Joe Doakes demanded he give up our key to the Yale lock (we had given him an extra key already) and use only the back door, which had only a bolt on the inside, thus requiring someone to come down to open it. John stood looking at him patiently until his oratory dried up, and then answered quietly, "We can use both doors, just as we do now," and went on his way.

"How can you stand him?" I asked when I heard of it. "I get so mad I could pop when he goes on like that."

"No use for two people to get mad at once," he rejoined. "A lot of the time he is not really responsible for what he does, Lu. You know he is suffering from cancer of the throat and probably half the time is taking Chinese [herb] medicine for the pain."

"No, really?" I cried. "Lord send me patience."

Poor Joe Doakes, Poor Joe Doakes.

Ah Bi's mother was sitting on the brim of a big tattered bamboo hat in the shade of Ho Jie's hopvine, resting after delivering our monthly ration of coal cylinders for the coal stove. Since her daily task was delivering the big baskets of coal, she was naturally rather coal-dusty, but she never failed to whisk the dust off her hat brim before sitting on it. Outdoor workers in South China nearly all wear big straw or woven bamboo hats, which are perfect protection against the sun and rain, and are also used to sit on. Although Ah Bi's mother wore inevitably soiled clothes, she wouldn't dream of sitting down on the ground and getting her trousers dirtier. If she sat down on the bench in Ho Jie's clean kitchen, she would normally blow imaginary dust off it first.

Her thin gray hair was gathered into a little knob on top of her head; her face was tanned by the sun and lined with years; her teeth were few and far between; her old-fashioned country-style tunic was patched and faded; her bare feet, gnarled and coated with coal dust. She was fanning herself with the folded newspaper that Ho Jie saved from the study wastebasket for her, and drinking appreciatively from one of our kitchen bowls what I hoped was a foretaste of today's soup. Unless you looked at her eyes, you might think she was just a dirty old peasant woman, pitiable perhaps in the hard life she obviously must live and have always lived. But if you were privileged to meet her on something approaching equal terms, you realized that here was a power in the land. She was a self-supporting woman. Neither her daughter, a medical worker in Peking, nor her son, Ah Bi, the carpenter, could persuade her to give up the independence and status that her labor, carrying coal, assured her. Her voice had to be listened to in the council of the *Jia-shu;* she had a say in the allocation of fuel, and she enjoyed her power. She and Ho Jie were enjoying a muttered discussion of Joe Doakes. I caught Ho Jie's words, "and they light the stove every mealtime in the stair hall, and you can hear Lok Sam [Cantonese for Mr. Lo] coughing a block away."

It was true. By now the Doakes family had taken over what had been Ho Jie's cubicle, to use as their kitchen, and Ho Jie was sharing Tientung's upstairs bedroom. In order to get a good draft to start the sulky coal cylinders, the Doakeses usually put the clay firepot out into the central stair hall, where a fine updraft speeded combustion and distributed the fumes and smoke into our quarters. If John was home, this would bring on a spasm of coughing most undesirable for his heart. The penetrating fumes were quite sickening to anyone, but really dangerous to him.

"That's bad, very bad," pronounced the sybil under the hopvine. She spat, averting evil. "Lok Sam is a good-hearted man." With that I fervently agreed in silence. She looked thoughtfully up at the window over the stair landing. My thought followed hers and inspiration came.

Ah Bi, the son of this powerful visitor, was a carpenter. (Incidentally, that she was known everywhere by the title "Ah Bi's mother" was a concession to country style, actually a courtesy title.) Ah Bi was a rough, tough character, but he was an independent craftsman, not answerable to any small group for what he might do in the way of odd jobs. He was clearly a working-class man, no capitalist, but he owned his own tools. Even after completion of the socialization of all industry and commerce in 1956, workers like Ah Bi—cobblers, repairmen, umbrella menders, and the like—were allowed to "serve the people" independently. Ah Bi could take on a job without permission of the Clock Tower.

I stepped down into the kitchen and greeted Ah Bi's mother, who was squatting by the open door. We exchanged courtesies.

"I suppose Ah Bi is very busy these days," I remarked, plucking and handing her a few clusters of hop blossoms from our vine (they are excellent in soup). And then in the time-honored way of China we proceeded into a negotiation for services that undoubtedly prolonged John's life.

It had occurred to me, all in a flash, that Ah Bi might enclose the staircase with plywood and ingenuity and hang a door that would firmly shut off our three upstairs rooms from the downstairs and funnel the undesirable smoke out the landing window. And so in a few days, with greater speed than I would have dared hope, timing his visits on occasions when Joe Doakes should be absent on revolutionary business, Ah Bi measured and plotted and all in one swift evening's labor accomplished our seclusion.

When Joe Doakes came home late that night to find the completed installation, there was eloquent silence. Ah Bi was putting the finishing touches on the door, which was equipped with another Yale lock, a good deal stronger than its surrounding plywood, but a clear indication of our intent. I could imagine Joe Doakes at the foot of the stairs looking up at Ah Bi and I rejoiced in the reflection that Ah Bi was a good deal bigger and had a fearsome reputation. Nothing was said by either. Finishing his work, Ah Bi walked slowly down past Joe and out the back door, leaving us happily locked within. I have seldom seen anything more beautiful than the inside of that locked door.

September 1966

"HAVE WE GOT an old knapsack anywhere? I mean a really old one." Tientung was rooting frantically in her locker box. It was a steaming summer morning at the end of August. Our clothes stuck to us, and our search through our resources for warm clothing seemed too insane to examine, but it had to be done, for the word had gone out that all the student masses of Zhong Da were to go to Peking to take part in the third great mass reception of Red Guards by Chairman Mao in Tien An Men Square. The first and second receptions in August, when the Red Guards had been officially recognized, had aroused tremendous enthusiasm. The present widening of the scope to include all students, whether Red Guard elite or merely masses, had started a frenzy of organization in Canton.

A few lucky ones of extraordinary virtue and zeal had gone from Zhong Da to the first two great meetings, and on their return they had passed the word that it was COLD in Peking, a thing hard for Cantonese to imagine in summer; they normally shiver when the thermometer goes below seventy degrees.

"Now here's your light sweater; that ought to be enough. What about bedding?" I had packed the children off to country duty many times by now, and knew pretty well what would be needed: a mat to lay on the floor (or ground) to sleep on, a mosquito net and a quantity of tape and some clothespins to hang it up with, a sheet or terry-cloth blanket in summer, washbasin, cup, bowl, spoon, and, for a trip longer than a weekend, a pail in which to carry water—to bathe and wash clothes.

"We're not supposed to take much, no more than each can carry herself, of course. We're to stay at some school, I hear—we won't know till we get there. I'll see what the other girls at the dormitory take. But I *must* have a knapsack for my clothes and odds and ends . . . like everyone else's."

"Probably there are thousands of knapsacks piled up at Chang Ping." Every time Mingteh came home from the commune for a visit, he took back a full bag, and never returned it to Canton again, though he never came home empty-handed. His welcome offerings of sugar, fruit, fish, and whatnot from the commune came wrapped in old newspapers or lotus leaves. "Can you buy something at the Phoenix [the slightly inflated name of the local State department store near Zhong Da]?" I inquired.

"Well, I'll look. Angel wanted to go shopping after lunch."

"Do you have enough money for the trip?"

"Oh, yes, plenty. We don't have to pay for our fare, and the University will transfer our meal tickets from the student canteen here. There won't be time for much shopping, anyway. Every minute will be organized, I expect."

"Hadn't you better take some extra money, just in case of emergency?" I had never outgrown the bourgeois notion that money equaled security when you left your home base. I had not ever really shared the children's experience of moving about taking my home base with me. From first grade onward they had been accustomed to being organized for large group maneuvers, whether for all-day excursions or for prolonged stays in the country at villages or at mass worksites. Before they were in their teens, they had already had considerable experience in managing their own affairs as members of their age group or class, and they felt perfectly secure in the context of their team. Everyone took the same equipment; no one took more than his comrades did. Everyone had the same amount of money. To have more would have been shameful. I didn't press the point. But I did suggest, "Do you want your cousin's address in Peking? I know you won't be likely to have a chance to visit aunt and uncle, but you might drop them a postcard just for courtesy."

"I could do that. I'll write it here in the back of my Little Red Book."

I felt better when that was done. I had no idea of what she was going into, but the security of a family connection was the best I could offer under the circumstances. After all, I told myself, she's twenty-four, and has traveled before.

After lunch she came in again, more than a little ruffled. "The only bags they had at the Phoenix were these." She tossed on the table a rather pretty gray plastic shoulder bag with zipper pockets. It looked all right to me, just the right size, modest, and rather pleasing.

"The girls said that would never do, it's too bourgeois. But Sue had an old army packsack of her brother's and she'll lend it to me, only it needs mending. Could you . . . ?"

"Okay. Hand it over. I'll absorb the bourgeois one for my knitting; then it won't be wasted." I got busy with patches and darning thread and plugged up the more serious holes in the rather dirty khaki backpack. It looked satisfactorily proletarian when I had finished. While I sewed, Tientung was gathering together some notebooks from her trunk.

"Can you put these somewhere safe?" she said, wrapping them up in a bit of old newspaper. "Destroy them if you have to, but don't let anyone get hold of them."

"What on earth are they?"

"Oh, just some of my own poems, and the story of the Green Mouse I made up for Mingteh when he was little. Goodness knows they aren't political, but I hate to think of some people I know trying to interpret them. It could be very inconvenient for me if the wrong guys try to figure them out." I agreed and undertook to do my best. So far we had only experienced that one rather ludicrous house visit by the Red Guards looking for the Four Olds at the onset of the Cultural Revolution, but I had seen and heard enough since then to become cautious. I thought it likely that Mingteh's poster on the front door had disarmed other eager searchers after that first visit.

"Good-bye now. We'll start early tomorrow. The Algerian teacher from the French Section is going with our small group. I'm in the 'weak and feeble' contingent as usual," she sighed.

It was taken for granted that in all mass activities there would inevitably be a few comrades with physical disabilities. Instead of leaving them out, the University always provided at least one unit that would have somewhat lighter duties. In the competitive days of adolescence this had rankled, but by this time Tientung accepted the fact of her lameness. (Like me, she had a congenital dislocation of the hip and could not carry heavy loads or walk great distances.

Instead of attempting the impossible, she had learned to develop other skills—cooking, repairing things, first aid—that made her a welcome member of any work team.) I was relieved to hear that the French Section teacher (who suffered from heart disease) would be in charge of her group. Under his leadership they would not have to carry heavy loads or walk too far.

"Well, have a good time and take good care of yourself. I *won't* worry," I lied cheerfully, anticipating her usual injunction when she was about to disappear into the depths of the People's Republic, beyond my reach, with no possibility of writing, certainly no phone calls or telegram upon arrival.

"So long! Trust the masses!" And she was off, swinging her appropriately patched bag. I set to work to repack the locker box and find a safer hiding place for her literary efforts.

I heard from Ho Jie, who knew everything, that Tientung and her classmates had got off early in the morning, and that she was riding in the truck on top of the baggage. The others were walking, marching, with banners and cymbals and slogans, to the railway station, some thirty minutes by truck across town.

"There's going to be a film tonight, Lok Tai," said Ho Jie, "showing the second Tien An Men reception. Wouldn't you like to go? They say you can see Chairman Mao real plain."

Regardless of that aspect of the treat, I appreciated her understanding of my anxious interest in seeing what Tientung was going into, and thanked her from the bottom of my heart. "Are you going?" I asked.

"Of course. All the *Jia-shu* are going. Would you like to come with us?" This was most tactful. She knew John would not feel at ease— he was "off the wall," but you could never tell what might develop in a crowd.

"I'd love to."

"Good. We'll take your bench and go early and get a good place."

And so we did. Free movies were normally shown every Saturday night on a big square field near the front gate of the University compound. On two sides were student dormitories—lucky souls who lived there could sit on their windowsills and enjoy the show. A

pretty little red-painted pavilion with curling eaves occupied a platform at the south side and served as a projection booth. The screen
was hung from poles in the middle of the field, and the audience sat
on both sides—nobody seemed to mind which. Everyone who could
walk or be carried went to the community show on Saturday, and
the general atmosphere was very pleasant and neighborly. Traditionally, the high brass sat on the platform on chairs arranged just in
front of the projection booth. For one very brief period I had occasionally been privileged to sit there; but when John was "hatted,"
of course he could not, so thereafter I would not. The *Jia-shu*, the
primary school pupils, the various University classes and depart-
ments sat on the ground in their accustomed places, or brought
along small bamboo stools or straight-backed, exceedingly uncomfortable wooden chairs. These last were a great menace to the un-
wary in the homeward-bound procession after the show. People
carrying them would set them down in the path and the small sleepy
children would stumble over them, and the careless dropped them
on other people's bare feet. All round the outside edge of the crowd
were bicycles, which gave a slight advantage to those who cared to
perch on them for three hours. What seemed like ten thousand
babies regularly attended, strapped on their mothers' backs; at first
they shouted hilariously, then wailed a little from fatigue, and usually
were sound asleep by the end of the first newsreel. Students attended
in groups; dating by couples was sometimes in fashion, sometimes
severely frowned upon.

   It seemed queer at first to see no students at the show—they were
all in Peking of course—but the field was packed just the same.
People from the street outside the compound had been invited to
come in to see the historic event on screen. Slightly off-key, but at
maximum volume, the strains of "The Helmsman" and "The Eight
Disciplines" alternated to entertain the crowd until the film should
arrive. It was being shown at another open-air cinema down the
road, and would be rushed to Zhong Da by motorcycle. As soon as
the showing at Zhong Da was over, the reels would be hurried off
to another waiting audience. Crowds in China don't seem to mind
waiting. People mill about and chat, children run about underfoot.
Tired people slip off their shoes and fan themselves and enjoy the

refreshment of the steady south wind blowing, blowing through the bamboos. A few children may have brought along their after-supper piece of candy to enjoy while waiting, but there is not the general eating and drinking in such gatherings that one would see in America.

At last, "The East Is Red" (not the national anthem). The Great Portrait of the Great Man appears on the screen, to preface the Great Event. There is a scattered shouting of *"Mao Zhu-Xi Wan Sui"* (Long live Chairman Mao) and a respectful quieting down, then the familiar scenes of Peking streets leading to Tien An Men Square. We see orderly throngs of Red Guards filing in to take their places.

One thing is immediately clear. This is no mob scene. I could almost guarantee that every person of the tens of thousands of people pouring down all the side streets into the Square is authorized to be there, known by someone to be there, and responsible to someone above him *for* being there. The organization of so many people for such a meeting is staggering. Many people in PLA uniforms can be seen among the crowd, but there is no visible military presence managing the multitude. Everyone seems to know where he is going; there is no pushing into empty spaces reserved for some other group, no disorder. Those already at their assigned spot sit on the ground, many small groups reading The Little Red Book in silent devotion; some burst out shouting slogans or quotations, some sing revolutionary songs. It is not a carnival atmosphere, nor is it exactly tense; one feels the excitement and enthusiasm building up. Those who arrived first had obviously waited for hours before the reception began. The inevitable question of how one gets through an eight-hour wait is answered by the presence of army sanitation trucks coming and going at strategic spots.

Now a wind seems to blow through the Square. Everyone is on his feet, shouting *"Mao Zhu-Xi Wan Sui."* Then the great moment, as the tall stout figure in army uniform becomes visible on the rostrum, waving and beaming. Cameras pick up faces of Red Guards in the crowd—rapt, ecstatic, and so young—in this moment of unparalleled solidarity with their generation. I think of my daughter as one of that mass and forget to watch the screen. What is it doing to all of them? Will the girl who comes back be the same?

I didn't receive the postcard from Peking until the actual day Tientung returned. Weary and travel-stained contingents began to trudge down the lane past our house, and presently the truck with the baggage and "feebles" rolled by and I knew she would be checking in.

Soaking in a tub of hot water (to celebrate her return, Ho Jie allowed her three thermos bottles), she shared bits of the experience, somewhat incoherently. "It was awfully hot and noisy on the train—continuous broadcasting—but we took turns sitting down and sleeping," she reassured me. "We waited hours at the Peking Railroad Station, then we were taken in trucks to various universities and schools where we were put in classrooms. Only it was so crowded when we got there, we had to sleep in a drafty corridor. Not until after the reception did we dare go out on our own for fear that we'd miss it. Oh, I forgot to give you and Daddy your presents! After the reception we had three days when we could go sightseeing; the Forbidden City, the Summer Palace, the historical museums, and so on. At first we were in our groups, very organized, then we got more independent and went around as we liked. I think almost everyone brought back some kind of souvenir and there must have been millions of photographs taken of 'me at Tien An Men.' People were lined up to get pictures with the historic background."

"Did you get some pictures?" I knew how she hated ceremonial picture taking.

"Well, you know how some of the boys are, absolutely daft about taking photographs. They'd rather take a picture of something than look at it." I knew. Everyone I knew had a photograph album filled to overflowing with the socially required pictures recording identical moments in their personal histories: the primary school classmates en masse, complete with teachers in the front row; "our class picnic at the park"; our best friend; the graduation pictures; and now for this generation everyone would have "me at Tien An Men."

"What about our presents," I reminded her.

"Well, I got Daddy some Chinese medicine. It's a kind of plaster that's supposed to be very good for lumbago. They call it 'dogskin,' though it isn't really," she insisted, "but you can't get it anywhere but in Peking."

"Daddy will be really pleased. How did you think of it?"

"On the train going north we discussed what we would buy, and all the girls thought that would be the best thing to get for him. They remembered how he had lumbago last spring when he lectured to our class and they thought this might help it."

The implications of this, as to "mass attitudes" toward John, soaked in. "And what did you bring for me?"

"Everything I wanted to buy was too expensive," she regretted, "and not suitable for the occasion. In the end I just brought you a picture of the Temple of Heaven."

And the implication of this also soaked in. For well she knew the family story of how her father and I had become engaged at the Temple of Heaven in 1936. A lifetime ago in another world. I no longer feared that our daughter had come back alienated.

"How was it at the reception?"

"Crowded," she answered succinctly. "We were alerted to eat breakfast very early. I was smart and didn't drink anything. I took my *man-tou* [steamed bread] and a canteen full of water, but some foolish souls tanked up on *hsi-fan* [watery rice gruel]. They regretted it by the end of the morning! Some spent most of the time standing in line to get into the sanitation trucks. It was comparatively easy for us to get to the Square, because Comrade Lin got the use of the PLA truck to take us near and then ran interference for us through the crowd. We all hung onto each other's shirt-tails like kindergarteners. We had a pretty good place, too, and when we got there, we just sat down and waited."

"Was it thrilling?" I pressed.

"Yeeess. It was exciting to think that I was one in a million for once," she said slowly. "But never again! It makes you feel that you are dissolving. Of course, at the reception I wasn't with my own group, but with the whole set of feebles from the University," she added.

As often before, I wondered at the quality and degree of her identification with her "group." Mingteh had the same capacity for integration with his peers. The experiences they did not share with their own group lacked reality. Nothing in my experience came near it.

"After the reception was over, I found Sue and Angel and the other girls in our room and we went together for our sightseeing and shopping, and that was more fun," she continued. "The Red Guards were having meetings, of course, but we masses got a good look at the old palaces and parks. The city was just packed with students, and the local people were very nice to us, though it must have been an awful nuisance to them. Buses were so packed you couldn't get near a conductor to pay your fare, and eating places were hopelessly crowded."

"What did you eat? Did you like Peking food?"

"I lived mostly on *man-tou* and noodles—no hardship for me— but the other girls got hungry for rice. It was interesting being part of a historical event in a way."

"How did you feel?" I pressed the question, trying to ask what I really wanted to know: "Did you feel at home there? That you belonged with the masses?"

"When I was with Sue and my other roommates, I just felt I was with Sue and my other roommates. But at the reception I felt like an observer from outer space."

The reception at Peking marked the beginning of a new phase of the Cultural Revolution at Zhong Da. In the previous months there had been a breathtaking series of events. First the rather formal announcement that the Cultural Revolution was beginning, then the phase of the pre–Four Olds Campaign, when the threatened leadership tried to divert the aroused students into criticizing the old professors; then the Task Force's redirection of the attack and the Red Guards' leading the masses to bring down the local "monsters." The mass organizations developed, merged, and polarized into two factions, which struggled, sometimes with leading figures in the University, then with the city administration, and then more and more often with each other. The autumn of 1966 and the whole of 1967, at Zhong Da, in Canton, and all over the nation, saw a series of confrontations of increasing sharpness: clashes between groups of Red Guards, between Red Guards and the authorities, and between the mass organizations under Red Guard leadership.

In the midst of chaos a kind of revolutionary order soon developed. Students continued to live in their dormitories, they ate at their usual dining halls, and, most important of all, they drew their stipends and meal tickets as usual. Not everyone, certainly, enjoyed "making revolution" as a way of life, but no one seemed to want to go home. To do so would make one a political nonperson—and separate him from his ration book. Students drew their rice ration at the University. If they returned home without leave, they would have no rice to eat, and their families might not welcome them.

Teachers continued to draw their pay, but did not teach. Instead of going to classes, students, members of the mass organizations under Red Guard leadership, studied the Little Red Book and the directives from Peking, went to meetings, wrote *da zi bao*'s, took part in demonstrations and parades. The elite inner circles quickly developed a bureaucracy rivaling in quality the one they had just overthrown.

No one was supposed to spend revolutionary time studying ordinary classroom subjects. The only book to read was the Little Red Book of quotations from Chairman Mao. Everyone carried his own copy with him all the time, as if to be ready to refer to it in emergency for guidance, or to be able to use every leisure moment in absorbing its wisdom. Every day in the dormitory began with what presently became almost a devotional ritual of reading the Red Book and "exchanging experiences" of the enlightenment it had brought. Among teachers and students alike it was an indication of political virtue to be able to quote long passages from memory, and capping quotations was a popular leisure-time practice. The morning ritual reminded me of the ceremonial required under the Kuomintang (KMT), when public meetings and classes all began with a recitation of Dr. Sun Yat-sen's "Three Principles" and a ritual of bowing three times to the portrait of the political leader. The memorizing of long passages and the exchanging of quotations was rather amusingly like the behavior of fundamentalists identifying bits from the Bible.

Imperceptibly the cult of the personality and the Red Book grew on everyone, until it reached absurd lengths. All newspapers printed a kind of Text for the Day in a box on the front page, and it was a rare edition that lacked a picture of Chairman Mao, usually an old one, reprinted. When the cult was at its height, it became an almost criminal offense to use a newspaper in which Mao's words appeared for such ordinary purposes as wrapping fish to carry home from the market or scouring a pan. Ho Jie had always enjoyed her perquisite of keeping each day's newspapers to use or to share with Ah Bi's mother. Now she reluctantly stacked them in a carton under her bed and went back to using banana leaves for wrapping. Personal letters between friends now began with quotations from the Red Book, as it became correct revolutionary procedure to preface any written document with reference to Chairman Mao's Thoughts. Chairman Mao was supposed to be in everyone's mind, and I expect he actually was for a great many. For self-protection even nonbelievers had to develop an ability for glib quotation.

Everyone had long been wearing the little red Chairman Mao buttons—to appear in public without one would have been almost counter-revolutionary. Now they began to increase in size and vary in materials. They appeared in metal, foam rubber, plastic, and porcelain, some as big as saucers, and collecting them became a mania.

But making revolution was not the only occupation of all "the masses" at the dormitory. Some of the girls on the campus had started crocheting, of all things: beginning with netting little bags in which to carry their Red Books when on a march, then going on and on, into the manufacture of dresser scarves, tablecloths, and full double bedspreads. Tientung had tried it, and made me a quite usable beret—then tired of it. "They really just want to talk about their trousseaux, and if I begin making things like that, the girls will talk . . ." she told me.

Tientung and I were sitting on the floor in The Room, as we called our combined living room and dining room, surrounded by little heaps of scraps of cloth. In them could be read the history of our family's wardrobe for the past decade: the last remnant of the good pair of pants that had been scorched beyond repair in the campaign to make steel at school during the Great Leap Forward of 1958; the indestructible cuffs of the handsome shirt (sent from Hong Kong by a devoted aunt) never worn in public for fear of being criticized for bourgeois style; a writhing mass of neckties, never to see the light of day around anyone's neck again—for sure (the universally worn Zhongshan uniform, what Westerners persist in calling the "Mao suit," had made ties the certain badge of bourgeois life); piles of neatly trimmed squares of cotton prints (I saw bits of the lavender shirt), the best bits of school blouses and childhood shirts. I reflected on the natural history of each item. First it had been part of a length of cotton cloth, anxiously selected at the cooperative store by Tien-tung and me after much planning and measuring and calculating of cloth ration tickets. There would be the agonizing moment when the shears would cut irrevocably into it, the hopeful try-on, the pinnings and snipping, the first self-conscious wearing to school, the gradual fading under Ho Jie's powerful scrubbing, the first tear, the downgrading to a nightshirt, the remaking of the solider parts for underpants, the ultimate reluctant dismissal to the kitchen of the more hopeless shreds for use as dish rags, and the careful salvaging of buttons and the brighter bits for this scrap collection. What to do with it?

Tientung had an inspiration. "Let's make a patchwork quilt!"

The very thing. It would give us a soothing occupation during the hot days of summer and help Tientung keep out of the way of mass demonstrations. The quilt, to be made at home, seemed ideal. But I had no experience in this kind of work and no clear idea how to go about it. Inspired by some ancestral spirit, Tientung seemed to know just what to do. In a trice she had paper, pencil, and ruler and was blocking out a design, sorting out the available bits and measuring them. I could see her great-grandmother, in her cabin in the Michigan woods a century ago, laying out her scraps and planning her pattern with just the same expression I now saw on Tientung's face. "We'll make it in diamonds," she muttered happily, "big ones made out of little ones, with the brightest all round the edge, so . . . we need more red here. Have you anything else we could use?"

I debated. I had. I had kept it hidden in a variety of places all during the Cultural Revolution, not because I felt it wrong to have, but because I couldn't bear to think of Red Guards or anyone else mishandling it. When my father left China in 1950, he left in my hands an American Flag, one that had flown over the grave of his father, a Grand Army of the Republic veteran, now at rest in far Wisconsin. How better preserve it from desecration than to incorporate it, even though in little pieces, into our patchwork quilt? We talked a little about the old Captain and his pioneering wife, and then lovingly cut up the relic into the shapes and sizes that would blend most happily into the monumental work. We spent many satisfying hours together, snipping and combining, and when the whole was finished, it was a triumph. How did she know how to make a classic diamond-pattern quilt cover? She had never seen one, I was sure. But it was a beauty! The final touch was a border cut from the old Christmas stockings, bright red and still furry flannel.

"Will you use it this winter at the dorm?" I asked when we had finished admiring it, all lined and pressed and ready to cover the padded cotton inner quilt.

"No. I think this is for Mingteh," she answered slowly. "It's big enough, for one thing, and I think he ought to have the flag."

April 30, 1968

IT WAS THE eve of May Day.

I could tell that John's blood pressure was up. Around holidays like October First (National Day) and May Day (International Labor Day) there was always additional political tension; more meetings, more demonstrations, more likelihood of bloody confrontations between the factions. Although he said nothing about it, he was worried about Tientung and the possibility of her being dragged into some situation of real danger. And on her side Tientung was always anxious for fear something she might do would bring the attention of the warring factions on her father. In recent weeks, however, the situation on the campus had been comparatively quiet, as the students took more active part in the struggles in the city. On this warm, humid April evening she had come home after dark, hoping her absence would go unnoticed. It was fairly certain that on May Day all the masses would be called out to take part in some kind of demonstration in town, and she didn't want to be involved. We had hoped Mingteh might have a holiday, but when, by nine o'clock, he had not shown up, we all decided to turn in and get a good night's rest.

Some sound outside disturbed my uneasy sleep and I looked at my watch by the feeble glow of my flashlight. It was never a good thing to show a light at night. It was just past eleven. I heard the sound of a lot of people running, in step, curiously threatening. Who could they be? A Red Guard hit squad, no doubt, out for some kind of night raid. Where were they going? Oh, not here, not to our house!

Up the front walk, still not a voice to be heard, the unmistakable sound of bamboo pikes beating at the door. Now the voices, yelling, "Open the door, come out, come out. Give up your Black Material. The masses demand that you give up your Black Material!"

Now John was awake and sitting up groggily, and Tientung was standing in the bedroom doorway, hastily pulling on her clothes. I could see Ho Jie peering out from behind the mosquito net of her bed.

For a moment I half hoped that Joe Doakes's enemies had come to deal with him but that faded instantly as the voices took up the cry, "Lo Chuanfang, come out. Give up your Black Material."

We heard Joe Doakes shuffle to the door downstairs and call something to the raiders, and heard them parley briefly. Then the door bar was being removed, the door was opened, and there was a rush of people into the downstairs hall.

I had been too paralyzed with fright to think of what to do, but now that I realized the mob had come for John, I was galvanized into action. Quickly I pulled on a kimono and turned on the light. No use pretending we hadn't heard anything now.

"Just lie down, dear," I told John, pushing him back into bed while he fumbled about for his clothes. "Just lie down and pay no attention. I'll see what they want."

Ignoring his protests, I ran out into the hall and looked over the banister. The raiders were shouting and now someone began banging on the plywood door on the stair. Ho Jie half started down to open it, but I sharply called her back.

"They'll break it down, Lok Tai," she cried, more troubled at the picture of damaged property than frightened of the raiders.

"Let them," muttered Tientung, and then to me, "At least it's delaying them."

I ran back to the front window and looked out into the darkness. Suddenly, on an impulse, I screamed, in English, at the top of my voice, "Help, help—robbers! Help! Help!"

I didn't really think anyone would help. By now I understood all too well the Chinese philosophy of not being involved in other people's troubles. But I was under attack and felt maybe people would heed. I wasn't going to go down without at least a protest.

At the sound of my screams a stone crashed against the window frame—Tientung pulled me back. I turned off the light and ran into the hall, closing and hooking the bedroom door behind me. My chief thought was to keep John from a confrontation until, somehow, I got the invaders calmed down.

More crashing blows on the fragile plywood door and it gave way. There was a moment's push and scramble as those in front had to back down to open the door fully, then a quick rush up the stairs. The group was led by a young fellow wearing a mask. Those following were also masked and some carried pikes. All were yelling like fiends, "Come out, Lo Chuanfang, and give up your Black Material!"

I quickly stepped to the head of the stairs and, holding onto the banister, made a barrier of my walking stick. This unexpected obstacle halted the rush. I looked down on the leader and saw that he had a knife in his hand. I recognized him as a student in one of my classes and called him by name.

"What do you mean, breaking in here like a lot of hoodlums?" I scolded at the top of my voice. "You can't come in here like that. Now just get out."

The ones in back, who were pushing and shouting, suddenly halted, a little disconcerted by this unexpected resistance.

"We want your Black Material!" shouted one in English. I recognized the onetime pretender to Tientung's bicycle and realized that this was not, perhaps, an entirely politically pure excursion.

"What do you mean, Black Material?" I half turned to Tientung, who was standing behind me, steadying me. Without my stick I was apt to fall down. "What do you mean?" I asked again.

"Let us in," they badgered, and to my hysterical amusement I could also hear John, locked inside the bedroom, calling, "Let me out!"

Seeing that Tientung was there, they knew that they would be recognized. Those behind began to push harder; then there was a general scramble. Someone grabbed my arm and pushed my stick away and the mob rushed in. Instinctively I turned into Ho Jie's room. Some followed me, while others rushed past into the living room. Ho Jie screamed and the invaders backed off from her. She was a "member of the working masses" and they did not intend to tangle with *her.*

I continued to scold and yell like a fishwife. "Who are you, coming in here like this? Are you gangsters?" They really were rather startled at my fierceness. I had always been known as a very mild-tempered person and perhaps they had counted on my timidity.

I was even surprised myself to find I was literally seeing red at the thought that anyone should break into my home by force and threaten John and Tientung. I was ready to scratch, kick, and bite.

"We are a revolutionary mass organization," rather pompously announced the masked leader with the knife, "and you must cooperate."

"If you call it cooperation when you go after an old woman with a knife and force your way into a private house in the middle of the night, then I *am* cooperating," I shouted. "What's your name, anyway?" I knew it and he knew that I knew it, but he answered. "Li Ming."

"Li Ming!" I snorted. "Li Ming! Li Ming is *nobody!*" Li Ming was the name of a character in the dialogues memorized so painfully by the first-year students in English. I had created Li Ming myself and the ridiculousness of it brought me some self-control.

"We intend to find your Black Material," he repeated woodenly.

"Go on and hunt," I answered. "I don't know what you mean."

I don't think they were too sure themselves what they expected to find. (To this day I am still not clear what was truly meant by Black Material—it changed according to who was demanding it.) They now began a desultory, rather aimless search, turning over papers on John's desk, ruffling through the book shelves, opening and closing drawers at random. Suddenly someone realized that they had not yet seen the innocent object of all this uproar.

"Where is Lo Chuanfang?" they demanded now.

"He's very ill," I replied, "but if you must talk with him, I'll see if he can come out."

By this time the twenty-odd young men were scattered about the living room and balcony; some tried to search Ho Jie's room, only to be fiercely repelled by that enraged, though frightened, inmate.

I unhooked the bedroom door and found John sitting on the edge of his bed, fanning himself gently. "Why did you lock me in?" he reproached me. "What do the boys want?"

"Black Material," I answered. "Can you come and talk to them? They're somewhat calmer now." I led him, resisting my exaggerated aid, to a chair in the living room, waving aside the inquisitors who pressed around.

"Tientung, get your father's medicine," I commanded. "And a

glass of hot water." She obeyed and we fussed around him, keeping off the visitors, who by now were getting quite tired of it all, and some, who were really embarrassed, tried to keep out of the way, hoping not to be noticed.

For the next hour or so they interrogated him, first in a bullying manner. "Why don't you come clean and tell the people what you have really done?" Then little by little, his calm, patient replies completed the disintegration of morale begun by my unexpected resistance and ferocious scolding. Presently the interrogation deteriorated into a dialogue between John and one of the more senior students, as far as I could understand, mostly about John's foreign education and his contacts with Americans before Liberation. Since John had not written or received foreign mail for many years, we could not produce anything to satisfy them. I had kept my own correspondence with my family in America to an absolute minimum and never kept letters after reading them. The only English letters in the house were a few from Mingteh to me, which I had sentimentally treasured for their evidence of his growing skill in expression. I didn't mention them to the interrogators.

Tired by their own exertions, the raiders now gathered themselves together and made as good an exit as they could, stopping at the head of the stairs for one more organized slogan shout, and then departed, warning us, "The eyes of the masses are upon you. You can't get away with anything again."

Since we had not gotten away with anything as far as we knew, and they had found nothing to seize, this was a little hard to understand.

They padded off down the stairs and I heard Joe Doakes close and bar the door behind them. Ho Jie crept down to the broken plywood door and pulled it to, and she and Tientung tied it together with bits of string and wire. Not that it would be an obstacle to further invasion, but just so it would make a warning noise in case Joe Doakes should take it into his head to come and make a search on his own.

Before the raid, Tientung had been sleeping on a bedboard on the floor in the room she shared with Ho Jie when she could get away from her dormitory. Now she came and lay down beside me. I

stretched out my hand to put out the light and she saw the black
and blue marks on my upper arm where the Guard had grabbed me.
"Don't say anything," I whispered. I had got John back into his own
bed under his net and I didn't want anything to upset him. "It
doesn't hurt a bit. Luckily no one really got hurt." I thought of the
lad with his knife. I thought of how John might have fared if he had
been pushed and hustled about, and I began to shake.

"Mother, what's the matter with me? I can't stop shaking." Tientung was also feeling the after-effects of shock and fright. We clung
to each other and shivered uncontrollably; though we knew in all
common sense that the raid was over, we lay until dawn listening and
trembling. We could hear Ho Jie for a long time, rooting about in
her innumerable bundles and baskets to make sure none of her
private property had been disturbed. John, that wonderful man,
went peacefully to sleep.

From beginning to end I was more angry than frightened, and I
was astonished at the violence of my feelings of outrage, not so much
at the fact that the students had forced their way in, but that they
had done so without any kind of search warrant. The English rose
in my veins at the thought of my home being violated. Moreover,
the fact that my cries for help had gone unheeded shook my confidence in the world I lived in. I saw the students with their masks,
their knife and pikes, as silly, irresponsible kids, rather than a serious
threat, but the realization that society had disintegrated to the point
where we were at the mercy of such actions shook me to the depths.

In the morning, as we talked over the incident, John's chief
reaction was combined amazement and amusement at my uproar.

"I didn't know you had it in you, Lu." He shook his head and
twinkled. "I'll have to watch my step." (He hadn't seen the bruises
and we didn't intend that he should.) "I don't think the boys really
had anything in particular on their minds. They are so ignorant
about everything before 1949. I hope I was able to enlighten them
a little."

Tientung looked skeptical. "It would be hard to enlighten some
of those guys," she muttered. "I think they were just out to make
mischief. No one is doing house searches on campus anymore; the

main struggle is in town. Unless they're starting something new with this demand about Black Material. Are you quite sure you haven't kept anything you ought not, Lu?" she queried earnestly.

"I'm not sure of anything now," I replied. "But I did go over the whole house thoroughly, and I think I've got rid of anything that might bother the most sensitive soul."

Indeed I had. The experience of my neighbors who had been searched more intensively than we during the Anti–Four Olds Campaign had made it clear to me that, in the opinion of some Red Guards, anything associated with religion of any kind was suspect. I had hunted out the few treasured books of prints and such souvenirs of home as the Christmas crèche and had grimly destroyed them. I could not bear to think of unfriendly hands touching them. What would not burn, I battered to bits and buried in flowerpots —a perfectly unnecessary bit of melodrama, but emotionally very satisfying. Recalling Professor Lao's difficulties with his Cupid, I had also burned pictures of classical statues, even souvenirs of the sculptures in the Huntington Gardens. Gramophone records had been a problem. In the end I left a few mangled bits in sight and hid Mingteh's favorite Beethoven, the Christmas carols, and the 1812 Overture under a paper in the bedpan under the bathtub. Thus they survived. I felt I could reassure Tientung about the contents of the house.

"If you're sure there is nothing to find, I think I'd better tell the Commune leaders about this search. It really was very irregular," she said. "If you don't tell them and someone else does, it will make trouble." And with that thought she hurriedly left and went back to the dormitory to report.

After lunch, exhausted, I took a nap, only to be roused by a gentle knock at my door. Two former girl students were there.

"We are from the Red Flag Commune," they said. "We're sorry to disturb you, but we were told to check on things here. Have you anything you want us to see?"

"I don't know," I answered. "Look around for yourselves."

They glanced around the room without touching anything, and then left, apologizing again for disturbing me. Tientung told me afterward that they had behaved the same way to John in his study, and had made it very clear that "we" are correct and that "they" had been very wrong.

That night, at the usual hour of nine, came the most welcome sound in the world—Mingteh shouting from below for Ho Jie to come down and let him in. While he satisfied his hunger for bread and Ho Jie hovered about urging him to eat, we told him the tale of the two house searches—the one so terrifying, the other so mild.

"That's not so good," he commented. "I think it points to a renewal of factional fighting here on the campus. Things are getting more tense in the country, too. Some of the fellows at the Homestead think we ought to be ready for trouble—there have been some fights in other villages between the factions. Not in Chang Ping, though," he assured me.

"I hope not," I said. "Do be careful. Now let's call it a day. There surely can't be any more trouble tonight."

But I was wrong. At midnight there was a third search. This time the raiders came to the front door very quietly indeed, and were admitted at once by Joe Doakes. Before we knew what was happening, they had cut our makeshift security arrangements at the stair door and were swarming up the stairs; this time in a dead silence, which was somehow more terrifying than the melodrama of the previous night.

Before I could raise the alarm, several girls pushed me back from the doorway into my room and locked me in. I was not afraid of their hurting John this time because Mingteh as well as Tientung was home. Also, this group seemed to be composed mostly of girls, rather little ones, led by the student who had been foiled in his attempts to get Tientung's bicycle. Everything went on very quietly. I could hear people moving up and down the stairs and rustling through boxes in the next room. No one spoke aloud. Presently I managed to get the door open and found two little teen-agers standing as sentinels outside. They were looking as sternly revolutionary as little girls in pigtails could.

"Who are you?" I asked the one in the pink flowery shirt. I still had the illusion that it made a difference who did things. "You're not Zhong Da girls; that I know. What are you trying to do?"

They put their fingers to their lips and shook their heads, indicating that I must not talk, and politely pushed me back inside. I concluded they were probably middle school girls recruited for this job by the would-be bicycle thief. I went back to bed, but not to sleep, for in a few minutes three more girls entered and proceeded to search the room with revolutionary thoroughness for "Black Materials." In dead silence they shook up my pillow (happily not noticing the bundle of currency I kept there against emergency needs); they rummaged through my dresser and seized with looks of triumph the bundle of Mingteh's letters written from Chang Ping . . . aha! foreign language correspondence! They took my reading notebooks, the work of years of self-study of linguistics filled with diagrams, maps, all those queer-looking characters (phonetic transcriptions)—probably to be interpreted as secret code of some kind —and happily turned in their loot to their leader.

When the girls had finished, they all went out and down the stairs. I got to the bedroom just in time to see the bicycle boy on the stairs, carrying my tape recorder on his shoulder, followed by another lad with my portable typewriter.

"Hey," I shouted, "what are you doing with my typewriter and recorder?"

"We are taking them to headquarters to be checked," answered the leader blandly.

"Well, give me a receipt," I demanded (quite hopelessly), but they made no reply and hurried on their way. I never thought I would see these precious tools again, but as a matter of fact, years later, when "incorrect actions" were being reviewed and rectified, a couple of sheepish-looking students returned both items to me; both typewriter and recorder were nearly worn out, but eventually the University actually paid for their repair.

After our visitors were gone and we had secured the useless door once more, we took stock of our losses. John said they had not interrogated him at all—he was almost disappointed not to have had occasion to enlighten their darkness. But when he looked over his desk, he allowed himself an exclamation of dismay. The manuscript for his book was gone. All during the preceding year he had been systematically working over his notes on different kinds of language change, comparing modern British English with modern American.

It would be, he thought, a useful tool for Chinese teachers of English, and he had spent many comparatively happy hours on it. Just the week before, he had finished making a fair copy, in Chinese of course, all by hand, and had destroyed his rough notes. All during the long months of factional fighting, he had worked away at it. It had comforted him to think that when the madness quieted down, he would be able to contribute something of use.

Now it was all gone.

Tientung, Mingteh, and I could not meet each other's eyes. We all knew how much it had meant to him to have some work like this to do for a future that seemed now impossible.

"Well, that's that," John said, turning from his disordered desk. "Did they take anything of yours?"

I told him about the loss of Mingteh's letters, and both the children broke the tension by laughing. "They won't get much out of those," said Mingteh, "with my kind of spelling."

"And they were *so* virtuous," added Tientung. "I thought you sounded unbearable in some of them."

"Did they find your poems?" I asked Tientung.

"No. They were in Ho Jie's peanut basket." She grinned. "But they took some of Mingteh's electronics magazines and all the readable books."

"Never mind," said Mingteh, "they need them more than I do."

Before Mingteh left the next morning for the early train back to the commune, he talked with me privately and very seriously.

"We really must get Tientung out of here before something more unpleasant happens," he said. "She's very vulnerable and if there should be a real battle here on campus, like there have been in colleges in the North, she will be in danger if she stays in the dorm and will put you and Daddy in danger if she comes home. I can't come and go so easily now because there is more fighting among the young people in the country. It would be of no use at all to have her come to stay at the Homestead, so we must think of a way to get her clear out of town until things settle down."

Summer 1968

MINGTEH CERTAINLY WAS right. It was high time for Tientung to be elsewhere.

It was a year now since the University community had been stunned by the news of the first casualty in the struggle between Commune and Committee. Tientung had announced it without comment: "A boy in the Biology Department was shot and killed today."

"How? When?"

"He was working on the fortification of the Biology Building, putting sandbags in the windows, and someone shot over the wall. The Commune will have a big funeral procession for him in the city." Tientung's voice was noncommittal.

"Must you go?"

"I'll go to the meeting on campus, but everyone knows I can't keep up on a march." I had never looked upon her lameness as a blessing but now I did.

All during the summer, fall, and winter of 1967, Red Guards of the two factions had led their followers into confrontations in town. Enlisting the sympathies of the townspeople in the struggle between Commune and Committee at Zhong Da naturally resulted in further fighting. Workers from factories and stores struggled with each other to seize power from those in authority and Canton was paralyzed. Grim stories circulated of street corner hangings, and people only ventured out of their houses to market hastily for necessities. The streets were deserted by daylight, and no one went out at night. While the fighting centered in the city, it had been comparatively quiet in the University. But those May Day house searches suggested that factional tension on campus was increasing. The Commune for some months held power on campus, although, incomprehensibly to me, Commune members still shared dormitory quarters with their sworn enemies of the Committee. Now both sides were fortifying buildings as if they expected a real battle. There was talk on the public-address system of laying land mines near the entrance gates, and armed guards were posted. Where did they get their arms?

I thought of the poor lad from the Biology Department and trembled for Tientung. He had not been attacking anyone when he was killed.

I could hear girls' voices down by the pond at the foot of the lane and went to peer out of Tientung's window to see if she was there. Only, of course, it was not Tientung's window anymore; when Tientung came to see me, she came as Ho Jie's guest, and I could no longer provide the shelter of a home. I threaded my way through the many objects that Ho Jie stored in boxes, bundles, and heaps, to look down the lane. Half a dozen girls were working with shovels, loading sand into a truck by the pond. Tientung was one of them; I recognized her walk. All the girls were "masses," members of the Commune in name, who always found themselves doing such chores as this. I took care not to call attention to myself at the window, but stood and watched for a while. Presently Tientung looked my way and waved her shovel. I hoped that meant she would come over soon.

The truck drove away with its load of sand, and the girls headed back to the dormitory. A few minutes later Tientung appeared at the back door and quietly came up to the splintered door on the stair. I was ready on my side and untied the rope that had replaced the now useless lock.

Over a cup of coffee in my bedroom, Tientung brought me up to date. The Commune was fortifying the former Engineering Building, well inside the campus, and the sand was for filling sandbags to defend the windows.

"The Red Guards seem to be expecting that the campus will be attacked from the outside, and when that happens, there'll be a warning signal like an air raid alarm on the public-address system and everyone is supposed to run to the building. They say a lot of the students have got hold of guns—but from who knows where," mused Tientung.

"This is awful." Everything was awful. "What will you do? What are the other girls going to do?" My anxiety was beginning to show.

"Angel is going home to stay with an aunt—indefinitely. And Sue says she won't join in any fighting and no one can make her. She's a peasant and has such good class background nobody can say anything, no matter what she does. She's going to go to the library and sit in the reading room. She couldn't go home now, and anyway, she intends to stick it out. She says she was sent to college and until she is sent to a job she won't be pushed out."

"Well, I admire her spirit, anyway. But what about you?"

"I don't know. I'm supposed to be on the sandbag-filling team tomorrow. If only Mingteh could come. Maybe I could go to the commune at Chang Ping with him."

"I doubt if you could buy a ticket without a certificate from someone, and no one would give you one now." I was dubious, anyway, about the safety of Chang Ping. City youths settled in the country were now in conflict with the commune authorities, and Tientung, as a university student, would be under suspicion there.

"It looks so bad that I feel in my bones he'll come soon. He always does. If he shows up tonight, shut the bedroom window for a signal, and if it's shut, I'll try to come over at noon tomorrow." I went silently down the stairs with her and tied the door as she slipped out through the kitchen.

Faith was justified. At nine that night there came the familiar hoped-for hail from the lane, and Mingteh was at the back door. Ho Jie hurried down and untied the rope to go down to the kitchen and let him in. She stopped short to listen to Joe Doakes and family, who were at home, carrying on a loud argument in the kitchen. Ho Jie hid behind the door and, as soon as Mingteh got in, followed him into our bedroom, eager to share her discovery.

Before Ho Jie could start talking, I jumped in and asked the usual question of Mingteh. "How long can you stay this time?"

"My pass is good for overnight, but everything is in a state of upset at the commune. I am sure nobody will miss me if I stay longer." I felt a sense of relief.

Ho Jie burst forth, "Joe Doakes is going to send his whole family away. He says there is going to be serious fighting—he ought to know

—and he's sending the children to the country to their grand-mother, and his wife is moving to the factory where she works. The sister-in-law is going to some relatives in town."

"Then there really is going to be big trouble here," said Mingteh. "That's just what I expected. Tientung *must* clear out." He said nothing about his father and me. We had already settled our policy. John was not strong enough to travel anywhere, even if he had been able to get permission. I, of course, would not leave him.

Early in the morning we closed the bedroom window to let Tien-tung know that her brother had come, and I got busy. I unstitched the pillowcase where I kept emergency funds, sewed a safe pocket into the inside of Mingteh's shirt, packed a change of clothing for Tientung in a small khaki book bag, and awaited her arrival. Luckily she came in before lunch and we explained the plan.

As I have already mentioned, one of the peculiarities of the Cantonese life-style is the midday siesta. In that hot and humid climate it is quite true that survival requires sleep in the middle of the day. Between twelve and two-thirty, no one ever does anything. Ridiculously enough, although there was something very close to bloody civil war going on in Canton, even the faction fighters appeared to shut up shop and take a rest at noon.

On the campus all paths were deserted, no one would be about. So it was during these hours that Mingteh planned to escort Tien-tung through back lanes to the River Gate, get on the little steam launch that could be expected to call there about half past one, and go with her across town to a hospital where we knew a remote family connection was working. Although this young man was connected to our clan only because his wife's sister was married to a cousin of Mingteh's in Shanghai, in time of stress the family bond could be counted on. Once in touch with "cousin," they hoped he would be able to help them get a certificate with which to buy tickets to Shanghai. Once there, First Uncle (John's elder brother) could be counted on to give them shelter as long as necessary. When it was necessary, and possible, for them to return, I was to send them word. Mingteh even planned to relieve my anxiety about their journey by writing and stamping a postcard, which he would mail upon their arrival in Shanghai.

In all this planning and preparation John had no part. It would have been perfectly impossible for him to tell a convincing lie if anyone had asked him where Tientung had gone. If he didn't know, he couldn't say. The children agreed with me that it was best to wait till the postcard came before telling him.

After a hasty lunch the travelers went quickly down the stairs, through the common kitchen, and, carrying only their modest book bags, casually walked down the lane and out of sight. Providentially, Joe Doakes had gone out before lunch and had not returned, and all his numerous household were seizing the chance to nap.

And that was the last we saw of our children for about ten weeks. But not the last we heard, for the promised postcard came along after a week, and we knew they had safely reached Shanghai.

Later Tientung told us how they had managed it. They didn't see a soul all the way to the ferry dock. Although the morning had been notable for a broadcast about a land mine blowing up, during the siesta hour all had been quiet. Thanks to the land mine alarm, mothers had corralled their children, and there were no witnesses to the departure of our two. On the launch, only a few peasants from a nearby commune were squatting on the deck with baskets of vegetables for the afternoon market in town. A few river boats drowsed at anchor in the hot sunshine, and a couple of sampans one-oared their way jerkily against the current. Everything seemed in a state of suspended animation.

In town it was the same. Normally, even during the lunch hour, there would be shoppers on the streets, but on that day it was ominously still, streets deserted. Avoiding the main avenues, they took off through side streets and alleys. An old woman, peering out of a basement window, eyed them sharply, then gestured to them to turn down a narrow lane. Silently they obeyed, hurrying to the next cross street. They heard a noise. Firecrackers? They kept on, hurrying and breathless, dripping with sweat, until they reached the gate of the hospital compound.

Almost at once they found "cousin" and explained their need of two tickets to Shanghai on the next train. "Cousin" promised to do what he could, and they spent an uneasy afternoon waiting for him to report. Toward ten in the evening he sought them out in the empty office where they had been keeping themselves out of the way and triumphantly produced two tickets. "We'll leave at once," he said. "Some friends will go with us to the station."

At the hospital gate they picked up a couple of young fellows and the five of them walked hastily down the middle of a dark, deserted avenue. At the station the escort disappeared and Tientung and Mingteh boarded the Shanghai express. In a few minutes they were moving with accelerating speed through the suburbs of Canton, headed for Shanghai and safety.

Forty-odd hours later they reached their destination and proceeded across the city to Urumchi Road, where First Uncle and several cousins lived. Fresh from the horrors of Canton's street fighting, they were amazed to see people thronging the roads, shops filled with customers, everyone going about life in a quite normal way. Shanghai had been through the phase of violence now paralyzing Canton and had achieved a degree of order, at least on the surface.

At last the sign on the street corner—Urumchi Road—and they knew that the next turn down the lane would bring them to First Uncle's gate. A polite and timid knock and good First Aunt was welcoming them with embraces and tears and hurrying questions as she trotted to and fro providing a much-needed breakfast.

Tientung said that the most wonderful thing to her was to feel safe behind a great big gate in a house occupied only by the family —no Joe Doakes. Housing distribution had not yet come to First Aunt's neighborhood, so the family could still enjoy being alone.

First Aunt's little patch of grass, ringed by a border of portulaca, looked like the Garden of Eden, and the little white stucco house, narrow and tall and overflowing with the furniture of several previous homes, was a haven of safety. But soon she noticed that all was not well with First Aunt. As always, perfectly groomed, not one black hair out of place and a small jasmine flower tucked into her chignon, there was something unfamiliar about her appearance: no favorite rings, earrings, brooches, or bracelets adorned her plump person, and her dress was a strangely penitential blue cotton. Though wreathed in welcoming smiles, her round face showed signs of strain, her eyes had dark circles from sleeplessness. Soon the cause was revealed. First Uncle had just been "taken up," not arrested, but detained by the revolutionary organization in the hospital which he had administered for years, to be interrogated and accused. As an "authority," a surgeon, a technical expert, a foreign-educated scholar, a man of means and professional prestige, he was bound to fall under suspicion. His top-rank salary had been cut to a subsistence allowance of fifteen yuan a month "until he should be cleared." It was indeed fortunate that Tientung and Mingteh had come along with the contents of the pillowcase in their secret pockets. When John heard of his elder brother's fifteen-yuan allowance, he laughed aloud: "For once I'm ahead of First Brother," he chuckled. "They've allowed me twenty yuan."

The family in Shanghai had a dreamlike summer, drifting from day to day never knowing what might happen next. Superficially calm and under control, the city was seething underneath, but being unattached to any organization there, Tientung and Mingteh could enjoy exploring the parks and museums, which were open but mostly deserted. They helped First Aunt with the housework and gardening, sharing her concern for the welfare of four hens kept to provide the household with eggs. First Uncle had not discarded his collection of *Life* magazines and *Reader's Digest*s (mostly dated from 1948 to 1953) in spite of the Anti–Four Olds Campaign, and the attic study made a pleasant reading room on rainy days.

Back in Canton, life was not so idyllic.

The morning after the children's departure I looked out the front window and observed a pedicab draw up, while an increasing clamor below stairs told me that at least part of the family Doakes was about to leave for safer quarters. Amid enormous confusion, the crippled aunt, who did the cooking, was carried out on Joe Doakes's back and set in the pedicab and baggage heaped on top of her. Joe Doakes then emerged with his bicycle, his year-old son strapped securely in the baby seat in front, his three-year-old daughter tied to the luggage rack behind. Interior doors in the house were locked and sealed. More relatives than I had known lived there—they all came forth and the procession went off down the lane, for an undisclosed destination for an unpredictable period of time.

The feeling of liberation was indescribable. To have the whole house to ourselves, even though only for a few hours perhaps, even though all the downstairs doors were locked, to be able, even, to use the front door without a confrontation! It was wonderful!

When Ho Jie came home from the market, she was radiant at the change. Then her face fell when I conscientiously explained to her what that change implied. One of the most active of the factional fighters had moved out because he obviously expected the house to be in a danger zone.

"Ho Jie, if you want to go to stay with your brother for a few days, you go ahead," said John. "There's enough in the house to eat for several days, and when it's peaceful, I can go to the market after a bit."

Ho Jie looked at me. She knew as well as I that he might walk as far as the market, but he could never walk back carrying a heavy basket.

"That might work out," I interjected, "or Ho Jie's nephew, Ah Cho, might leave some vegetables when things are quiet."

"Nonsense," said Ho Jie briskly. "I'm not afraid of anything. No one is going to bother me, and I won't leave you. What would Mingteh say?"

That night we bolted both the front and back doors downstairs inside and had the best night's sleep we had enjoyed since May first.

This was just as well, because after that there were few nights quiet enough for sleep. We could hear machine guns rattling, first from one side of the island, then the other, as faction battled faction. The fighting now spread to workers' groups struggling to take over factories; the battles made the efforts of the students appear amateurish in comparison. News bulletins on the public-address system sounded like military communiqués. Night and day the Commune-operated broadcasts in the University blared out news of skirmishes and sieges, interspersed with patriotic militant music and slogans, to an ever emptier campus. Rows of faculty homes were vacant, their occupants either taking part in the struggle or, more frequently, "gone to visit relatives in the country." The Red Guards and student "masses" of the Commune were now concentrated in their fortified building. A remnant of the Committee had gone into a state of siege in the library, where they waited day after day for their comrades in the city to come and capture the campus and rescue them.

Every day Ho Jie had to go farther afield to find any food, and often came back in a great flurry, to tell me that the street had been closed because of shooting near the market. She had to pass under the gun emplacement of the tractor factory near the University to buy fish, so we ate less fish, and Tiger and Buttons, our two dear cats, developed an unnatural ability to live on eggplant. At night, when the guns from the tractor works blazed, we watched the red tracery over the lane as they shot up the neighborhood.

At such times I always felt better sitting on the stairs, well away from the window. In Wuchang during the air raids in the days of the Japanese invasion, back in 1938, we had formed the habit of sitting in stairwells. It was generally believed that when houses collapsed the stairwells remained standing. I remembered the many hours John and I had spent in dugouts, trenches, and carefully selected angles of walls, during the days and nights of bombing Guilin, and pondered the contradictions of our life together—so serene and joyous within, so violent and dangerous without.

During the hot summer nights in 1968 while I sat on the landing, John would go calmly to bed and sleep peacefully through the shooting. I had blocked the window facing the lane with the winter cotton quilts, in the hope that they would at least delay the entrance of any ricocheting bullets. Naturally the bedroom was terrifically hot and airless, especially under the mosquito nets, but often my hands and feet felt cold.

One night when it was particularly noisy and it seemed likely that the besieging forces would enter the campus (possibly by the gate in front of our house), I said to John, "Do you ever feel sorry we came back to China in '47?"

"Well"—his gentle voice sounded amused—"we certainly would have missed a lot if we had not!"

I thought of some of the things he might have "missed"—the destruction of his health, the frustration of his career as a writer, the loss of friends, the years of exile from his old home, the years as a political outcast, above all, the waste of his talents.

As if reading my mind, he continued, "I know that sometimes it seems like a terrible waste. . . ." He paused. I thought of his confiscated book manuscript. "But no effort is ever really wasted, you know. We can't always see the results but they exist in the world somewhere. They are there."

A burst of machine-gun fire in the street interrupted us. Then I said, "So far we have always come through okay, but we may not always make it, you know. Our luck might run out sometime. Do you think we'll get through this?"

"This will pass," he answered. "We'll get through it one way or another."

I considered the implications of this calm appraisal, realizing that one of the ways might conceivably be fatal.

"I know this," he went on. "I never could have survived this far without you." He smiled. "And I think I could do better right now if you could scare up a cup of Ovaltine for me. I'm really hungry. I'll hold the flashlight."

And diverted by the satisfaction I always felt in feeding him (as he well foresaw), I headed for the food cupboard.

I am thankful to have these words to remember.

September 1968

"WHAT'S GOING ON?" I called to John. "Are a lot of people moving out? It seemed to me they just moved back in."

The Committee had victoriously taken over the campus, and Joe Doakes and family had returned. I was, as so often, looking out the front window toward the big iron gates of the compound. From it I had seen the Red Guards with their banners parade past and had watched the walking wounded with bloodstained bandages straggle along after the first violent encounter of the factions on the streets of Canton. I had seen faculty families hurrying out, carrying their bundles and bedding, fleeing before the violence expected at Zhong Da. And I had seen students armed with automatic rifles standing guard while the sirens wailed a warning of impending attack by the "enemy" factions. And now I saw a procession of bicycles, all laden with bundles and boxes, radios and stacks of books, and even tables and chairs. They were being pushed along by blue-clad young men all wearing white plastic crash helmets. As I watched, a couple of the white-helmeted men approached our front steps; they hesitated, looking at our door. I gathered that they must be friends of Joe Doakes, as they nodded and waved to him standing in the doorway. Immediately I heard him come in and close—and bolt—the front door.

"Tientung will be back for lunch," comforted John. "We'll ask her what's up." The children had only got back from Shanghai that day and the campus was still in a state of suspense. However, the siege of the library had been lifted and now the power was precariously held by the Committee faction. The graduating classes were being organized for the distribution of jobs. Mingteh had not yet returned to the country; he wanted to stay with us until things were more orderly and Tientung's assignment was decided upon. At the moment he was out in the campus somewhere visiting his friends, picking up what news he could.

Suddenly there was the family knock at the kitchen door and in burst both Tientung and Mingteh. They had met on the doorstep and had both come at top speed to warn us.

"Quick," cried Tientung as Mingteh tied up the plywood door more securely. "Needle and thread! We'll sew up those new sheets and towels and Daddy's new winter sweater into sofa pillows." I obeyed without asking questions, and as we rapidly did up the more irreplaceable textiles, disguising them as pillows, she hastily explained.

"There are gangs of looters going through the compound," she said. "They've got little Mrs. Ma's radio and her boy's bike, and they are working their way down our lane. They've just been through The Cat's home and taken every stitch of clothes they had, and practically all their furniture, too." ("The Cat" was the nickname of one of Mingteh's most intimate friends; his father had been under a political cloud for years, having unfortunately been a teacher of aesthetics in the Department of Philosophy. After Liberation he had spent most of his time being ideologically reformed, but it appeared to be a hopeless task as only the Marxist philosophy was respectable. Of all our neighbors he was obviously one who could be looted with most impunity. Who would dare defend him?)

The loot-laden bicycle parade was now explained. We all worked frantically. Our anxiety focused on sheets and clothing because such things could only be bought with cloth ration tickets.

Mingteh at the back window reported that the looters seemed to know pretty well where they wanted to go. I wondered if our monster-neighbor was being visited. And I wondered if Joe Doakes would be. The morning wore on, and we still wondered. It was a little quieter now, fewer posses of white helmets passed by, and fewer loads went out the gate. The main force seemed to have moved on.

"Listen, there's the loudspeaker." We strained to hear. An authoritative voice announced something about Workers' Propaganda Teams being formed in Canton. We had heard that they had already functioned successfully in Peking and we felt they would provide much-needed proletarian revolutionary order here and unite the squabbling factions under their working-class leadership.

"We could do with some kind of order, I might say," observed

Mingteh. "Probably these visitors are just jumping the gun. We'll keep things well battened down just in case."

"It seems remarkable," Tientung said, "which people were looted and which were not."

"It's the only time I ever have been glad to have Joe Doakes downstairs," I commented, and we left our conclusions unspoken.

It was a very strange sound that wakened me before dawn the next morning. A continuous, rustling, moving sound outside, below in the lane. Not daring to risk a light, I cautiously sat up and pulled aside my mosquito net. I inched myself up to the window at the head of bed and very carefully peered out from behind the half-drawn curtain. It was too dark to distinguish much below, but the cause of the sound became apparent; masses of people were marching silently through the big gates, and the sound was the unavoidable rustle of their rough cotton clothes as they moved along. It was the slight, unmistakable whisper betraying an army on night march. Not a word, not a footfall, just a barely audible rustle.

I sank back into bed, a prey to the familiar cold feeling of the kind of panic that makes your insides shake up and down and your outsides shake back and forth. I dared not call John—I didn't want to risk making any sound to call attention to our having noticed people who were making such a total attempt to conceal their presence.

Minutes passed. The sky was getting a little lighter now. I ventured to look again. Ranks and ranks of white-helmeted figures filled the lane as far as I could see in both directions. They were standing now, in perfect silence. What discipline! When John whispered my name it sounded like a shout.

"Lu, what is it?"

"It must be the Workers' Propaganda Team," I answered, coming close to his bed and whispering through the mosquito net. "I heard them march in, hundreds of them, and now they're all standing out in the lane. I guess they are waiting for daylight to rush in."

He sighed. "If they're really the Workers' Propaganda Team, they're here to stop the fighting," he reassured me. An incredible man—he turned over and peacefully went to sleep. I did not. I waited and watched until the sky was nearly blue, then slipped out and woke up Mingteh. He was sleeping on the floor in the other room.

"Mingteh—wake up! I think the Propaganda Teams have come."

"That's what they must be," he said when he had peeked out the balcony window. "There must be thousands of them. I can see white helmets massed all the way to the crossroad. They seem to be very well organized in groups and most of them are carrying pikes." As he spoke I heard a slight but clear, bell-like sound. Nothing is really like it—a bamboo staff ringing as it strikes stone. "Somebody dropped his." Mingteh grinned. But no sound of words came. No one moved or spoke.

"Call Ho Jie," said Mingteh. "Is Daddy awake?"

"He was, but he went back to sleep when he figured out who it was."

"Best thing he could do. We'll just keep still till we see what happens. No use to call attention to ourselves unnecessarily."

I tiptoed out (always aware of the recently returned Doakeses sleeping under my feet) and tactfully roused Ho Jie, cautioning her to keep still. We all got dressed as quietly as we could.

Full daylight now showed the masses standing silently in the lane. White helmets, white T-shirts, blue pants, no red armbands. In every small group of ten or so, several were armed with bamboo pikes. Then the loudspeakers blasted off with the morning hymn to Chairman Mao and the authoritative voice began (first in Standard Chinese, then in Cantonese). It was announced that the Workers' Propaganda Teams had entered Zhong Da and would conduct a house-to-house search for arms, supervising the "voluntary disarmament" of the factions. Everyone was to remain where he was, no one was allowed to move about. Everyone must obey the orders of the Workers' Team. No resistance would be tolerated. Revolutionary discipline must be maintained.

Then as we watched, squads of Team members deployed into the residential area to begin their search. As I learned later, still more and larger contingents were assembled at all the other gates, to cover the other faculty housing units, the student dormitories, and mass organization headquarters. We waited our turn, thinking we would be among the first as our house was in front of the gate. But no, it was a couple of hours before a squad marched smartly up to our door.

I seated myself at the top of the stairs, my *Peking Review* in hand. I think all the family were more terrified that I would repeat my performance of resistance than they were of meeting the Team members. I reassured them over and over that I would be good, but my reputation for manners was gone forever, and they hovered anxiously in doorways, ready to suppress me if I got out of hand.

As soon as the anticipated knock at the front door was heard, Joe Doakes answered it, speaking in his somewhat unctuous "official welcome" voice. However, the spokesman did not respond with courtesy phrases, but began to read a search warrant aloud—first in Standard Chinese, then in Cantonese—explaining again who they were and that their purpose was to search all premises for weapons or anything used in factional fighting. I could hear the men moving about below in Joe Doakes's bedroom, opening boxes, searching through his papers. No one below said anything. Then the Team captain grunted. He had found something. There were consultations, then the captain rapped out an order. Joe Doakes began explaining, protesting, was silenced, and then agreed.

Now it was our turn. The Team marched up to our plywood door, knocked. Mingteh opened it. The captain walked up to the landing and saw me. He looked a little surprised, but, not nonplussed at all, he began to read his search warrant again, in both dialects. Then he turned to Mingteh and asked if I could understand what he had said, that it was essential that no one be searched without understanding who was doing it and for what reasons. (What a contrast to our earlier searches!) Mingteh said he thought I understood, and I smiled cheerfully at them, waving my *Peking Review.* But still Mingteh was asked to translate it into English for my benefit, which he did in short order.

All the searches we had experienced before were amateurish compared with this one, but this was the one I didn't mind. My heart was satisfied by the search warrant! These workers were seriously looking for weapons to prevent any more bloodshed, and I felt perfectly at ease in their hands. To them, we were not the enemy. The enemy was factional fighting, not factions or individuals. It was no small part of my comfort at the moment to hear, outside in the garden, Joe Doakes being directed to burn a pile of posters and pamphlets he had concealed. This propaganda encouraged violence and was considered to be a kind of weapon.

When the searchers came into our bedroom, they politely asked me to unlock our trunks. They swiftly rummaged through, feeling for weapons, and came upon the metal box in which we kept the housekeeping cash and such papers as my old passport. They fished it out and opened it, then handed it back to me as if it burned their fingers.

"Don't you want to look through this?" I asked.

"No," replied the leader, "we are looking for weapons. We will not disturb the masses or interfere with their personal possessions."

I thanked them and watched their further research, with a growing apprehension as I realized that the next thing they would look into would probably be a cardboard carton under my bed. It was not that I was concealing a hand grenade in it, not even a pistol, but my poor cat Buttons had moved in and deposited her latest family of kittens there, and I really didn't know who was going to be more surprised in a couple of minutes.

My feelings were very complex. I didn't want my dear cat to be frightened by a strange hand intruding where she had chosen to keep her precious kittens under my bed, obviously the last safe place in her world. And I didn't want the Propaganda Team man to be bitten. But most of all I didn't want him to feel that he was being made to look foolish, because who knows what complicated reactions might result? I was further blocked by the consideration that anything I might attempt to say about cats in Chinese might sound to the ears of the searchers like a remark about Chairman Mao, because my poor pronunciation could not be trusted to distinguish "mao" (cat) from "Mao." All these thoughts flashed through my mind in the instant while the worker was closing the trunk and bending down to reach under the bed to pull out the box. I reached out my hand as he reached out his: he froze and looked up. His sun-bronzed, wrinkled face was a mask of suspicion, his growing friendliness reversed. I stammered in English, "Let me . . ." and pulled the box out so he could see the innocent contents, a fat and foolish white and yellow tabby defensively surrounding her squirming yellow kits. Three pairs of eyes looked at each other: round amber cat eyes full of fright, black Cantonese eyes narrowed in suspicion, and my blue ones apprehensive and amused. Then the amusement dawned in the black eyes, too, and the fright disappeared from the amber ones, and for a moment three personalities met in a memorable harmony. The worker rose from his knees and prepared to leave. He and his assistants checked our name and address off a list and they pattered off down the stairs, turning at the door to wave a gesture of farewell, backed up by the ghost of a twinkle.

All morning long the campus swarmed with little detachments of Propaganda Team members. At every house they read their warrant and with the residents' permission searched the premises for weapons. Never afterward did I hear anyone complain of their behavior. Clearly they were not to be confused with the looters who had taken advantage of the situation earlier in the week. My admiration for the real Workers' Teams grew as the day wore on and I could see some of the things they had to contend with.

Just opposite our front door, on the other side of a high picket fence, was a research institute. Often, during the long days and nights I spent at home, I had amused myself by watching the goings-on among the scientists in the volleyball court in front of our house. I could only guess why they did what they did. It was like watching rushes from a film with a random sound track. The scientists were acting like schoolboys running amok. Sometimes little groups gathered on opposite sides of the court and shouted slogans at each other. For a week, every night from midnight to 2:00 A.M. someone in the otherwise empty assembly hall practiced singing "The Helmsman," solo, always breaking down at the same place, hour after hour. One night the Institute's Red Flag Commune faction seized power. First a group of a dozen young men and girls sat on the steps for more than an hour, reading The Little Red Book as if in prayer. Then they closed their books, stood up, shouted a slogan, and started across the courtyard toward the one-story office building, where in one office a single light bulb glowed. Halfway across their nerve failed and they retreated in confusion to the steps, squatted down, and went into meditation over their books again. This happened several times before they finally made it to the office, banged on the door, and hauled out the occupant—a rather stout old man. They seized him by the arms and hustled him off to the assembly hall, from which I soon heard slogans and shouting and all the tumult of an accusation meeting. Later, from time to time, I saw the stout old man, hoe in hand, aimlessly chopping at the weeds along the path, guarded by a small posse with red armbands. Now, today, the same stout old man was in conference with the Propaganda Team members. I saw some of the white-helmeted workers coming out of the building carrying armloads of materials—could they be guns? Their findings were stacked neatly on the steps and a young woman member of the Team set to guard them. I could see clearly a revolver in an army holster on top of the pile. Were the scientists really only schoolboys running amok?

The loudspeaker blared again, this time with shocking news. At the Polytechnical Institute in another part of town where searches were also being carried on (this was clearly a coordinated citywide effort, determined to stamp out violence in every student center at once), a member of the Team had been killed. It seemed that a student had set a booby trap in his desk, pasted a label on the outside warning "hands off," and then had gone away. The worker had opened the desk and the homemade explosive went off and killed him. As news of this tragedy spread, the mood of the searchers hardened. "Dictatorship of the proletariat" came to have new meaning, as the aroused workers made a clean sweep of student quarters.

Factionalism did not die with the advent of the Workers' Propaganda Teams, although active fighting ceased. Hostility took on new forms, which seemed to me even worse than the confrontations on the street. Shortly after our house had been inspected and warranted free of offensive weapons, a second inspection took place, this time by very serious-faced Workers' Team members. The first I knew of it was when I heard a scrabbling sound in the attic over the hallway, where a screen ventilating panel was set into the ceiling. In all the years we had lived there we had never opened it up, contenting ourselves at housecleaning time with poking at it with a broom to dislodge the larger cobwebs. Thinking that Buttons had somehow got into the overhead space, I went to check up. Through the dust I could see that someone was peering down. "What do you want?" I called. But the answer, muffled by all that dust, conveyed nothing.

Presently Ho Jie came up the stairs, scarlet with rage. "Lok Tai, some of Them [she could no longer bring herself to name the hostile faction] told the Propaganda Team that Lo Tientung had hidden hand grenades in the attic, and they sent a search party to find them."

"Good heavens!" I was really scared. Not because I thought my daughter had done anything of the kind. She had resolutely refused to take part in violence. But it would be so easy for anyone to go into the attic from the other side of the common wall of our double house and plant anything there—to incriminate Tientung, and worse still, John.

"You don't think it was . . ." I nodded to suggest our hostile housemate, Joe Doakes.

"No." Ho Jie was almost disappointed, but had to be truthful. . . . "It was that girl who used to come here for you to teach her. [I thought back to June 1966 and the meeting that melted away. She was the pretty one with pronunciation problems.] She just did it out of spite. You didn't know it but she used to come here to the Doakeses' often and once she tried to ask me about Mingteh." I could imagine how far the spy would get along that line with Ho Jie.

Was it jealousy? Was it factionalism? In any case it was a prime example of the kind of false accusation tactic that was to wreck lives in the Clearing of the Class Ranks Campaign. It was appalling enough that an apparently quite nice young woman would accuse an acquaintance of what was a very serious crime, on no grounds whatever. But even worse was the fact that everyone accepted the tactic. No one else seemed to feel as I did that when it was possible for anyone to lay false accusations with impunity, all society broke down. It was now an accepted thing, a political weapon, and the one who used it was not censured. Indeed, the ones who came eagerly forward to the Propaganda Team members and accused others were welcomed and praised for their zeal.

In principle, the Party always undertook to investigate any charge brought against anyone, and in fact, as in this case, I know they often did. But anyone who volunteered information was rewarded. It was undeniable that such things could and did happen in every society, but at least, I thought, one ought to have the option of despising the informer.

September 1968

TIENTUNG CAME HOME one morning with a gleam in her brown eyes that warned me of trouble ahead.

She and Mingteh had been back from their trip to Shanghai only a couple of days. She had been to a meeting in the student dining hall and had heard a cadre inform members of the classes of 1967 and 1968 that they were about to be distributed to "suitable" employment. They had been waiting for this for a year and a half at least, but had not expected to have to choose so fast. There was a stunning silence when they discovered that they had two days to make decisions that would influence their whole lives.

Tientung explained: "There aren't really enough jobs to go around. For the eighty people in all the Foreign Languages Department classes there are eight jobs in Xinjiang, seven in Gansu, five in Guangsi, two in Shandong, six in Honan, and three in Yunnan. Those who don't want to go to places so far from Canton will all be enrolled as workers in the State Farm in Swatow, under army management, for who knows how long?"

"Great guns!" Mingteh exploded. "Xinjiang? Yunnan? Gansu?"

John looked pale and distressed. "Have you any idea of what kind of work will be assigned?"

"Only at Swatow. That's a big state farm, so the work will be outdoor farm work, rice and sugar cane, I expect."

"That's impossible for you," Mingteh put in. He had had a good deal of experience at that kind of work. "You can't stand that kind of job, out in the sun all day; heat does you no good."

"I know," she agreed mournfully. "I sweat buckets sitting still in the shade. But that wouldn't be the worst of it in Swatow. Most of the people I know are going to choose that, so as to be near Canton. Some of them advised me to go there, too. They think they can come home sometimes."

INTO THE BRIAR PATCH

"They're fooling themselves," said Mingteh. "Once you're in, you're in."

"I know. But it isn't just that I know I can't stand the heat, it's the idea of going on and on in the same way, for still another year, living in a dormitory with all the same people, every moment organized, everything regimented. I've been a student all my life: I want to get out and be free at least some of the time. I want to feel like a grown person. I don't want to go on being a student forever."

She really sounded desperate.

"Well, let's make a list and look up all the other places on the map and see which is most practical." Mingteh pulled down his book of maps and began making notes. "Since the pay will be the same wherever you go or whatever you do, and you don't know what the work will be, all we have to go on is the place."

"That's right. They told us we just go to the place they give us a ticket for and report to some office or other and the local authority carries on from there."

John's face looked grim. To think of his darling child being shot off into space this way—out of sight, out of touch. Perhaps the bitterest thought to him was that he could not ever write to her without endangering her politically.

Mingteh pressed on for a solution to the problem. "How about Guangsi? That's the next province, not so far, although the transportation there is not direct."

"That's a vile climate," I broke in. John and I had spent a miserable term there in 1938–39, as refugees from the Japanese invasion. "It was horribly cold in the winter and horribly hot in the summer. Guilin is pretty but you don't know that you'd be assigned to Guilin. You might be anywhere, and it's a very backward place in spots."

"No, not Guangsi." She was decided about that. "A couple of the boys in the class want to go there because that's their native province. They have first grabs for Guangsi." She was looking in the book for Yunnan, the place where she was born in 1942; that was where John and I had spent most of the war years, after the destruction of Guilin drove our college west on the refugee trek again. Tientung could certainly not remember beautiful Yunnan, but she always claimed that she felt the high mountains calling to her.

"Yunnan?" She brooded over the map, tracing the line of the

railway, locating Kunming, following the tortuous twists of the Burma Road, till she put her finger on Hsichow, the tiny village of her birth. "Someday, perhaps. But not now. Angel and her comrade want to go there, and I've had enough of chaperoning them!" She grinned.

"Anyway, it would take you weeks to get there, and there is still too much factional fighting going on. Forget Yunnan." Mingteh was still looking at the national map. "Honan, Shantung?"

"Those jobs are classified." No more need be said. "Classified" jobs were for the children of families of good class origin, poor peasants, proletarians, Party members—not for ours.

"That leaves Xinjiang and Gansu."

"Now Xinjiang is next to Tibet." Tientung was tempted. "I always have wanted to see Tibet. If I have to leave home, I'd rather go a good long way and see something interesting."

"Don't be romantic," Mingteh remarked acidly. "Have you any idea how far that really is from Canton? How long you'd be traveling? You'd have to go to Urumchi, and after you get there, there is no telling where you'd have to work."

Tientung sighed. "Well, how about Gansu?"

"Now there'd be some sense in that," Mingteh approved. "Look, you'd go by rail through Wuhan . . ."

"Oh, maybe I'd get to see Uncle Jamie in Wuhan," Tientung interrupted.

"Not impossible, though difficult. Once you get on the train you have to keep going." Mingteh brought her back to earth. "You go on to Zhengchow, and change trains there for Lanchow—that's the provincial capital of Gansu. The classmates who are going on to Xinjiang would have to go that way, and you'd have company all the way to Lanchow."

"That sounds more reasonable," put in John. "There'd be a good-sized group going all that way—it would be safer." He knew, we all knew, that there was safety in numbers on the road.

Tientung was absorbing the topography of Gansu. "That'd be right on the Yellow River," she gloated. "And look, there's a section of the old Great Wall right over there. I never knew it ran so far west."

"Yes," agreed Mingteh, "but you'll notice that while it's an inch from Lanchow on the map, there's a mountain range between and no roads marked. For goodness' sake, be practical."

"Okay," she sighed again. "I think it makes most sense to go to Gansu. After I get there, I can look into the Great Wall angle."

And so the great decision was made, and when next day she told her classmates that she volunteered for that remote northwestern province, they were dumbfounded, and the political instructor in charge of the distribution, puzzled. It was a choice that glowed with political virtue, to undertake to go to a place most Cantonese viewed with genuine horror, and her electing it helped solve the difficult problem of filling the undesirable posts. But why should a young woman who had lived most of her life in Zhong Da, the cultural heart of the South, consent to exile in such a place?

Her friends and teachers could not understand her action, but we could, very well. Hadn't I done practically the same thing myself when I opted for a job teaching English in far-off China, instead of settling for a post in familiar Illinois? Hadn't her father acted on a similar impulse when, in spite of the traditional Chinese love for home, he had seized the chance to go to distant America to study? Hadn't Mingteh when he left his comparatively comfortable home, his books, his music, his radios and experiments, to plunge into the utterly different life of a commune peasant? We had each in his and her own way felt the need to explore new horizons.

So now we turned to and concentrated on getting our pioneer ready for the new world. Speed was essential, for the graduates were being sent on their way within the next few days. Every traveler would have to be prepared to carry his/her own baggage, so no one could take much: a suitcase that could be locked, a duffle bag or bedding roll for bedding and winter clothes, a pail in which all last-minute objects would be stuffed, including a bowl and spoon, possibly a small book bag, and inevitably a wet towel tied to the handle. (In the service of cleanliness, it seems everyone in China carries a towel—preferably wet.) It was a fairly standardized setup. But for the group going to the far northwest there was a special problem. They were moving from the semitropical climate of the coast to the cold continental climate of the mountains, and once they reached their destination, they feared, there was little likelihood of supplementing their outfits. Every item had to be weighed and considered with utmost care. So I was surprised to find valuable space being allowed for a small box of seashells.

"Why these?" I asked, although I guessed.

"They're for the children," she explained. "There are sure to be children, and they probably never saw a seashell, so I'm taking them along to help make friends. Canton will seem like the ends of the earth to people in Gansu."

She was right, it would. And to people in Canton, Gansu seemed more strange and outlandish than even New York. Many Cantonese have relatives abroad, or at least know someone who has, but no one, *no one* ever went to Gansu! It was said that people there ate millet and corn flour buns and there was no rice; that they lived in caves carved out of the loess mountainsides; that there was never any fish, only mutton, if that. And it was *cold*. To most Cantonese, no combination of circumstances could be worse. But although Tientung had lived long in South China, to her the life-style of Gansu sounded delightful and the prospect of corn pone and mutton a welcome change.

The suitcase was packed. The pail, the inevitable last-minute container, was ready to go. A special little Cantonese basket was stuffed and wrapped carefully with plastic. The last thing to be done up was the bedding roll, with the quilt, the blanket, the mat, the mosquito net, and winter coat. Rolling up a bedding roll, roping and tying it, is a fine art. It was here that John unexpectedly excelled. The children couldn't remember ever having seen him do this before. But I had. How many times during our refugeeing days we had bent together over one of those huge, shapeless masses of all-essential textiles, and pushed, pulled, pressed, and roped it into a disciplined portable pack. Now we bent to it again, and before the admiring eyes of our young, displayed our skill with a diamond hitch. "Not bad," commented Mingteh as he shouldered it to carry it to the railroad station.

I was glad in a way that everything was so hurried. There was no time for feeling our feelings. Tientung and I had long since agreed that we would never indulge in tearful partings, but I felt like a very Spartan mother, indeed, as she went down those stairs for the last time, with her bag and pail, Mingteh following, shouldering the bedding roll. He had undertaken to get her safely to the station and promised not to leave her till she had made connections with the others of the northwestern expeditionary force. What he felt at seeing his lifelong chum and confidante going off into the blue, I dared not imagine.

Turning at the door to wave good-bye, our pioneer smiled up at us. "Don't worry! Brer Rabbit is going to jump right into the briar patch, you'll see!" And she was gone.

It seemed like a very long time that day before Mingteh came home. The realization that Tientung was gone, for at least a year but possibly longer, to an unknown place, with unknown people, into unknown dangers, flooded over me. I would not dare write freely; John dared not write at all—and there certainly was no telephone communication. I was not concerned about the physical hardships of the northwest—she was most adaptable about such things and would find no problem. But I began to imagine all the very real dangers possible in renewed factional fighting in that area of the country, and premonitions chilled my heart.

"Mingteh has been gone a very long time," I finally remarked to John. And I was shocked to realize from his face that he was just as worried as I was.

"Yes, it ought not to take so long," he agreed. "I'm really anxious about what might happen at the station." This was the first time in my knowledge of him that he had ever admitted to anxiety and I was accordingly in a panic.

When Mingteh finally showed up at dusk, we fell on him with questions and were only partially reassured by his answers.

"We got to the station okay," he told us. "It was packed with all the graduates from Canton, leaving for all over the country. We found Tientung's classmates after some hunting, and everyone milled around asking why they didn't start. I hung around just in case, and I'm glad I did. There was a loudspeaker announcement of an order for a general inspection of baggage. The security people for the station (or the Propaganda Team, I guess) came in and opened up all the baggage, suitcases, bedding rolls, everything, looking for hidden weapons. What a job! Then I had to spend the rest of the time helping tie up other people's bedding rolls with our diamond hitch!"

"I'm certainly glad you were there to help her."

"Oh, she'll get along all right," he assured us. "Trust her to land on her feet! [How proud she would be to hear such praise!] She was sitting next to the window with that girl who worked with her on painting walls with slogans. They looked pretty cheerful. Just before the train started, that guy from her class who used to come here for tutoring jumped on board—he didn't have a pack or a suitcase, just the clothes he had on. He'd been in a bad factional fight and didn't dare go back to get his things—his friends brought him his tickets to where he was hiding, and he just made it. Great unity!" He snorted. Although the Propaganda Teams had taken over and the fighting was supposed to be quelled, the bitter animosity of the factions persisted and it would be a long, long time before there would be peace and security.

Next day Mingteh also departed, going back to the commune at Chang Ping, where the autumn work would keep him busy for some time. He had long since overstayed his leave of absence, and while he said nothing, I knew he was a little apprehensive about his welcome when he should check in again at commune headquarters. Almost anything could have happened at the Homestead in his absence.

John and I felt very isolated as we faced the prospect of the next big campaign—the Clearing of the Class Ranks—without the benefit of their advice.

We had come to depend on both the children more than we had realized. Tientung's lightning visits and briefings on the progress of the complex political situation had been the bright moments of every day. Mingteh's unheralded but always timely appearances had saved many a situation. Even though neither of them actually lived at home anymore, we felt the warm assurance of their concern, and I always strengthened myself by the thought, "In case of real trouble or anything I can't handle, I can always get in touch with my children." Before he left for Chang Ping, Mingteh handed me a sheet of paper on which he had carefully written out in very plain Chinese characters a telegram addressed to himself at the commune saying "Need you" and signed "Mother." Pinned to the page was the precise amount of money needed to dispatch the message from the post office.

"Keep this safe," he instructed me, "and if you should run into anything very serious, have Ho Jie or Dick or any of the other neighborhood kids send it, and I'll come. With or without permission! But don't send it unless you really need me. I won't wait to come again till I hear from you, for sure, but I don't know how things are at the Homestead."

I understood. As order was being restored in the cities, there was more fighting in the countryside.

Yes, John and I felt very much alone.

But, in fact, we were not alone in being separated from our children. It was an experience we shared with nearly all of our generation and class. From the year of Liberation onward, all our family had been subjected to a continuous strain. All the powerful forces of the new revolutionary society were bent on winning over the rising generation. Family must never come ahead of revolutionary interest. Loyalty must be to the Party, to the State, to the work team. It was the reward and joy of our lives that somehow Tientung and Mingteh had neither rejected us nor turned their backs on the new society. While they did not accept the official judgment passed on John, neither did they become embittered outcasts in their own generation. Now, as Tientung took on the challenge of a whole new way of life, she saw it, not as a punishment or misfortune, but as a "briar patch" in which a determined rabbit could make a home.

However, although the children's loyalty and their ways of meeting misfortunes gave us great joy, it was a secret bitterness to us both that we were in a sense the cause of their difficulties. Our position in society was what it was because we were what we were, and we could not change that. But we could only be thankful that although we had to be separated, our inner solidarity as a family was not shaken.

Autumn 1968

THE YOUNG COUPLE next door were expecting their second baby within a very few days, so I was surprised to see the hopeful father assembling his backpack and traveling gear on the front steps, as if preparing for a long journey. I asked Ho Jie about it.

"He's an Investigator," she replied portentously.

"An Investigator? What's he investigating?"

"He's an Investigator for the Campaign for Clearing the Class Ranks," she explained. "The collective leadership of the University is sending a lot of cadres out to find out all about people who have problems."

I had been so relieved to have the shooting stop and so absorbed in my own family affairs, getting Tientung off to Gansu and Mingteh back to the country, that I had not fully taken in the magnitude of this movement to clear the (proletarian) class ranks of all persons who might be considered enemies of the people.

"Seems to me the young woman next door is going to have something of a problem, and very soon, if she's left alone right now," I commented. To my unreformed mind, the birth of a child appeared far more important than the investigation of Problematical Problems. "Is there anything we can do to help her out?"

Ho Jie gave me a despairing look. "They were both in the Committee," she began patiently, as if explaining something elementary to a very stupid child. "It would be for Joe Doakes and his wife to look out for her, not *us*. In any case, when her time comes, her fellow workers at the factory will see to her."

"How about the little boy?" He was a charming three-year-old with whom I had built up a shy acquaintance over the hedge. "Where will he go?" The notion that I might possibly find occasion to take him in for a bit was too attractive to drop, although I certainly did not dare let Ho Jie know what was in my mind.

"Oh, he'll stay with some of the folks at his mother's factory."

Still I was dubious. "But will her husband be away long? Doesn't he feel he should be with his wife when she goes to the hospital?"

Again Ho Jie looked at me pityingly. "What use would he be to her there? Having babies is woman's work. The doctors will look after her. He's on an Important Political Assignment."

I began to worry that this new campaign might involve John. He had been accused of various political misdoings, but every time he had eventually been cleared. How many times could one be tried for the same crime? Or would some new accusation be dreamed up?

Day after day now the public-address system bellowed forth accusations and exposés of horrendous plots involving most of the senior teachers, as far as I could make out. Some of the "discoveries" were so extravagant and preposterous that I couldn't believe anyone could take them seriously, until I began to hear from Ho Jie about some of the accused confessing, and more shocking than that, of several of the accused committing suicide rather than face the charges.

Investigators were on the move all over the country, traveling (free) from distant parts to find persons accused of political crimes and interrogate them. We soon became accustomed to a new routine. A knock on the door, a couple of students (sometimes one from each of the supposedly nonexistent factions), and a summons to John to go to the Department office to answer questions. Sometimes this summons would be "Lo Chuanfang, hurry up and come to face the people's investigators"; sometimes in English, "Dr. Lo, some people at the Department would like to see you." (As if courtesy in English would not count politically.) It depended largely on who was calling for him.

The next incident occurred on my birthday, October 12. There was no cause for celebration as far as I could see. I was having a bad case of "empty nest syndrome" and even resented John's efforts to cheer me up with the birthday greeting: "Grow old along with me, the best is yet to be!"

"That's all nonsense," I growled. "The older we get, the worse everything is."

"Maybe so, maybe so, but you might as well try to be optimistic," he rejoined.

"I really think that old saying is true." I looked out the window. "That a pessimist is an optimist's wife. I know what makes them get that way!"

We were interrupted by the now almost routine knock at the stair door, followed by the incursion of a posse of students.

"Lo Chuanfang, you are wanted at the FLD office to meet with comrades from an investigating team."

Nothing for it but to find his cap (the usual gray cloth worker's cap, which made him look as if he was in a kind of disguise, totally unlike himself) and wave him off to the morning's work. I only hoped the investigators would not be too nasty, and I felt ashamed that I had not encouraged the optimism he so bravely professed.

Alone in the empty room, I settled to my time-passing task of reading English poetry, searching out poems and bits of poems that would convey nourishing ideas to the absent children. Every day I carefully copied out, as legibly as I could, things that I hoped would help them, and once a week sent off an envelope to each that would be perfectly unintelligible to any other readers, yet explainable as being "Study Material" for English language lessons. We almost communicated in a code.

I was interrupted after an hour by another knock at the door and a determined entry by two more *very* angry young men.

"Why hasn't Lo Chuanfang reported?" they shouted rudely.

"But he has gone," I protested. "Two other comrades came an hour ago to summon him to a meeting, and he left with them at once."

"No, he couldn't have," they shouted. "Where is he hiding?"

"He isn't hiding," I declared confidently. "I saw him go and he hasn't come back."

"Well, if he does come back, tell him to report *at once* to the FLD office," they grumbled and went off.

What could have happened? I knew how ill he really was, and I had terrible visions of his falling unconscious on some bypath, or of his being waylaid by factional mischief makers. I went from window to window, as if looking up and down the lane would bring him into view.

Ho Jie came upstairs for my verdict as to whether bean sprouts or bak choi should appear for lunch, and I told her what had happened. She took it very seriously, which frightened me even more.

"We must go and look for him," she said. "He might have fallen crossing the causeway by the fish pond." A series of little artificial ponds lay between our house and the office building now used by the Investigators. To get there, one used a narrow footpath, often slippery and muddy, and it would be easy to fall—or be pushed—into the water.

I had not been downstairs and out of the house for weeks and the sun was surprisingly hot and dazzling to my unaccustomed eyes. Leaning on Ho Jie's shoulder, I hurried as fast as I could toward the ponds. I saw some people ahead and hoped they would turn aside and that I would not have to meet them face-to-face on the narrow path. I had not realized before that it might take sheer physical courage to walk down that familiar path in broad daylight, and I thought of how many times I had seen John start off surrounded by his sometimes unfriendly guides, and how many times he had come home after dark—silent and exhausted. And I had not risen to his effort at optimism. . . .

We reached the muddy edge of the pond and stopped. The path was overgrown with grass and weeds and too narrow for two to walk side by side. My head swam. "Ho Jie, you go across and ask at the office if he has shown up," I said. "I'll have to wait here."

"Stand here in the shade," she commanded, and I leaned against a tree and watched her stout black-clad figure, topped with the broad round bamboo hat, move briskly over the causeway and out of sight down a tree-sheltered path.

For several lifetimes I stood there, listening to my heart thud.

Now Ho Jie was returning. Alone. No smile under the big hat. "He hasn't been to the office. No one knows where he is. We'd best go home and wait."

The room that sometimes seemed so unbearably crowded with the two of us trying to keep out of each other's way now felt vast and empty. I never cried when Mingteh returned to Chang Ping; I had not shed a tear when Tientung left for Gansu. But now I did. John was gone and I didn't know where he was and what could I tell the children?

I quickly wiped my eyes when I heard another pounding at the door and a "Where is Lo Chuanfang?" The new relay of messengers was angrier than ever. "Two comrades have come here from Wuhan to question him. Why doesn't he come?"

"I tell you, he left when he was first called, and I don't know where he is." I was getting angry in turn. "I've just been out as far as the ponds to look for him, and there's no trace . . ."

The two students looked at each other and turned pale. I remembered then what Ho Jie doubtless had thought of, that a few days before, a despairing older teacher had ended his life by drowning himself in that very pond. It was not the thought of his despair and tragic end that made the messengers turn pale, it was their realization that they would be held responsible for "incorrect" handling of a "case" if another person should be driven to suicide.

I had no fear that John might have taken that way out. The first time we heard of a colleague's suicide during a political inquisition, we had discussed the rights and wrongs of such an action, and he made his stand clear: "My life is not mine to dispose of. And when things get as bad as they possibly can, they are bound to get better!" No. No fear he would take that way out.

The students consulted briefly. "We'll go and look. We'll send the comrades from Wuhan over here to wait for him. Mind you, treat them with all due courtesy!" And leaving me seething with resentment at this last shot, they hastened off.

The investigators from Wuhan, when they arrived five minutes later, proved to be two factory workers. They wore the customary workman's jacket of blue denim, not the Mao uniform of the cadre, and their little blue cloth visored caps looked perfectly right on them. Although they had not been in Canton many hours, they had already furnished themselves with Cantonese black plastic sandals, hard to get in Wuhan and considered very desirable.

Slightly disconcerted when they saw me, they relaxed when I spoke to them in Hubei dialect. We exhausted the normal inquiries about their journey, the comparative heat of Wuhan and Canton, how old I was and how long I had lived in China, where I had lived in Wuchang (surprise and growing cordiality when I could name familiar streets). They gave me an emotional description of the Russians' treachery in pulling out of factories and construction work in 1961 and became even more friendly when they learned I was not a Russian (as they had first suspected) but an American. We ran out of talk and looked at our watches. An uneasy silence developed. I could feel my interrupted tears accumulating and burst out, "Comrades, I'm so sorry my husband is not here to meet you, since you have taken so much trouble to come here. But I don't know where he is! He went off this morning and no one can find him. He's been very ill, and I'm afraid . . ."

Before my eyes the investigators turned into human beings.

"Now don't be upset, Elder Sister," they urged. "We'll go and look for him."

Remembering the students' stern instructions to be polite to them, I struggled for control and begged them not to disturb themselves, to wait and eat lunch. But while we were going through the politeness Ping-pong, voices on the stairs announced visitors again, and in strolled John with the two lads who had come first. In two minutes the group arranged a future meeting, and the two lads bore the visitors off to feed them at the canteen.

"Where *have* you been?" I cried, dissolving.

"With those FLD boys," John answered. "Why, what's the matter? Have those Hubei people been here long? Did they bother you?"

"No, they were quite polite," I answered him. "But no one knew where you had gone. People kept coming to find you . . ."

"The boys took me over to one of the offices and I've been chatting with them all morning. They were quite decent, in fact they walked all the way home with me." (A marked courtesy in China.)

Further discussion of the morning's confusions made it clear that a breakdown in the "great unity" of the factions had caused the contretemps. The first set of messengers had deliberately concealed John's presence from the other faction.

But not all hours spent with investigators were pleasant, by any means. One morning a pair of definitely "lumpen proletariat" types came storming in, pushed John into the living room, banged the door in my face when I attempted to follow, and bolted it from within. I heard a sound like someone pounding on the table with a heavy metal object—a gun?—and shouts. "You see this? We know how to use it. Come clean now, you so and so, or we'll make you."

I could only hover in the hallway, hoping they could not be as bad as they sounded. Then I heard John replying in his mild and gentle voice, asking them to sit down, as if they were honored guests. Gradually their tones came down in volume in response to the old teacher's tactic of speaking quietly to a noisy class. When I heard them burst out in a loud guffaw as John told them some funny story, I quit my listening post and went back to sit on the edge of the bed to await their departure.

"What were they after this time?" I asked John when he came into the bedroom to change back into his old tweed jacket. He looked and acted like himself in that coat, and he always seemed strange in the "blue" uniform. Lying back against the pillows, he beckoned to Tiger, who was waiting to be invited to sit on his knee.

"Lately they've all been asking about things that happened in Wuchang way back in 1935." He looked puzzled. "They don't seem to know anything. These fellows today thought London was in America. They were dumbfounded when I showed it to them on the map. They kept demanding that I confess that I went to London to study in 1933—they'd got me mixed up with someone else, of course, and it took a long time to convince them."

"Did they finally believe you?"

"I hope so. I think some former 'friend' must have been stirring up trouble in Wuchang." He sighed.

"Of course, all someone would have to do would be to suggest that you were someplace you weren't and leave it to you to clear it up. Meanwhile he'd get credit for being willing to inform and attention would be turned away from him." I sighed, too, but less from sorrow than indignation. I took a less generous view of human nature than John did, and I was less shocked at treachery. No, not less shocked, less surprised. I had a momentary nightmarish vision of Investigators running rapidly all over China quizzing frightened scholars about their past.

"The hardest part right now," said John, "is trying to remember what I did and whom I knew so long ago. When they ask me if I knew someone forty years ago, I really can't be sure. If I say I can't remember, they get mad. If I say no, they call me liar. And if I say yes, then they keep on trying to dig out more about the person." He rubbed Tiger's ears till he purred. "I don't want to get anyone into trouble."

"No, of course not. But look at it this way. If you can put some facts straight on the record, you might help someone *out* of trouble. These Investigators are really very ignorant about what was happening in China in the thirties. They know nothing of modern history. You can enlighten them quite a lot."

There was a hopeful gleam in his eyes as he reached for his notebook and gently put Tiger aside. "That's true. These young men are not stupid by any means. They just never had the chance for much education." The teacher's passion to inform was well alight now, and I felt that the Investigators were going to have an interesting time from now on.

October 31, 1968

"DO YOU THINK there's any danger they'll make you go to Cadre School?" The loudspeaker was blaring out lists of names and directives for the great hegira of teachers, staff, and students to the mountains.

"No, I really don't think so," John replied calmly. "The Propaganda Team workers know perfectly well how little I can do. They know I can't climb mountains and nobody is going to want to carry me!"

"But why haven't they called you to an accusation meeting for Clearing the Class Ranks yet? The teachers and everyone are leaving tomorrow. Today's the last day they'll be here."

"Well, today isn't over!" He lay back and picked up a book. Almost all the time now when he wasn't called out to meetings, he lay on his bed, reading and writing, warming his hands on his faithful Tiger.

I sat by the window as usual to understand the broadcast. Little by little I had been able to figure out the present situation. A national directive had specified that all teachers, staff, and students were to go to a May 7 Cadre School, where they would continue to carry on the Clearing of the Class Ranks Campaign. The school for Zhong Da personnel was situated on a barren mountain in the north of Guang-dong Province and was said to offer even more than the usual hardships for its "students." Everyone would live hard, work hard, and study hard (study the Little Red Book); only those medically certified as unable to stand the anticipated hardship were excused. The "accused" thus exempted from going to the School had been rushed through a series of meetings, with a climactic "accusation" meeting for each one. After this meeting, the accused had to write their "confessions" to the charges made and display their recognition of their political errors, whatever they might be.

The earlier meetings had been broadcast and I had listened to the angry roaring of *"Da Dao . . ."* (Down with . . . whoever was accused). Ho Jie had gone with the *Jia-shu* to one and had come home pale and shaken.

"They made old Professor Ma stand there on the stage in front of everyone, all bent over, with his hands on his knees. Every time he looked up, one of the Red Guards would push his head down. They kept shouting questions at him but they wouldn't let him answer. Then they cursed him for not answering." Ho Jie obviously felt this was not reasonable. "Oh, Lok Tai, if . . ." She dared not express her concern for John.

But as meeting followed meeting and professor after professor was accused, the broadcasts were stopped. More time was being used on the preparations for the Cadre School, and I had a feeling that no matter how much indignation was required of the accusers, it must inevitably be running down, for all of them faced a complex of personal problems with the hegira. Is it possible to yell with rage from 8:00 A.M. to 12:00 noon, from 2:00 P.M. to 5:00, and from 7:00 to 10:00 P.M. every day for a month? I began to entertain foolish hopes that somehow John would be overlooked.

Not so. Was that his name? I could hear the words "Foreign Languages Department" clearly enough. Surely he must have noticed. No. He was dozing quite peacefully, obviously not sharing my apprehension. Should I wake him, so he could prepare himself a little? Even as I wondered, the messengers arrived.

There was a slight scuffling on the stairs, as if they could not agree as to precedence. I walked slowly to the door and pushed it open. Four young men stood there—why so many, I wondered—but soon realized that there had to be two from each of the now "united" factions. The familiar shout, "Lo Chuanfang, you are wanted at a meeting." I looked over their heads, down into our former living room, and was momentarily paralyzed to see that Joe Doakes was holding a meeting there; the room was filled with blue-clad workers, all wearing the blue visored caps, all smoking, and now all looking up at me with expressions of cold curiosity. I started to turn and go back upstairs to get John, but the messengers wouldn't let me go in or speak to him. I stood on the stairs under the chilling gaze of the people in Joe D's parlor. Pride kept my head up. I heard the two who had pushed their way in shouting at John, and saw one of them follow him into the bathroom. I remembered that at an earlier meeting, one accused man had jumped out of the bathroom window when they came for him. These boys had orders to take no chances. Was it possible that John had to be accused by Joe Doakes?

I realized that at least he was to be spared that horror as the two guards pushed him down the stairs and past Joe's door. Facing me as he descended, he managed a reassuring smile, and though my lips felt stiff, I tried to return it. As he passed me he spoke. "Hope for the best!" "Silence," snarled the guard, and the five went on down, passed the Doakeses' open door and out into the lane.

I shut the door on the staring faces below and climbed back up to spend the longest morning of my life.

For a few minutes I sat by the window, trying to pull myself together. He will be all right, I told myself firmly. They can't hurt him. I went over in my mind the first time he had been accused of nameless political crimes—that was in 1952, in the Thought Reform in Wuchang. Then, all the former administrators of the old mission college had been accused at once, in a mass meeting. It had all seemed unreal and impersonal at first. Then as the campaign progressed in intensity, each of the senior teachers had the concentrated attention of the students, and met for the first time the experience of being publicly cursed and reviled, of being told to confess without knowing what they were accused of.

In 1958 there had been the Anti-Rightist Campaign. I had been with him at the Department meeting when our colleagues had, without warning, turned on him, cursing and reviling him again— for unspecified errors. Now he was going through it all again. I could only pray that he would come through unscathed physically, as I knew he would be untouched in himself.

The minutes dragged on into an hour. The public-address system was silent now. Joe Doakes's meeting broke up and the blue-clad group dispersed, chattering, down the lane. I tried hard not to imagine what might be happening. "Do something," I told myself. "Don't just sit." So I made some coffee and put it in a thermos, in case it would be needed, opened up John's bed and warmed it with a hot water bottle. I could be sure he would be exhausted when he came home, if nothing worse.

For the thousandth time I tried to guess what the current accusations would be. This game was perhaps the most trying aspect of the whole situation. The accused was supposed to be fully aware of his own wrongdoings and to confess in detail. If one had no feeling of guilt, it was impossible to know what to confess to. If one didn't confess, one was said to be guilty of stubbornness or insincerity or whatever anyone chose to say.

One of John's chief problems in the Thought Reform of 1952 had been his failure to realize that his interest in the Gallup Poll constituted a political crime in the minds of his inquisitors. Naturally he had not volunteered a confession about a matter which seemed entirely irrelevant and for weary weeks had to listen to criticism of his "insincerity" in "concealing" it.

In 1958 during the Anti-Rightist Campaign, for a long time the struggle centered upon the question of his alleged "anti-Party" motivations. This was because he had brought together a number of FLD colleagues in an effort to reconcile long-standing grievances that were destroying the unity of the Department. At the meeting some of the teachers had made critical remarks about Party members, for at this time criticism of Party members was being officially encouraged in the Hundred Flowers Campaign. It had never occurred to John that he should report such remarks made in his presence. This failure led to questioning his motivation and attitude toward the Party. Now, in the Clearing of the Class Ranks, what new problems would emerge?

By now we had pretty well grasped the fact that we belonged to a doomed species in the new order and could only hope for tolerance because of our usefulness. We even could see why people like John were considered a menace. To a radical, a liberal is more dangerous than an out-and-out conservative, just as a heretic is more hated by the orthodox than a heathen. The only way the dogmatist can deal with dissent is to suppress it totally. Our slow and painful learning of these conditions did not mean that we accepted them. In every political campaign we saw people break and join with their accusers to accuse themselves. Emotional conversions brought relief from unbearable psychological pressures. But John often told he was "stubborn" and could not confess guilt he did not feel. Nor could I. A properly progressive wife should badger and nag him to make the gestures that would stop the accusations. Such behavior was not for me.

The morning was nearly over. Would the meeting drag on or would the healthy hunger of the student masses be more potent than their required indignation? Even as I wondered, I saw a solitary figure walking slowly up the path. Looking up to see me at the window, he waved and nodded. I flew to let him in.

"Don't tell me anything until you've had a cup of coffee and rested a bit." I took off his coat. He swayed on his feet and sank on the bed. His hands were quite cold, and I hurried him under the covers to warm up. Tiger purred over the hot water bottle and that made him smile.

While he sipped the coffee, I picked up his discarded trousers. They were stiff with mud. I couldn't keep back the question, "Did you fall?" I meant, Did they knock you down?

"Oh that." He smiled again. "I'll tell you all about it. No, I didn't fall down. I had my stick, you remember." In recent months he had taken to leaning on a walking stick, his father's old-fashioned cane. It seemed to give more than physical support.

"I'm all right now, really. It wasn't too bad. As soon as we got out on the road, the guards began quarreling with each other. Two of them wanted me to hurry, the other two said I was ill and must take my time. It was the old factional fight, not really anything to do with me personally. I just walked along and paid no attention. When we got to the meeting hall—"

"Where was it?" I interrupted. If it was a big hall, the meeting would be more important, i.e., more dangerous.

"It was in that small mat shed in the old Department area," he answered. "As we came near, I could hear the cheer leaders warming up the crowd with slogans, and when someone saw us approaching, they began the chorus of '*Da Dao* . . .' " He seemed more amused than disconcerted.

"They led me onto the platform and the two who had tried to hurry me wanted to take away my stick. The others said I couldn't stand without it. The first two grabbed it away then and said I must stand like a prisoner. That was hard, on account of the lumbago."

I thought of the students who had got the "dogskin plaster" for him in Peking.

"So the 'good guys' brought out a bench and said I could sit down.

It was very muddy; that's how I got so dirty." I had to believe him. I hoped it was so.

"And that's how it was. They were more interested in arguing over me than with me."

"Did they bring out anything new?"

"Nothing at all. Just the same old stuff dressed up to sound as if they had just made some exciting discovery. More about my attitude than anything."

"Was it a big crowd?"

"Not very. Mostly the FLD teachers and a few students."

"How was the atmosphere?" Atmosphere could mean so much in this crazy game.

"Noisy when the cheer leaders signaled for noise, but I think they have had about as many meetings this month as they can stand. After all, I've only had one, today, but they've been at it continuously for weeks."

"I'll cry about that next week when I have more time." I was not as forgiving as he.

"Well, it's over anyway. And do you know, Lu, one time when they were all being led in their *'Da Dao'* shout, I looked up and saw at least one person looking straight ahead, with her mouth shut tight. At least it was not unanimous!"

"I'll bet I could guess who it was. But I won't." How it warmed our hearts to think that there was even one who did not bark on demand. "What happens next?"

"Tomorrow everyone will leave for the mountains for Cadre School, and those of us who have been left behind will study under the guidance of the Propaganda Team. I'll have to write another self-criticism and meet with the Investigators. Some time, when they are satisfied with my self-criticism, I may be 'liberated.' "

"That ought not be too hard—you've done it often enough. Take a little rest now and go at it slowly."

If no new or astounding things had been brought forward in the meeting and he could stay on at home, I now felt more sanguine.

November 1968–June 1969

"LU, HOW WOULD you like the job of going over this book and just marking the places where there are biographical notes? You know I don't read English poetry, but the lives of creative men and women are always interesting. I'll read them for recreation. I can't think about my 'self-criticism' all the time." He smiled ruefully and handed me the big, thick, blue-covered volume *The Victorian Poets*—a prized work by Royall Snow, the husband of Dorrie Carter Snow, my University of Chicago roommate in days long ago.

As he had intended, I rose like a trout to the lure and began leafing through it. "I'd love to. I'll draw a line along the margin to show where the biographical bits are and you can skip the literary criticism."

"Good. Then while I work on the self-criticism, you can do this for me!" He left the book in my hand and went back to his bed. There, surrounded by exercise books and little piles of notes, he now spent most of his mornings writing and rewriting the paper that must be accepted by the "study class" leadership before he could be "liberated," that is, restored to a position of comradely equality in the ranks of the working class.

Everything in our lives depended—we thought—upon John's finding the right thing to say and saying it in the right way. In spite of its being such a life-and-death matter to him personally, he could not help becoming interested in the technical problems of such communication and in spite of everything wrung a certain amount of satisfaction out of his labors. But it was with shame I realized my restless pacing up and down in the other room must have been disturbing him, and characteristically he had thought up a congenial occupation to keep me quiet while he worked. I laughed at the way he managed me and settled down to my assignment.

The departure of Tientung for Gansu and Mingteh for Chang Ping Commune, for an indefinite time, had left me very lonely indeed. Ho Jie was in a state of impenetrable gloom—some of her kin were in deep political trouble—and John had to be let alone to work on his self-criticism. I never went out of the house while he was working there, lest Joe Doakes take advantage of my absence to harass him. Weeks went by when I did not go down the stairs and out the back door even for a brief pacing up and down the secluded back lane. Since the bulk of the University population —students, teachers, and staff—were off at Cadre School, the neighborhood was deserted and silent. I felt uneasy even walking near the back door.

Sometimes John and I felt like two passengers on a deserted ship, sailing through a thick fog to an unknown port. I was grateful to him for suggesting an occupation to help pass the interminable hours. But soon I found an additional outlet in my task. The nice wide margins of the book inspired me to jot down notes—diary fashion —of the daily small events that I would have written to the children if I had dared to write. I consoled myself with the idea that when we all got together again, I could review these notes for them and bring them up to date. Although the events I had to record were not always very cheerful, it encouraged me to imagine referring to them at some future homecoming.

November: John ill, cannot eat much. Ho Jie discouraged about market—John wanted sponge cake, anything light, but none was to be found. Investigators looking for information about students we had back in Hsichow in 1942. Most lucky for one of them, found a snapshot he had sent me for Christmas, '43, showing him in Paris, conclusive evidence to the Investigators that he had not been involved in a certain political plot in Kunming at that date. Now who could have tried to involve him? Mingteh's "cousin" dropped in to see John, says Mingteh worried about his father's health. "Cousin" checked blood pressure, heart, etc., and mentioned "emphysema"—what's that?

Thanksgiving Day—salt fish, no turkey! But enjoyed feasts, recalled, at Brent House, in Hsichow, and with American friends. What wonderful people we have known.

December: Most unexpectedly my turn to be ill—fever and much misery. No doctor will come (most doctors in Cadre School—but those left will not visit a Rightist's house) —John in a panic. Ho Jie finally chased down a Chinese herbal doctor on her own, got some vile herbal tea, poured it down me, and smiled for the first time in a month when the fever broke. . . . Alas, poor Buttons is dead. Could a cat catch my fever? Ho Jie buried her with all honors under the hopvine, and on top of her small mound laid a ceremonial offering of rice in a broken bowl. . . . Christmas?? . . . But Mingteh home without warning for his birthday, December 30. Pale and silent. What goes on at Chang Ping? . . . Joe Doakes drunk and disorderly on the thirtieth, trying to break in to harass John. Mingteh kept him out. . . .

January: Tientung's birthday January 6; managed to send me a rare letter from Gansu for the day. She is working at a commune along with other graduates to prove herself to the peasants. Like John she has to be liberated. . . . Cold in Canton. Is she warm enough in Gansu? . . . Joe Doakes's wife absent—investigating—Joe celebrating something with a party of his cronies, a chicken dinner, and much wine and shouting. . . .

February: Chinese New Year. A hard time for John—homesick for Wuchang. Hope deferred maketh the heart sick. The preholiday study classes didn't include him. . . . Some teachers, mostly younger ones, newly liberated, back from Cadre School. Ho Jie tells me they have had terrible times there. So thankful John didn't have to go. . . . Tiger provided diversion by falling out of the second-story window. I braved Joe Doakes to carry him back, slightly stunned, but he survived it.

March: Very cold and raw. John ill. Cannot eat. . . . Tiger in great battle with Comrade Yuan's tomcat. Bloody but unbowed. John called out by student activists to join in manual labor. . . . He collapsed in the field, just as Mingteh came looking for him. M carried him home on his back. Propaganda Team leader sent message later exempting John from further field work. . . . M's unexpected appearance explained by his having to go

	to hospital to arrange for tonsillectomy. No choice. . . . Tientung able to visit a cousin in Sian over New Year. Sounds happy and loves the Northwest. Good old Brer Rabbit.
April:	Joe Doakes and his henchman pounced; we must move to positive hovel by the fish pond—impossible! But when John suddenly told to join "study class"—this could be the beginning of "liberating process"—this foiled Joe and henchman's moving plot. Alternative horror—they are putting a kitchen in our bathroom, WC at one end, stove at the other. *Mei yo ban fa* (nothing can be done). . . . Mingteh arrived in the midst of house rebuilding to recover from tonsillectomy. . . . Total chaos at home, but John oblivious—going daily to study class. Tientung assigned to teach near Lanchow.
May:	Again—hope deferred. John not called on before May Day, although several in his class were "liberated" for the holiday. . . . May 7—Hallelujah! John called out to evening meeting without warning, gave his "self-criticism," and came back to report he was "liberated—provisionally." . . . Continued factional dispute does not allow for full "liberation." John's first act—to write to his children. Liberation—even provisionally—will mean more meetings but under much less strain. He is very tired and cannot eat.
June 6:	An old family friend, traveling in Gansu, has seen Tientung. He dropped in today to bring us a present from her—a collection of stones she picked up on the banks of the Yellow River. Could anything be more pleasing? Or more typical of our girl? She also sent a letter, but he forgot to bring it—I must wait till he has time to come again.

John was still at his usual study class meeting in the late afternoon of that day. While I chatted with our guest, I noticed how much he had aged in the years since we had last met. But then no one in the Ninth Category could have come through them unscathed.

John came in rather late and very tired but revived upon seeing a visitor who was not an Investigator. Ho Jie managed to contrive a supper to do honor to the occasion, and watching John play the host, I realized how long it had been since we two had entertained a guest. Afterward, as we sat in the crowded little living room, I watched and listened while the men chatted. John was animated, cordial, encouraging our guest to talk about his impressions of the Northwest. I had not seen him look like this for years. The degree and quality of the gradual change in John during the weary years of isolation and harassment had never been so apparent to me before.

"I'll tell you more about what we were discussing tomorrow," said John, swaying a little. "I'm tired, too tired to talk anymore." His face was suddenly gray, and he once more looked like the man who spent his days going to meetings and who lived apart.

"Yes, get some rest now," I urged. "You don't have to go out tomorrow, do you? Just take the rest of this week off, why don't you?"

"Can't. There's study class tomorrow and Saturday. But that's the last. I'll really rest after that. I promise."

I awoke on Monday morning knowing something was terribly wrong. John was writhing on his bed in pain, and with every breath groaning uncontrollably, gasping for air. He couldn't speak.

"Ho Jie, Ho Jie, please go to the clinic and ask the doctor to come at once. I think Dr. Lo is having a heart attack! Tell them about his breathing this way, and hurry, please, hurry!"

Ho Jie didn't wait a minute, but threw her apron on the stairs and ran off. I waited, waited, for her return, doing whatever futile things I could think of to ease John's distress.

After a long hour, Ho Jie stumped in alone, her face crimson with anger and hurry.

"No one is willing to come, Lok Tai," she sputtered. "They say they can't make a house call unless the Department leadership writes the order and guarantees it is necessary."

"Then please go find someone at the Department," I begged her. "Tell them how he is suffering."

"I did go to the Department, Lok Tai," she replied. "No one there would listen to me. Then I met that round-faced teacher on the road back and I told her, but she just said the same thing—no doctor could come unless the Leadership wrote a certificate."

John had been trying to follow our talk. "Never mind," he whispered. "No use. Mingteh . . ."

"Yes." I turned to Ho Jie. "We'll just send for Mingteh. He left a telegram for me to use. Now where is it?" I rummaged in my bureau drawer frantically and found it. "Here, find Dick and ask him to take it to the post office."

Relieved to be doing something useful, Ho Jie scuttled off, and I heard her calling Dick to the door.

"Now it's going to be all right." I wiped John's face and straightened the sheet. "I've sent for Mingteh. He'll come tonight."

I hoped this would be true.

Suddenly we were not alone. Standing in the bedroom doorway, peering through her round spectacles at us, was the round-faced young cadre from the Department. Behind her several students were standing, shifting uneasily from one foot to the other. They had entered unbidden by the door left open by Ho Jie and presented themselves without ceremony.

"I have just seen Ho Jie on the road," announced the young woman coldly, to me. She was now a member of the leadership of the Department. "She tells me that Lo Chuanfang wants a doctor to come here. I have come to check to see if he is really ill."

I was dumbfounded.

Hearing the words "Lo Chuanfang," I thought with sick despair of the meaning of "provisionally liberated." "You can see he is sick," I said, striving to sound as impersonal as she did. "He is having a heart attack, and I fear his life is in danger. Please send for a doctor to come at once. I dare not leave him."

"I have no time to go," she replied. "But I will write a note saying that he is unable to attend the clinic. Perhaps Ho Jie can—"

"I'll go, Mrs. Lo," one of the uneasy students now broke in. "I've got my bike here. I'll go as fast as I can. Just let me do whatever your son would do if he was here."

The round-faced cadre glared at him but gave him the note, and he was off, taking the stairs two at a time. I ushered the inspecting committee out.

The doctor was accompanied by a rather frightened nurse and was breathless from being whisked across the campus on the back of the bicycle—and perhaps also from fright.

"I don't know what to do," the doctor whimpered. "Maybe I should give him an injection." Terrified of the responsibility of a serious case like this, she appealed to the nurse, an older woman who was more experienced.

Between them they painfully gave him what treatment they could, and after watching him writhe and moan for half an hour, they scurried off, avoiding my eyes as they chorused, "Tell him to rest."

John lay exhausted. I urged him to swallow a little tea. Then he roused himself, looked about to see that we were alone, and said, "Lu, isn't today payday?" It was, but I wondered how he could think of it. I nodded. "Lu, send Ho Jie to pick up our pay envelopes."

"Of course, she'll go right away." I didn't want anything to worry him, so I dispatched her at once; was he worrying that I didn't have enough money in the house? I sat by his side until Ho Jie came panting back and threw the two envelopes on the bed. He picked up his and opened it with some difficulty—it contained fifty yuan. He looked at it with a puzzled expression, then with an ironic smile. "So," he said, "my stipend is raised from twenty to fifty yuan because one side liberates me, but I'm not put back on full pay because the others want it to be 'provisional.' " So that was why he was so anxious. The real evidence of his status would be the amount in his pay envelope. Now he knew. The struggle was not over.

Exhausted, he slept fitfully throughout the afternoon. Tiger sat on the end of the bed watching him.

The hoped-for shout in the lane came at nine. Mingteh hurried into the house. John was dozing, but roused himself to greet his son. Speaking through the mosquito net, he asked, "How long can you stay with Mother?"

"I'll stay as long as you need me," he replied. "Don't worry about anything, Dad. I'm here now to take care of you."

Peering through the net, I watched John's face and my mind at last acknowledged what my heart had been denying for days.

At daylight next morning Mingteh outlined his plan: "I'll go first to the clinic and raise as much hell as I can, but I'll get someone to come to the house," he said. "Then I'll go right on from there to see if I can find Dr. Fu—she is the mother of one of the girls at the Homestead. I'll try to get her to come, or at least tell me what to do. Keep Daddy as quiet as you can, and try to get him to eat. I'll be back as quick as I can."

All that morning the monsoon wind moaned and blew through the house. John seemed in less pain, but he was far away. Toward noon, a young nurse from the clinic came in. "Your son said Dr. Lo was ill," she said gently, and took his hand to feel his pulse.

John tried vainly to sit up, then said with matching courtesy, in the old-fashioned way, "Your honorable name, Sister?" There were tears in her eyes as she replied and busied herself about giving an injection. She watched him for a few minutes until it took effect and he dozed again.

"What can I do?" I asked as I went with her to the door.

"Just try to get him to eat," she answered, not meeting my eyes.

He was still asleep when Mingteh came in. "Dr. Fu says he must go to the hospital at once," he reported. "He needs oxygen. I must get in touch with the Red Cross hospital. They have an ambulance and should come and get him. I'll go now and phone from the post office."

I was sitting on the edge of my bed watching John. He seemed to be sleeping. Ho Jie tiptoed in, followed by our recent visitor from the Northwest. He had found Tientung's letter and hurried over with it at the first opportunity, well knowing what it would mean to us. He was shocked to see John's condition.

Waking when he heard Tientung's name spoken, John held out his hand for the letter, but it seemed too heavy for him to hold. Our friend opened it for him and read it aloud—a letter full of love and hope and confidence.

John tried to speak but couldn't. Hoping to ease his difficult breathing, I slipped around to the head of his bed, and held him up, resting against my shoulder. His hand found mine and returned my pressure, to tell me he knew I was there. Everything grew very still. I knew that John was liberated at last.

I sat for what seemed an eternity, holding him close, hoping foolishly no one would notice what had happened. Then Ho Jie looked in, saw, and burst into loud wails. Our friend, who had been sitting as if frozen, hurried her out of the room. Everything began to happen at once in a frenzy of confusion. Mingteh was there, his arms around me; everyone kept trying to lead me out of the room, and my only thought was to go back to be with John. Then the Red Cross ambulance men were filling the house, the doctor was there, writing a certificate, then the *Jiashu* leader and faceless cadres were everywhere. Suddenly I realized that a van had stopped in front of the house and that the workers from the mortuary had come to take John away. How long it had taken to get the doctor . . . how efficiently the machinery operated now. Mingteh led me away from the window. The van drove off.

My mind was like an empty room, echoing with footsteps going down the stairs. I went into our room and sat on the edge of the empty bed. Outside in the lane was a sudden single burst of firecrackers. Joe Doakes was protecting himself and his family from the contamination.

Next morning Mingteh led me out of the house to walk by the pond in the quiet and solitude. As we went down the stairs, I could hear the Doakeses' doors being hurriedly closed. Sitting under the trees by the still water, Mingteh explained the procedures: John's body would be kept at the mortuary for one week before cremation. Mingteh hoped that Tientung would be able to get home before then; on the last day we would be allowed to see him once more and have whatever ceremony we wished, but Mingteh made it clear this was entirely a family matter. For twenty years there had been no church. For the "provisionally liberated" there was no revolutionary comradeship.

No, there was a little. On the Sunday I was visited by two of our former students, now colleagues in the FLD. Like John, the man had been too ill to go to Cadre School, but had been in the same study class as John. He had been among the first "liberated." Now, with the permission of the Propaganda Team leader, he and his wife came to offer their sympathy.

That same day came the reinforcement Mingteh and I so badly needed. Tientung came in from Gansu and seemed to bring with her a breath of fresh air from an outer world. Things began to click into place and we could communicate again. Mingteh and I had been too stunned to pay any attention to external appearances, and I neither knew nor cared what anyone might think about our family arrangements. John belonged to me, not to the society that had rejected him. But Tientung did not see it so.

"I know it doesn't matter to Daddy, nor to you," she earnestly pleaded, "but we must think of the family and do the little things that show everyone how *we* honor my father." So under Ho Jie's coaching and helped by her own observations, Tientung saw to it that there would be the appropriate funeral wreaths with white flowers and suitable inscriptions prepared for the final meeting. There would be the essential new white-soled shoes for John's feet, the new uniform, and the mourning armbands for us to wear. She kept Mingteh from shaving—the chief mourner must appear too distracted to think of his own appearance; she kept me from ironing her white blouse to wear—she too must not appear "dressed up."

I asked Tientung if Ho Jie would want to go with us, and she said, "No. Partly she is very afraid of death and partly she thinks Joe Doakes would break in if we all went out at once." So when the time came for our final visit, only Mingteh, Tientung, and our one old friend and I rode out to the mortuary at the edge of the city.

For John there could be no funeral ceremony with the comforting ritual of the church; the church had long ceased to function. There would be no gathering of affectionate and grateful students to honor a loved teacher, no friendly colleagues to speak appreciatively of his life's work, no kindly neighbors to say good-bye to a kindly man. Students and colleagues were at Cadre School reforming their ideology. Even those who might wish to come would not dare to show such opposition to the powers that now controlled their lives. Not wanting to embarrass anyone who still held human feelings, we asked no one to join us in saying our last brief farewell.

We climbed endless flights of stone steps to a terrace overlooking the treetops and sat on stone benches among the pots of flowers. Behind us was a row of small rooms, where friends and relatives could come to pay their last respects to the coffined dead, while a public-address system broadcast at intervals the traditional wailing funeral music and announced in businesslike tones that "Room . . . was now available for the ceremonies for . . ." Attendants would come and place the wreaths for the occasion around the door and, as soon as the ceremony was over, pick them up again and bring out the floral offerings for the next group. Small groups of mourners, some weeping, some silent, came and went; some, like us, sat around waiting their turn.

For the last time I heard John's name called on a public-address system, and I got up and, leaning on Mingteh's arm, walked into the small, empty, whitewashed room, where a very plain coffin stood on two trestles. What lay there beneath the blue covering on the coffin had nothing to do with John. The children bowed ceremonially, strangely. Then we were being ushered out, the wreaths were being hurried away to make room for the next . . . and our old friend, in a never-to-be-forgotten gesture, left us to accompany John on the last mile to the crematorium.

Mingteh was now the head of the family. He laid out the first steps of the longer plan he had in mind: Tientung must stay with me as long as she could during the summer, then return to her job in Gansu. Getting her moved back to Canton would be a long and difficult task, and this was not the time to attempt it. Mingteh would apply to his commune for permission to return permanently to Zhong Da to take care of me; for the son of a widow this was a traditional, allowable request. Ho Jie was to be urged to remain with me to take care of the home as before . . . and I was to ascertain my standing in the Department as soon as I could.

Opportunity to do this came sooner than I had expected or would have wanted. Within a few days I saw once more the same round-faced cadre from the Department coming up the stairs, and called on all my reserves of pride as I greeted the visitor.

She had the grace to be slightly embarrassed as she explained her errand. "The students have asked me to come and call on you, to express their sympathy. They hope you will not be too sad. That you will soon be able to help them with their studies again."

I thanked her for the message and waited for her to go.

So I was still to be a teacher. And I was not to be too sad. How sad was just sad enough? What could you teach when the only thing in your head was an echo saying "gone, gone, gone"?

July 1969

"WE'RE GOING TO put a man on the moon, Mother."
Mingteh extracted my little portable radio from the bedside
cupboard where it lived modestly hidden under a towel. Ho
Jie knew perfectly well that it was there but preferred to be
officially unaware of it. "I think I can fix this up so you can
hear the broadcast—from the moon, mind you!"

"Really?" I was not so much unconvinced as not much
interested. All that got through to me was the "gone, gone,
gone" feeling. There was nothing to catch hold of at all.
Tientung was there. Mingteh was there. But I was not at all
sure that I was.

However, a lifetime of responding to the enthusiasms of
the children brought forth a kind of reaction to my son's
improbable statement. I knew that he was trying desperately
to rouse me, bring me back from my retreat. I half suspected
him of playing a joke. But if he wanted to pretend that he
could listen to the man in the moon, and it gave him some
satisfaction to do so, I could only go along.

"That'll be fine," I commented abstractedly. All I really
wanted was to be very still and go on trying to reestablish
the contact that had been broken off so abruptly. Sometimes
it almost seemed that I could. I wished Mingteh would go
away and leave me to my groping into another dimension.

But he persisted. "They're on their way right now," he
told me. "And on the nineteenth, the moon-landing vehicle
will come down on the moon, while the mother ship circles
around. They'll broadcast to earth. Just think of it!"

I had to think of it. My first thought of course was, "How
interested John will be!"

For so long it had been my habit to treasure up every little
bit of news that would divert and amuse him. Because of his
"political problems," John, of course, was not supposed to
listen to foreign broadcasts, but no one had ever suggested
that I could not. So I listened regularly to the news from the

BBC and the Voice of America with the ear plug device Mingteh had bought for me, and then shared what I heard with John. It helped keep our sense of perspective alive among the mad events that were going on around us. Just hearing the English language spoken was a companionship and a comfort in our solitude. We had heard about the early preparations for the moon-landing expedition, but events closer to home had crowded it out of our minds. And since John's death I had stopped listening altogether and the outside world had ceased to exist.

But in spite of myself, I felt my imagination stir at the prospect of Americans landing on the moon. That night I looked out at the nearly full disc, riding high over Canton, and thought how many people's eyes would be fastened upon it, all around the world, at the great moment of the landing—what a unique concentration of attention. It would be an almost palpable connection between earth and moon. Then a chilling thought occurred to me—what about the differences in time? I called to Mingteh in the other room, where he was tinkering with my receiver. "Whatever you do, don't try to explain to me about what time it is happening," I begged. "Just plug me in when there's something to hear."

It was a long-standing family joke that I was totally incapable of comprehending time zones. I could hear John patiently explaining the implications of a turning planet, and laughing at my obtuseness. And now Mingteh would . . .

"There, there, Lu, don't worry, I'll listen on my set and tell you when to tune in to the rebroadcast," he reassured me. "But it really is not so complicated. It's—"

"Stop. I'll listen to the man in the moon if you want me to, but I can't stand having it explained."

Mingteh chuckled—just like John—and went off to tinker some more, highly pleased—like John—with his diversionary tactics and his success in managing Lu.

Voices from the landing vehicle preparing to launch from the mother ship. The countdown. What came to my ear was the roaring of space itself. Blurred voices. A giant step. We came in peace and for all mankind. My thoughts soared to Michael Collins so alone on the far side, the indispensable backup man, most courageous of all in his solitary responsibility. I pictured that flag against the lonely surface of the cold white plain. I told myself, "There are things up there now that were made by human hands, in America. There are human footprints in that dust. Forever after when I look at that moon, I will be looking at a part of home, even though I can't quite see it."

A bit of home was on the moon. And home was on the far side of the earth. No longer here. There were still some things that had to be done in China—the children's situation must be secured. Tientung must be helped to return from far-off Gansu. Mingteh must get back into the family orbit, freed to choose his own way. And then?

I had concentrated so intently for years on the complexities of my life with John, with the struggle just to keep alive at all, that I had not considered any possible future for myself alone. Without John I didn't feel like a person. I was my children's mother, my husband's wife, my students' teacher, but in China I didn't exist separately. It was a daring thought. Was China farther from America than the moon was?

I laid down my chopsticks and contemplated my handsome son across the table. He had dispatched his first bowl of rice, white, that is, without eating any of the so-called *sung,* the simple vegetable dishes that constituted our dinner. "Do take some fish," I urged, "I've finished."

Ho Jie had provided us with a small fish, about eight inches long, including its head and tail. The sauce was delicious, but as usual one look at its staring eyes had ended my appetite for fish for the moment. After so many years in China, I was certainly not unaccustomed to the appearance on the table of fish complete with their expressionless faces, chicken and duck with eyes and beak and scaly feet bobbing about in the soup tureen, and most of the time I could take it with the "philosophical detachment" John had recommended at my first experience. But at times of physical depletion or depression I still had problems.

"Has Ho Jie taken her share?" inquired Mingteh, spooning up stir-fried Chinese white cabbage.

"She hasn't had any fish," I replied. "She knows that we always leave some for her, but she takes what vegetables she wants when she dishes up." I never could learn to feel comfortable that the cook had to wait for leftovers, although that was the custom in the few local families where a cook was still employed and ate separately.

The Cultural Revolution had greatly altered old Chinese family ways of eating; few people now employed a servant, and household workers were considered members of the family, and very often were distant relatives. The relationship of servant to employer could be a delicate and complex thing in the old extended family, and under the changing conditions of socialist revolution, there were many contradictions and adjustments to be made. In our family we had always followed the general pattern of John's old home, assuming that the cook-housekeeper, whose help was essential because of my full-time teaching load, was to be treated like a member of the family. We called Ho Jie "Jie," meaning "Elder Sister," and her combination of loyalty and independence had made possible a very harmonious home for years. But life-styles were changing. It was in the air.

"The fact is," I said slowly, watching Mingteh's face, "I just don't like to eat fish when I have to see its face." There. After years of loyal suppression of my feelings, I had said it. I was self-confessed a foreigner.

"Is that all?" Mingteh was amused. "I don't like to eat a fish head myself, but in the country you can't be squeamish. Here, I'll just divide it." His chopsticks dexterously cut the fish in half and he carried the dish to the kitchen, where I heard him tell Ho Jie firmly that hereafter, the head and shoulders were for her and the rest for us, and to divvy before serving. She sputtered slightly, but as she particularly liked the head and shoulders, it was a halfhearted protest.

"Now after supper," Mingteh announced, well into his third bowl of rice, comfortably mixed with sauce, cabbage, and bits of fish, "I want to make a list of what foods you *really* like and honestly *don't* like, and I will see to it that you get what you can and ought to eat." He fixed me with an appraising and very observant eye. "You aren't eating enough and you are not getting outdoors enough. We are going on a health program for *you.*" I trembled inwardly, but it was a warm and comfortable tremble. I felt that I was being taken into a benevolent protective custody, and I recalled the Chinese saying about a woman's three obediences: before marriage, obey father; during marriage, obey husband; and in old age, as a widow, obey son. Well, I thought, here we go again.

Mingteh, at twenty-four and a half, had been away from home for five years, and I began to realize that he was in many ways almost a stranger to me. Like his father, he was a rather silent man, observant and thoughtful, but very reserved. Because of painful experiences and life away from home, he was, if possible, even more reserved than John in his contacts with an alien and often hostile world. After all, John had become an outcast late in midlife, but Mingteh had never known anything else. But like his father, Mingteh had a great capacity for friendship, and I was constantly being surprised at the extent and ramifications of his acquaintance.

We had all grown accustomed to depending on him to solve all the practical problems of the household, and his brief and unscheduled visits at home were fully occupied with repairing everything that had broken down since his last visit. Now I was the thing that had broken down, and he was obviously going about analyzing the breakdown and planning the procedures for repair.

Since Tientung's return to Gansu (she had overstayed her leave of absence by a good month), Mingteh had taken over the management of the household, including me. He had entirely rearranged all the furniture in our small living room, made Ho Jie's impossible kitchen usable by putting up shelves and hooks low enough for her to reach. Somewhere he had found a tin baby bath big enough for me to sit down in, so that it became possible for me to take a more satisfactory bath than I could get standing on one leg over the drain hole in the WC cubicle.

He adjudged it to be "inconvenient" for Ho Jie not to have a room to herself (meaning inconvenient for him as well as Ho Jie) and fixed himself a bed in the living room, which took on the "cultured" appearance of a couch by day. I got used to seeing him sit looking at a piece of furniture with a dreamy expression, and then presently finding it transformed into something more convenient and usable, after a session during which the living room would be adrift with sawdust. Thus my desk plus two very handy little side tables turned into an extension of his couch to accommodate his five-foot-ten frame. Ho Jie believed implicitly that he could do anything he thought of, and I was beginning to approach that attitude myself.

"Lu, I've heard from my cousin in Shanghai," he announced one day after meeting the postman in the lane. (He always anticipated his call lest Joe Doakes get our letters first.) "He says that he can send you a wheelchair by freight. It will cost 364 yuan including carrying charges. You can propel it yourself on a smooth sidewalk, and I can push it up hills. You'll be able to get out and see something different, even if it's only going to the clinic." What a dizzying prospect!

I was stunned by the idea of such a daring change in my life-style. Since our move upstairs in the autumn of '66, I had hardly ever been more than twenty steps from our door. I thought with sudden longing of the lovely smooth drive through the campus, shaded with flowering orchid trees, running from the South Gate to the banks of the Pearl River, where one could see boats, boats that had been out on the big South Pacific and would be going there again, and the distant peak of White Cloud Mountain, White Cloud Mountain where the airport was.

"It seems very expensive," I faltered.

"Nonsense." Mingteh was brisk. "We have plenty of cash on hand in the pillowcase. It's far safer invested in something useful. If you agree, I'll send off the money order before lunch."

I did. He did.

Looking forward to the arrival of the liberating wheelchair, I felt the days slipping by more quickly. The notice from the freight office came. Ah Cho was alerted to help and the two young men set off to collect the prize. Ho Jie and I were too excited to settle down to do anything and spent most of the afternoon peeping out the window to see if they were in sight. I showed Ho Jie the picture of the chair that Mingteh had made for me—pointing out all its anticipated glories of bicycle wheels, plastic cushion, and safety brakes.

"Ah, that Mingteh." She glowed. "A good son. But he does like to joke. He told me the other day that the Americans had landed an airplane on the moon!" She cackled aloud at the exquisite humor of his wild imagination. "What a thing to say. I told him I had showed him the rabbit in the moon when he was just a little fellow, but he needn't try to tell me there was an airplane there!"

A tricycle delivery van appeared at the bend of the lane, the driver pushing at the handlebars and Mingteh and Ah Cho laboring behind. I realized that they must have pushed it clear across town, some twenty minutes by car. On the van bed was a huge wooden crate, intricately tied on with straw ropes. Ho Jie hastened down to open the front door and to satisfy her curiosity, returning at once to get a bowl of water for the driver, who sat on the steps mopping his streaming face and shoulders with the towel he carried in his belt for that purpose. Mingteh and Ah Cho came in for water and to get tools to open the crate. "It's too big to come in the door," Mingteh explained, mopping himself and gulping hot water from the rice bowl. (No experienced laborer in Canton would drink cold water when he was sweating.) "We'll have to undo it in the front yard and assemble it and then bring it upstairs."

He and Ah Cho set to with joyous dedication, while Ho Jie hovered about, collecting each nail as they extracted it, with little squeaks of sheer pleasure at the length and newness of this trove of hardware, interspersed with sharp reprimands if she thought Ah Cho was being careless and bending one unnecessarily. She dared not reprimand Mingteh, but she kept a watchful eye on him, too. There was a deep silence behind Joe Doakes's windows, where we all knew his family of women folk would be gathered watching with agonized curiosity while the unpacking went on.

Since John's death they had kept their doors into the central common hall closed, to prevent my bad luck from entering their quarters, so now they could not feast their eyes on the spectacle of the new wheelchair coming upstairs. Bump, bump, bump, up and in and into the narrow space of the living room. Ah! The beauty of it! Gleaming nickel, white enamel, yellow plastic cushion and backrest, bicycle tires, and handles to push it with . . .

"Sit down, Lu, try it," Mingteh commanded and I quickly did so. My hands over the armrests could grasp the outer holds of the big wheels and easily push it along. Crash, I was involved with the bookcase. I reversed. Crash. I was up against Mingteh's couch.

"Never mind, you see how mobile it is." Mingteh was filled with satisfaction. "It's a little crowded to move it up here. No! don't go out into the hall, you might roll yourself down the stairs." He seized it from behind just in time. "Now, where can we park it?"

This was a considerable problem. Even folded up, it occupied space, and space we had not.

"I know," Ah Cho put in. "I'll bring up all the wood from the crate and we can build a stand onto the top of the stairs." And so they did. There was just enough space to squeeze past, and the chair was invisible when the plywood door was opened. A good point.

While we ate a late supper, Ah Cho and Mingteh not exactly sitting down with me, and not exactly sitting in the kitchen, but hovering between, bowls in hand, Ho Jie made absolutely certain she had collected every nail, every splinter of precious wood. This she stashed in her bedroom, under her cot, and I could hear her sorting the nails long after I had gone to bed that night.

But what was going on in the front yard? I got up and peeked out. It was Joe Doakes with a flashlight, carefully combing the ground, in case a single nail had been overlooked.

November 1969

I SOON REALIZED that Mingteh's determination to get me a wheelchair had more significance than met the eye. All during that autumn of 1969 the reports of growing tension on the Sino-Soviet border became more and more alarming. They permeated the newspaper and the radio news and were the topic of discussion at political study classes, even at the *Jia-shu* level attended by Ho Jie. Members of recently antagonistic factions could agree to unite in the face of what was presented as a national threat, and instead of placing land mines to kill each other, erstwhile enemies joined in digging air raid shelters and elaborate systems of tunnels. I was used to Ho Jie's going off to do various bits of community manual labor and I had not paid too much attention when she mentioned that the women of the *Jia-shu* were digging an air raid shelter. Presently she asked me tentatively if I thought I could walk from our house to the new shelter assigned to our area. It was an impossible distance for me, and I said so. She made no comment then, but I now began to put things together and to grasp why the wheelchair project had got under way at that time.

Now she was presenting me with a smudged mimeographed form to fill out. "What's this?" I asked her.

"At the *Jia-shu* meeting we all have to hand in a report like this," she answered, "to let the leadership know where we would be able to go in case we have to evacuate Canton. The Russian revisionists want to drop atom bombs on Canton, and all the old people and little children must be able to go to a safe place."

"What about the shelters you've been digging?" I asked as I tried to figure out what answers to put on the form.

"They are not safe enough. I told them that if there was an alarm, I'd carry you on my back, but they said that it would be better to go right out of town. At least they have to have it on the list where you could go if you had to."

This combination of circumstances was too much. My stout little Ho Jie undertaking to tote me piggy-back to a shelter to escape an atomic bomb dropped by the Russian revisionists; the inescapable bureaucratic mimeographed form prepared, filled, and filed by the unshakable powers that still seemed to function in spite of Cultural Revolutions, factional fighting, or imposed union. "China, you are too much for me," I said in my heart, and to Ho Jie, "Where on earth could I go? Chang Ping, Mingteh's commune?"

"No, because he is trying to move his *hukou* out of there. If you got in there, it would be inconvenient. [I knew what that meant.] No, I still have a house in my husband's family village. [Surprise to me.] There are relatives living there, of course, but it is my house and I put down on the form that I'd go there. I think the best plan would be for you to come with me and be my guest."

I was overwhelmed. "Ho Jie, that is too good of you. But what about Mingteh?"

"Well, of course, if there was a bombing, he'd be with the other young men." Well, of course.

"Ho Jie, we'll fill out the form that way, and I thank you very much. But I don't really think it'll come to that."

"Good. I'll just tell our leader that you'll come with me then."

And so it was that the form went up the bureaucratic ladder announcing that Professor Xia Lu-teh would return to the native village of her friend Li Chun Ho, as she was not a native of Guangdong Province and had no other place to go.

Affairs of this sort were being handled by the new University collective leadership composed of Propaganda Team members, representatives of the former mass organizations, Party members, and, more and more, the PLA. Most of the faculty I knew were still at the May 7 Cadre School; I had been invisible and out of sight and out of mind for some time, and to the new management I was an unknown quantity. When Ho Jie's report filtered through to the responsible officer, it must have raised some question as to my identity and status and, most of all, who was responsible for me, a foreign professor, in a situation now overseen by military authority.

I can imagine the conferring, the investigation, and the decision by a responsible comrade that must have preceded the next step.

Mingteh came back from a trip to market filled with his news.

"They want you to move, Lu," he announced.

"Not again," I moaned. "Where? To Ho Jie's village?"

"No, that's just the point. They don't want you knocking about in rural Guangdong, and they realize that it is out of the question for Ho Jie to tote you about here, so they have decided to move you into Number 6 in the northeast district of the campus—to the house the foreign teachers occupied in 1967. They say it has a deep cellar and you could take shelter there. Besides"—he grinned—"the Clock Tower cadre wants to assign this flat to a friend of his!"

This was the beginning of a very hectic week. That evening Mingteh loaded a protesting Ho Jie onto the back of his bike and wheeled her off squealing across the campus to look at the new house. They returned breathless and perfectly beyond communication. I got the impression they had seen a stone fortress with numberless rooms, far from any human habitation, with incredible advantages in the line of security, cellars, water tanks, and, above all, solitude. For once Mingteh's ability to make drawings and blueprints failed him and I had to agree to the move, sight unseen.

Things happened faster and faster. Although the next day was Sunday, somehow Mingteh got the key and in the late afternoon we two ventured out to inspect the new home, although already committed to it willy-nilly.

It was a dramatic exit, bumping the wheelchair down and out, through the tense silence of the Doakeses' closed-off hallway. Out onto the road and away across the campus in the gathering dusk of the November day. It was very still and deserted and we passed no one on the way. I had not been out on the parkway for so long that it was all unfamiliar and I enjoyed every inch of our progress. The chair turned down winding paths and climbed little slopes, then plunged down a rather steep hill, where the sidewalk was nearly obstructed by the untrimmed shrubbery of the garden adjoining. "We're almost there," Mingteh panted, holding back the heavy chair as it bumped over the many cracks in the paving. "Now, it's the next one."

We were passing the kitchen courtyard walls of a double house and now turned abruptly under some overhanging banana trees and up the front walk of a fat, square little building with a huge arched wooden door at the top of a short flight of stone steps. There were no lights in the other half of the house, no lights anywhere in fact. The large residence at the foot of the hill was all dark, and beyond that was a deserted swimming pool and bamboo gardens. Behind "our" house stretched deserted gardens toward a deserted football field. We were the only people in the world.

Mingteh concealed the chair behind the banana plantation and, taking out a huge brass key, opened the heavy door. It was reinforced with iron bands and great studs and, with its arched top and the fanlight over it, made a melodramatic entrance into a rather small house. We tiptoed through and found ourselves in a living room crowded with what appeared to be the furniture from several class-rooms, offices, and living rooms. It was an impenetrable jungle of chairs and tables. Dim light filtered through dirty French windows opening on a thicket of bamboo growing right to the walls of the house. These windows, like the outsized front door, were arched and impressively dignified.

"What's to do with all this furniture?" I asked.

"They'll take it away tomorrow," Mingteh assured me. "We're to live upstairs. Come on and see that. There's still some of the furni-ture that the English family used and the Clock Tower office offered it to us, but I think we'd better not get involved." (It is better to do without a material advantage than to inspire envy.)

The stairs had a helpful iron railing and halfway up passed another arched door that led into a dark, cavernous pair of rooms, lighted by dormer windows and skylights. "That's a kitchen for the upstairs apartment," Mingteh told me. "Ho Jie is delighted with it."

Around the corner and on the second floor we found two enor-mous bedrooms, each as large as the total space we were now occupy-ing, and a third smaller one in the middle, opposite a bathroom that made me sob with desire. A tub, a sink, a Western-style WC, and, incredibly, a medicine cabinet with a Mirror. "All this," I said. "I can't believe it."

"There's more," he gloated, "a *closet.*"

There was. No one who has never lived without a closet for a lifetime can appreciate the glory of having a closet—and one with a tiny casement window, too. A place to put things out of sight. In Chinese houses you store things folded in boxes and store the boxes under beds or use them to sit on.

Like those downstairs, the rooms were crammed with furniture, a bed, a piano, desks, huge chairs, and bed boards. Apparently Red Guards had been camping there at some time and someone had written large patriotic slogans on some of the walls. Papers torn up and discarded drifted about the dirty cement floors. Inside the closet, a stool and a table, ink-stained and scarred, suggested that someone had been incarcerated there to write a self-criticism. Mingteh picked up a sheet of paper torn from an exercise book, glanced at it, and grunted. "It seems our neighbor spent some time here . . ." The page bore the name of a teacher whom I had last seen paraded as a monster back in 1967. Possibly she had been obliged by the Red Guards to spend some time in this house, writing her confession. Mingteh stuffed the page into his pocket. "What are you going to do with that?" I asked. We both knew very well that there ought to have been some items in that confession about some of our family's misfortunes. "Burn it," he replied, "and forget it. That's what my father would do."

"It's getting too dark," I said. "Let's look at the air raid shelter in the cellar while we can still see."

The way to the cellar led through a dining room, a pantry with the unheard-of magnificence of glass-doored built-in cupboards, a kitchen with the remains of a once tiled sink, and down a winding stair, again with overwhelming arched doorways, into a laundry room and a series of small cement cells. It was like the dungeon of a ridiculous little castle. The first cell contained a decaying straw mattress. "Is this where they kept prisoners?" I murmured, joking.

"Yes," replied Mingteh in a matter-of-fact tone. "It was really too funny yesterday, when the man showed it to me. Just as we came down the stairs into the cellar, a huge yellow tomcat jumped out of this cell and rushed past us up the stairs and the comrade nearly fainted with fright! I suggested it was the ghost of someone who had died there, and he acted as if he believed me. In fact, he just hurried us out and wouldn't go back."

"I don't mind that kind of ghost," I said, remembering how

delightfully John and I had been housed in an ancestral temple one time, because fear of ghosts kept everyone else from enjoying its otherwise very comfortable premises.

Very early in the morning of moving day, Mingteh again bumped my wheelchair downstairs, for the last time, and I climbed aboard. This time I was carrying a basket with a packet of sandwiches, a thermos bottle of tea, and a pillowcase filled with a terrified and unwilling Tiger. We had not mentioned our plans of moving to the Doakeses, of course, and my exit with Tiger must have occasioned much painful curiosity. The plan was simple. I was to be trundled over and deposited in the now emptied (and somewhat cleaned) upstairs flat, while Mingteh and a squad of his loyal friends packed the contents of our place into a handcart borrowed from the Clock Tower office and onto bicycles and ferried our goods across the campus. Ho Jie occupied herself with preparing an enormous meal for the young helpers.

Tiger sat on my lap as we rolled down the deserted paths and roads. It was so early in the day, all was silent except for the steady howls of distress from Tiger and Mingteh's occasional grunts when we went up hills. Alone in the new home, I locked Tiger in the closet with a fish head to console him and sat in the wheelchair looking out the bedroom windows into the junglelike garden below. It was all still except for the birds, no human voices, no one passing. The whole south wall of the three rooms was a series of big windows, and the south wind rustled through the bamboos and parted them to give glimpses of a huge garden and lawn stretching back to the road that ran past the athletic field. I could see hibiscus bushes with crimson flowers, and a giant flame-of-the-forest tree standing in the center of a lawn. How someone must have loved this garden, I thought. How I am going to love it.

The cheerful chaos of the boys' unloading and unpacking filled the afternoon, and when night came, even the discovery that 100 million mosquitoes shared our quarters did not spoil our satisfaction. Ho Jie was in glory at having the exclusive use of the small middle bedroom, the biggest space she had ever occupied, and right opposite the marvelous bathroom. Mingteh set up his bed board in the middle of everything in the room we decided was to be used as a living room, and I sank exhausted onto my bed in the largest room I had occupied in years. But not to sleep. I was too conscious of the open staircase in the hall, the unoccupied rooms below, the fantastic number of French windows onto the dark garden, and the as yet uncounted outside doors. I was glad when Tiger, released from the closet, mewed at the edge of the mosquito net to be allowed to join me.

Early in the morning, before breakfast, the first day in our new home, Mingteh was up and about, concerned with the duty of returning the heavy wooden cart to the Clock Tower where he had borrowed it the day before. It was the poorest excuse for a cart I had ever seen, clumsy and falling apart, heavier than its contents. The boys had had to spend half the morning repairing it to make it usable at all, and they had declared with wrath that it had square wheels. Now Mingteh was eager to get it back to its proprietors, to avoid any further conflict, knowing that if it came in later than 8:00 A.M., there would be unpleasantness with the Clock Tower people. I looked out to see him trundling it off.

It was really too big for one man to move, even empty. At the end of the garden there was a little rise of ground leading up to the athletic field and paved road. I watched him approach it slowly, calculating the pitch and weight. He put on speed and moved more quickly, almost to the top, then, halted by the steepness of the rise, he had to swerve the cart quickly to avoid being run down as it slipped back. Retreating, he started again. The same thing. Trying a different angle and going faster, the same. It was a desperate, a heartbreaking struggle: no matter how hard he tried, he couldn't be strong enough. Should I go and help by putting stones under the wheels when it got part way up so he could get a second wind? Even as I thought of this, he thought of it, too, and I saw him laying out bits of brick to act as brakes. Should I call Ho Jie? No, a man had his pride.

I thought of his father trying time after time to do the equally impossible, writing and rewriting his self-criticism, spending his last strength hopelessly, but determined to do what he had to. I could hardly bear to look. Mingteh had stopped and was resting, wiping his face, looking at the slope, at the cart. He got up and made one more adjustment of his bits of brick, picked up the handles of the cart, squared his shoulders, and lunged—to the right, pause, to the left, zigzag up the hill, a final heave, head down, back bent—and the wheels had gone onto the pavement. I took it as an omen of eventual victory.

Within a day or two of our moving in, Mingteh and Ah Bi connived to build a doorway at the foot of the stair, using the wood of the wheelchair crate for the framework. To their infinite glee, when they explored the attic space overhead, they had found an unused wooden door, two inches thick, complete with hinges. It took all their united strength to get it out through the small trap door and down the stairs, but once in place, it was a barrier that no one could pass. Ah Bi put in a new Yale lock and added a stout wooden bar, so that even when quite alone I felt safe at last. To accommodate Tiger and make it unnecessary for me to go up and down, the boys cut a small cat-sized exit in the frame, and we all enjoyed a combination of freedom and security unknown for years.

For weeks after we moved in, the neighborhood was quite deserted; both the nearby houses were dark. No one passed our door and I could wander in the jungle garden at will. My first exploration revealed nineteen different kinds of flowering shrubs and trees and promises and hints of a succession of flowers with the seasons: gardenia bushes big as trees, spicy cassia, hibiscus glowing with big pink blossoms, and many I could not identify. Leaning on my stick, with Tiger close behind me for company, I spent long mornings poking about and reestablishing contact with the earth. At one end of the lawn there was a gigantic eucalyptus tree. Mingteh and I together, reaching round its trunk, could not quite touch hands. It stood at an angle, revealing the terrible power of some typhoon that had nearly uprooted it, but it had survived—its partly shattered trunk caught and supported by two young pines that had grown strong in its shelter. We named it Disaster Defeated and many times I went and drew some kind of strength by touching its moss-covered trunk.

The hazy early winter days slipped by peacefully, and the healing atmosphere of the garden and the security of the house began to make me come alive. Ho Jie also began to relax a little now that her days were undisturbed by battles with Joe Doakes . . . although she daily mourned the hopvine she had had to leave behind at Number 48. The glories of the "high-class house" consoled her, especially her own room. Mingteh spent days rearranging the furniture in the other rooms and offered to help her get settled. Once her bed was set up, she refused to allow a single change among her countless baskets and boxes of salvaged nails, bits of wood, discarded clothing too good to throw away, paper in every shape, bundles of envelopes carefully cut open and turned inside out to serve as notepaper. She expanded joyously in the new room, banging nails into every wall and hanging up her clothes at random everywhere. The great glories of the new room were two—it had a wonderful big south window admitting the cooling monsoon wind and allowing for hanging clothes out under the eaves; and it was directly across from the luxurious bathroom. It is no exaggeration to say that doing the laundry is one of life's biggest problems in Canton. Tourists often like to take candid shots of people on the city streets scrubbing out the day's shirt or a pair of pants in an enamel washbasin, or of bamboo poles sticking out of upstairs windows, with garments dancing over the heads of passers-by. They see it as "local color," and smile superior smiles. I only wish they had to live in Canton's climate, with rationed clothing, crowded housing, and fixed working hours. They would cease to smile, and only wonder how the Cantonese contrive to be as clean and good-natured as they usually are, in the face of such continuous exasperation.

To begin with, it is usually so hot in Canton that clothes are soaked with sweat within an hour of putting them on, and it is so humid that they must be washed immediately or they will "spoil." No one wants to risk ruining a garment, for cotton cloth is strictly rationed. A shirt that mildews or dissolves into shreds is a real disaster. People living in the city cannot leave their irreplaceable garments in their back yards to dry while they are away at work. The solution is to hang things out the windows, beyond the reach of thieves.

Zhong Da's inhabitants were comparatively better off than city dwellers, because there was more outdoor space for drying clothes in the sun, and a good many houses like ours had little courtyards. But even so, few were so rash as to leave their precious garments unchaperoned, even in a courtyard, during working hours.

Washing bedding was even more difficult than the daily scrubbing of clothes. No one had washing machines, certainly, and even built-in laundry tubs were undreamed of. The great value of having a "foreign bathroom" was the big bathtub. No one could ever afford enough hot water to fill it for a real luxurious soaking bath, but it was a great convenience to have a tub, with running cold water, big enough for the washing of sheets and mosquito nets. The solution of the mechanical problems of washing a double-bed-sized mosquito canopy, in a bucket and two washbasins, with cold water and sticky yellow soap, and then getting it dry between dawn and dusk, when the mosquitoes come into action, is evidence enough of the real genius of Canton's working millions. Every national holiday, May Day, October First, even the half holiday of International Working Women's Day, had to be dedicated to the urgent problem of those mosquito nets.

The great convenience to Ho Jie of washing the clothes in the bathtub could not be denied, and before long most of her noncooking time was spent in the cool of the breeze, slowly and happily scrubbing the few clothes we had. Sitting in the midst of the household this way, she had everything totally under her observation and control. The bathroom became the control room of our spaceship; it was the Heart of the Home!

Spring 1970

THE MOVE INTO Number 6 North East was an accomplished fact, and I am happy to say that I never again laid eyes on Joe Doakes. But his baleful influence continued to haunt us. I sometimes fancied that our name must have been high on some private hit list of his in the Clock Tower, to prompt his henchmen to continue to obstruct and harass us whenever opportunity might present itself. The fact of our having been assigned to better quarters instead of worse suggested that I personally was now in a somewhat stronger position in the intricate interplay of policy and politics, but it did not guarantee any very great security for Ho Jie (who had clashed personally with Joe Doakes most bitterly) or for Mingteh, who was in a vulnerable situation because of his lack of a *hukou* permitting him to live at Zhong Da.

The *hukou* is a little paperbound booklet that registers one's legal existence at one's legally assigned residence. Excepting peasants living in agricultural communes in the countryside, every person in China was (as of 1970) registered in some *hukou* book, records of which were carefully kept by the local government. Without a *hukou,* one could not get a grain ration book. Without a grain ration book, rice, flour, sugar, meat, fish, and cotton cloth could not be purchased.

When Mingteh moved to the Chang Ping Commune, his name was struck off our family *hukou.* As a commune peasant he had no *hukou,* and therefore no ration book. When he visited us at Zhong Da, he had either to eat our rations or to bring a bag of rice with him from Chang Ping. This, of course, was possible for short periods of time, but could not go on indefinitely. Tientung's name had been removed from our book when she went to Gansu. John's name was struck off when he died. Only Ho Jie and I had the necessary tickets for food. Even though the peasants in Chang Ping Commune agreed to let Mingteh leave, in consideration of

his duty to take care of me, unless he got a *hukou* allowing him to
live in Zhong Da, he would be without food, without work, without
legal status. Worst of all, he could be picked up by the police at any
time as an unemployed youth and sent back to the country. (The
Jia-shu women were supposed to report to the police the presence
of *any* unaccountable persons.) Because of the unsettled conditions
in Canton at that time, security officers made frequent house
searches, looking for illegal residents.

It was an uneasy situation to be in. The problem was only partly
economic. Although my salary would have been ample to support us
both, money alone could not buy his food. It was also a political
problem: an unemployed young man with no work unit was a nonperson, already politically suspect. And perhaps most painful of all,
it was a kind of moral problem. Mingteh himself felt unhappy when
he had no work and no work unit to identify with. He was by no
means idle. Settling into the new house, repairing, and cleaning kept
him busy from morning to night, quite aside from the ambitious
program of study he immediately embarked on. But he was so
accustomed to being a part of a work team that he was miserable
when detached.

We had gone together, in September 1969, to the Clock Tower
to petition the authorities there to help get the essential *hukou* for
him, but all in vain. I got the impression that his case was not going
to be solved with any very breathless speed. Moving a person's *hukou*
did involve complex issues in 1969–70, and it was not surprising that
it took nine months from Mingteh's first application until the final
solution. The settling of educated youths in the communes was a
national movement, and resettling anyone in a city meant reversing
national policy, so each case had to be considered in the light of its
special circumstances. While the peasants in the communes raised
no objections to people moving out, the responsible officials in the
cities had every reason to be very conservative about letting people
back into the overcrowded streets where factional fighting was still
apt to break out. No one could be very certain what would be policy
from day to day, and so officials delayed and avoided decisions that
might get them into big trouble. Thus, in spite of the greater comfort of our new home, we were not able to enjoy it fully.

Then one day Mingteh came in jubilant. "A guy from the Clock Tower just told me that I should go to Chang Ping tomorrow to see about getting my *hukou*," he announced. This could mean only one thing—that the officials at Zhong Da were getting ready to approve his return. Glorious. "Once I get in here," he continued, telling me what we had discussed so many times, "I can hope to get assigned a job and I'll feel like a human being again."

"I'll get a pass from the Office," he went on. "They're guarding the gates again. While I am gone, don't let *anyone* in."

I promised.

But how could I refuse admission to the kind of visitors who came banging at the door the next morning after he had left for his early train? Looking out the staircase window after the first shout, I saw the white uniform of the local security officer, several khaki PLA uniforms, as well as the familiar shiny black tunics and bamboo rainhats of recognizable women of the *Jia-shu*. What could they want, coming in such strength at nine in the morning? Ho Jie was at market. I felt extremely alone.

"What do you want?" I called out the window.

"Is Ho Jie there? We want to see Li Chun Ho [Ho Jie's formal name]," answered the police officer.

At least it was not Mingteh they were looking for. But what could they be after Ho Jie for?

Since she was not at home and might well delay her return till the coast was clear, I went downstairs and opened the Door.

It was raining hard and they were all quite wet and their shoes and/or bare feet were all very muddy. Some apologized for this in a neighborly way and I began sorting out the sides. The *Jia-shu* women were obviously ill at ease; the PLA types were official and stern; the Clock Tower cadre—I had seen him but he had not come into my life officially before—was probably on the Other Side. The police officer was being very official.

I invited them all into the living room, the biggest room at the end of the hall. Tiger ran howling as they approached and hid under Ho Jie's bed behind several baskets.

"Do you understand Chinese?" sternly asked a PLA man.

"A little. Please speak slowly in *putong hua*," I replied.

"Is Li Chun Ho living here?" he asked.

"Yes, she has lived with me for more than ten years," I answered.

"True, true," one of the *Jia-shu* women volunteered and the other two nodded confirmation. "Ho Jie has worked for Professor Xia for a long time. We all know her."

"She must go back to her native village at once. All nonessential persons are being moved back to their own places. She must be ready to report at the Security Office on the street at seven tomorrow morning," the security officer contributed.

"But this is impossible," I protested. "Can't you give me a little time to find someone else to stay with me?" I was not going to mention Mingteh at this point, certainly.

"No, she must go." The Clock Tower official was very fierce and determined. He looked toward the PLA officer.

"Some very serious questions have been raised about the woman Li," said the police officer, speaking carefully to make sure I understood. "She has no right to be on the Zhong Da *hukou* list. She should be in her native village taking part in productive labor. There can be no idlers occupying places here."

"She isn't idling," I said. "She keeps house for me. I am old, past sixty, and lame. I can't go out to the market."

"That is true," said one of the neighbor women bravely. "Professor Xia couldn't walk from here to the market."

The PLA men conferred in tongues unknown, while the Clock Tower official with difficulty suppressed a smirk. The white-uniformed policeman looked impassive.

One of the *Jia-shu* women, after listening to the colloquy, broke in, "Professor Xia, I'll buy your vegetables for you at the market and bring them up. But can you manage the stove?" (A Cantonese coal stove takes a lot of managing.)

"Oh, thank you, Elder Sister. If you could do that, I could surely cook for myself."

"Can she cook?" snorted a PLA man in surprise.

"Of course I can cook," I replied with a surge of indignation that surprised me myself. "I'm no old-fashioned *tai-tai.* I'm a working woman. I can't walk far because I'm lame, but I would be ashamed not to be able to do housework." It shocked me to realize that they thought of me as a "bourgeois intellectual," almost by definition scorning manual labor of any kind. I was torn between the feeling of being alien to their world view and a deep need to make my own view understood.

"All right then, if your neighbor can help you by buying your vegetables, there's no problem. The woman Li must go tomorrow morning." The Clock Tower man was warming to his work. "She mustn't be late. Seven o'clock sharp. All the other unmentionables will be there and we'll rid Zhong Da of all this kind of rubbish. . . ."

At this point Ho Jie came in.

Her jaw dropped as she saw our guests. She said nothing. She didn't have to. The police officer stood up and glared at her. Tucking his thumbs into his belt and striking a pose very reminiscent of characters in operas, he launched into a tirade in Cantonese that I was all too happy not to understand. Ho Jie turned red with fury, then pale. When he concluded, the PLA men and the *Jia-shu* representatives stood up and swept out of the room, the *Jia-shu* ladies looking rather timidly over their shoulders at me in a kind of apologetic farewell.

"They certainly brought in enough mud," was all Ho Jie said and went for the mop.

"What in the world is happening, Ho Jie," I said, allowing her time first to work off a little steam with the cleanup operation. "Why do they say you have to go?"

Ho Jie sat down heavily on a stool and began to wipe her eyes with the back of her hand. "It is all Joe Doakes, I know it," she cried. "You saw that man from the Clock Tower? He's one of Doakes's cronies. They fixed this up between themselves the day we moved out of Number 48."

This was the first I had heard of it.

"That morning, after you left, that security man came in and asked me a lot of questions about my husband's family and whether we were poor or lower-middle peasants and whether I still owned that walnut tree." (I knew that the ownership of a walnut tree had been very important to Ho Jie; the question was whether, if she claimed it, it put her in the class of well-to-do middle peasants, rather than the now more prestigious poor peasants' category. If her *hukou* registration as a lower-middle peasant could be questioned, it would be enough under present circumstances to make it possible for the zealous official to demand that she move out.)

"And with Mingteh away," I groaned. "It's raining and I can't even go out to telephone—if I knew anyone to telephone to." Ho Jie could not be expected to cope with a telephone.

"Just as well Mingteh is away," rejoined Ho Jie. "I'll bet they knew he would be out, that's why they came today." There was no way of proving that, any more than there was any way of proving that the walnut tree was involved. It was enough that the blow had fallen and there was no one to turn to.

At that point in came another influx of visitors, tramping in more mud and leaving a trail of splashes on the walls from their raincoats. It was the PLA team again and the police officer. They had been conferring.

"Please, can't you move a little more slowly on this," I begged. (They had sat down without waiting to be asked, a bad sign.) The senior-looking PLA man launched into a long speech in a dialect none of us understood. He was stern but somehow gave me the impression that he was anxious to do precisely what his orders required, and that he wanted to be sure I knew that this was not a personal matter as far as he was concerned. This suggested to me that he was not entirely sure of the case at the local level. The police officer stood by, looking the very picture of a loyal subordinate admiring his superior and backing him to the death in a dangerous situation.

Concluding his speech, the soldier stood up and meticulously wiped up a small splash of rain (we are alert to the needs of the masses), somehow combined a bow and a salute, and clumped off. The police officer could not resist the opportunity for a final outburst in Cantonese at Ho Jie as he followed them.

"There's no help for it," Ho Jie frankly sobbed as the door banged behind them. "If I don't go, they'll make more trouble."

"Could your brother help?" I thought of her very sensible brother, a Party member and a worker in the post office. "Could you go and find him and tell him what's happening?"

"He isn't at home," she answered. "He's been sent off on some business and, anyway, I would not want to involve him in the affairs of the Wang family." (After marrying into the Wang family, Ho Jie no longer had any real claim on her own kin, although there was a warm and constant communication between her and all her own family members. She had even adopted this brother's son, Ah Cho, because she had no child of her own. But in a crisis both loyalty and custom demanded that she should not embarrass her brother with something involved with her husband's estate, especially because of her brother's responsible position as a Party member.)

I wracked my brains to think of someone who might help. I knew that if Ho Jie once got back to the commune, it would be well-nigh impossible to get her out. And if Mingteh should be kept at Chang Ping for an indefinite time, what could I do?

On a sudden inspiration I remembered that a former student of mine, a Party member, had just come back from Cadre School. At least I could talk to him and he to me, and he would be able to tell me what I could do. I hastily wrote a note to him in English, just asking him to come see me, and gave it to Ho Jie, hustling her off in the rain to find him at the Department office. She was gone a long time. I went to the kitchen and looked about in despair, regretting all the things I had neglected to do that might have made it more convenient for Ho Jie, although in all justice I knew she was very pleased with it as it was. I foresaw myself bending over that concrete sink, fanning that coal-cylinder stove under the tiny window, spending hours of solitude cooking a hank of cabbage, for a solitary meal.

Ho Jie did not return alone. She brought with her my former student, a tall, sunburned, barefoot young man, his muddy blue trousers rolled well up on his sturdy legs, a broad smile on his round face. He carefully put his dripping bamboo hat on the floor. Ho Jie ushered us out of the kitchen into the parlor and turned the occasion into a ceremonial call by a twitch of a chair into position. I told my story to a sympathetic audience of one, and when I finished, my listener said, "Don't worry. I'd better talk to Ho Jie a bit and learn more about the whole thing. Meanwhile, help her get ready to move. It is true, it is Party policy for nonessential residents at Zhong Da to return to their villages. There are lots and lots of people hiding here who have no *hukou* and it is necessary to restore order. I'll look into it and see what is right."

This reserved promise of action gave me more confidence than lavish promises to fix everything up. This was a man of principle.

"Thank you, Comrade Chen," I said. "I know you will do what ought to be done. I understand the necessity of clearing suspicious characters out of the University. There has been a long period of disorder and the Propaganda Team people can't know who is who here. They have to obey orders."

Satisfied that I was willing to be reasonable and after a long conference with Ho Jie, he departed and I went to the kitchen. Ho Jie was preparing lunch. Life must go on.

"That's a really good Party member," she said emphatically as she dished up. "I went to the office first to look for him, but he wasn't there. There were a lot of people sitting around drinking tea and talking, but *he* wasn't there. They said because it was raining they had called off the manual labor that had been planned for the day and no one knew where he was. So I went to the field over the road where I could see some of the Department students working repairing the ditches, and there he was, up to his knees in mud, leading the work to fix the pathways. Now that's the kind of Party member I respect!"

"Me, too. He's a good lad, and if there's anything to be done, he'll do it. He told me that we should prepare for you to go anyhow, and that's what we must do. After lunch I'll help you pack."

All that cold, rainy afternoon we sorted and stuffed her multitudinous belongings into baskets and bundles while she told me sporadically some of her personal history, which explained the walnut tree. She had been, actually, sold in marriage to a man much older than herself who was a confirmed opium addict, a middle peasant who owned a small field or two, but who did very little work himself. "He was so soaked with opium he couldn't give me any children," Ho Jie said bitterly. "You don't know how lucky you are, Lok Tai, an obedient, modest daughter and a filial, clever son. And Lok Sam never raising his voice." Shortly before Liberation her worthless husband had died. She was entitled to a share of his property and was a member of his family irrevocably. When she elected to leave the village and come to Canton as a housemaid, the clan had allotted to her the produce of the walnut tree, in return for the use of some of the house. Her precise status was difficult to determine at the time of the Land Reform; as the exploited wife of a bad character, she had the sympathy of the cadres and neighbors, and in the spirit of not pushing things too far but allowing a slight gray area, the tree remained in her name, a source of equal pride and anxiety. She loved owning a tree, but she feared that owning it might make her almost a capitalist, and that was against both her newly developed political conscience and her interest.

Neither of us wanted much supper, but we went through the motions and then sat together on the edge of Ho Jie's bed, surrounded by her bundles and baskets. We would strip the mat and quilt off in the morning and fold up the mosquito net and stuff it in on top of the baskets. Her carrying pole leaned against the wall in readiness.

"It may not be for long, Ho Jie," I tried to comfort her. "As soon as Mingteh comes home, he'll think of something." Before she could answer there was a rap at the door. Not a bang.

Ho Jie looked out the window and went slowly down to open up. I knew it wasn't Mingteh. She moved so slowly. Then I heard a somewhat familiar voice, speaking in Cantonese, a good deal of ha-ha-ha, then someone coming upstairs. I stepped out to the head of the stairs. There stood the white-uniformed police officer, beaming benignly. "I just came round to let you know that it won't be necessary for Ho Jie to go tomorrow morning." You would have thought he had spent all the day struggling to bring about this happy conclusion. "Good-bye, Professor Xia. Good-bye, Ho Jie." He bowed and beamed himself out.

"Well." Ho Jie dragged herself up the stairs and sat down on her bed heavily. "Well." We were both speechless. We shook our heads. We sniffled a little. Then we began to laugh. We laughed till the tears ran down and we were helpless. Then Ho Jie got up and began briskly to unpack.

Next day in the evening Mingteh came home on the usual train. The three of us sat in the living room and told and retold our tales and rejoiced as he showed us his officially stamped permit to live at home again. "Tomorrow I'll take this to the Police Office and get entered in the *hukou* book again," he said. "I just wonder how that man will look!"

"I can tell you," I answered. "He will smile so happily you will think Ho Jie and I imagined all this. He won't be embarrassed in the least."

"No, I know it all happened all right," he replied seriously. "I think we were very lucky. Probably someone knew I had to go to Chang Ping and took the chance to act while I would be away. They didn't think you'd be able to do anything."

"I'll never forget how good Comrade Chen was. I don't know what he did or even *if* he did anything, but I think he's one good guy."

That night there was a *hukou* inspection at midnight. What's so special about midnight? I heard the banging on the door and my heart leaped into my throat. Then I remembered. Mingteh had that precious stamped paper. Ho Jie's name was still on the page of the brown book. I heard Mingteh open the door and the neighbor woman's voice, "Sorry to wake you, Comrade Lo, but we have to check, you know . . . yes, yes, everything is in order. No, don't disturb your mother, we needn't look upstairs."

A world of understanding not expressed, everything known but nothing mentioned.

1971–1972

MINGTEH HAD WANTED a TV for a long time; even
when he was in middle school, before he went to live in the
commune, he would raise the subject occasionally. However,
it did not seem to be the kind of thing he wanted very
intensely, at least in the immediate present. I was accustomed to his way of feeling "needs," going all the way back
to early childhood when he "needed" an old broken alarm
clock to take apart, needed it so desperately that when,
against much disapproval from neighbors, I had let him
disembowel ours (thereby "wasting it"), he had cried with
joy. From time to time there were other needs of major
importance to him: a scooter that gave him the mobility and
speed he craved, an electric soldering iron that put him on
a professional level in his radio assembling, a secondhand
violin that he could take apart so as to comprehend the
curves of the sound box. When he "needed" something, I
knew, and tried my best to provide.

Now, back at home and unemployed, in the summer of
1971 he began talking TV again, and I knew I was in for
it. There would be a transparently casual comment on some
program someone else had seen and we had, of course,
missed; a remark on how confined my life was, and how
much good it would do my spirits if I could watch interesting TV programs in the evenings. Then I would hear about
how much cheaper secondhand parts were at the junk market in town, how someone had found really first-class gadgets
for a few cents. I was not too responsive at first, for several
reasons. I wasn't sure whether this was a real "need," or just
the effect of having no job. As to my own profiting by the
acquisition of a TV, I couldn't have cared less. I had only
seen a TV program once in my life, back in the United
States in 1947, and I really didn't entirely believe in it even
then and there. I couldn't think it likely that in the midst
of the Cultural Revolution there would be programs that

would prove much refreshment to my spirits. I imagined a succession of model operas and political speeches and felt I could live happily without them. I feared that if we bought such a conspicuous luxury, it might cause trouble. I had seen and experienced the petty malice that just plain envy could excite. And most of all, I felt reluctant to put out such a large sum of money from our dwindling reserve fund in the pillowcase. My pay was sufficient for our daily needs, but what if it should be stopped? Anything could happen.

But one day while we were working together on the translation of a list of electronics parts for the Department, he raised a new suggestion, one that startled me and made me feel that I had sadly misjudged him.

"You know, Lu," he said, "I know where to buy all these parts. I could build a TV for you myself, if only I can get a tube—that's the hard thing to come by. It isn't that I want to *have* a TV; you ought to know that. Anyone who has money can *buy* one. It's that I want to *make* it myself."

"Could you?" I was used to seeing him stir up functioning radios out of his numerous boxes of minute hardware for the pleasure of it—but a TV? "Do you mean you could put one together from scratch? Without taking one apart first?" (I was used to his methods.)

"I think I could," he replied. "I've studied it all out in the books Grandfather sent me from America and I think I understand how it works in theory. I'd make a blueprint first and check out with my friends. It shouldn't cost very much. I'll make a budget. . . ."

He could see that I was coming over. This put a new aspect on his project. If making it would be useful to his education, it would be worth it, no matter what the cost. I felt very sorely that he had been unjustly deprived of the scientific training he could have used so well. The TV represented education to him; it was no status symbol or leisure plaything.

So we made some adjustments of the marketing budget and he began a long, patient hunt for the necessary parts. When it was peaceful in the city, he could be gone for hours, prowling through the junk market, inspecting mysterious gadgets in the radio stores. He seemed to know hundreds of youths "temporarily home from the country" who also spent their days sorting over bits and pieces of what he called "electronic garbage." He wrote numerous letters to friends and classmates and cousins scattered all over the country, and all of them apparently entered enthusiastically into this project. All during the spring and summer of 1971 his little boxes filled up with the essential bits and pieces, and the worktable he now built for his project developed extra leaves and expanded clear across the big room, which was now my classroom, his bedroom, and our dining-living room.

The assemblage developed from chaos into something that drew pleased cries of *"Wah!"* from visiting chums, and finally the great moment came when a sympathizing cousin found, who knows where, a small, green-tinted oscilloscope tube, which was to be pressed into service for the picture screen.

At that time, the TV station in Canton only broadcast for a couple of hours in the evening, and was not entirely predictable even then. The receiver could only be tested at inconvenient times, and one could not be sure whether failure to show a picture was due to the set or to the broadcast. But the night finally arrived when the last gadget was in place and the moment of truth was upon us. The makeshift tube glowed, the sound of "The East Is Red" came over the loudspeaker, and there were, there *really* were, moving figures on the screen.

"It works!" What a triumph!

Ho Jie, hailed in from the kitchen to see the achievement, looked at it critically. "Of course it works," she snorted. (Her faith in his ability to make anything was absolute.) "He's spent enough time and money on it. But why are the people green?" This minor defect did not discourage Mingteh in the least, as he had anticipated it, but it worried Ho Jie so much that she refused to stay in the same room with green people and never really enjoyed the TV until presently a proper tube of larger size was procured and built into a second version.

Green or not, the pictures looked wonderful to me. I was pleasantly surprised to find that the greater part of the broadcast consisted of newsreels and I was delighted to see documentary films on the Red Flag Canal, the DaQing oil fields, and the commune at

Dazhai—parts of China I had not seen before. The glimpses of cuttings from foreign newsreels were like letters from home. Moreover, Mingteh's great technological breakthrough happily coincided with the exciting moment in history when the United Nations finally restored China's place in its assembly, and we saw the PRC delegates enter the great hall. The sight of New York streets made my heart pound. I wondered if Mingteh would ever see those tall buildings, some familiar to me, but many new since my days there.

The climax of our viewing came with the Nixon visit in January 1972. Rumors of the preliminary negotiations had been in the air for days before it was announced that we could see the actual pictures of the landing and reception. No one in the West has ever been able to explain how it is that news, especially secret news, circulates so fast in China, and at the same time how secrets can be known by everyone but mentioned by none. The very nursery school babies who passed my door on their morning walk, each holding the shirt-tail of the baby in front, knew that the American Big Man was visiting Chairman Mao and that somehow that meant they should wave to me.

The night the news pictures were first shown, worker-peasant-soldier students, the first class to be enrolled since the Cultural Revolution, crowded into our room, all eager to see. First, the usual identifying shots of Peking, the airport, the representatives assembled to greet the foreign visitor, the guard of honor drawn up with dramatic precision. Then the big silver bird circling down, the opening door, and the tall American on the steps. I had scarcely ever seen even a smudgy news photo of Nixon, and my first glimpse of his political face left me unmoved, but when I heard the Chinese band play the ceremonially required national anthem, the blurring of the picture could not be blamed on the oscilloscope tube. My tears at the incredible sight of the American flag against the skies of China, even though green, again, nearly obscured the most thrilling sight of all. Premier Chou Enlai, a cordial smile on his well-loved face, stepped forward and took the offered hand of the American visitor, and by that act of magnanimous forgiveness of insult and affront, began a new era in the history of China and the United States.

Other pictures followed and for several nights we saw the events of the crowded schedule, as the guests were photographed seeing all the things that people are taken to see in Peking. The presidential couple at dinner, meeting officials, the ceremonial pictures with Chairman Mao, at the gala performance, etc. etc. But the one that gave our little audience the most satisfaction was Mrs. Nixon in the kitchen congratulating the cook.

At the time of this historic visit I was not in a position to see many of my colleagues; I was not well, and was not expected to attend meetings, so I did not hear much expression of opinion about the significance of the breakthrough. But the spontaneous comments of the worker-peasant-soldier students when they saw the historic handshake, Ho Jie's observation that Mrs. Nixon was "not proud," and the speed with which urchins on the road picked up the tunes of "Home on the Range" and "Oh, Susanna" after hearing them played on the radio broadcast about the State banquet for the American guests led me to believe that the visit met with genuine "mass approval."

People in America often ask me about anti-American sentiment in China, and I am puzzled how to reply. I was certainly aware of the periodic anti-American propaganda campaigns, from 1949 on, but I never felt that my colleagues and neighbors identified me with unpopular actions by the United States government. For one thing, Chinese government propaganda draws a clear line of distinction between "the American government" and "the American people." This makes possible a high degree of flexibility of behavior.

The closest to an anti-American experience I ever had was my personal struggle to maintain the use of my native American pronunciation in the classroom. Some members of our FLD preferred British as a more prestigious dialect, and wanted me to change my speech, but I resisted this for years, partly on linguistic and pedagogic grounds, but equally, I admit, out of a stubborn and unreasoning allegiance to my mother tongue.

Whether or not the events were related, I will never know, but shortly after the Shanghai Communiqué, it became possible for us to collect, through the Bank of China, a modest legacy in American money left to me by my parents in 1964. I had been in correspondence with the lawyers about it for years, off and on, whenever it seemed plausible, but only now did all the parts of the machinery get into gear and the various agencies function to hand over the money. We had long given it up as a practical resource; in fact, it had become a family joke. So when we were notified that we should go to the Bank of China down on the Bund by the Pearl River to receive an overseas remittance, we were incredulous. It happened in early spring, when Tientung, happily, was home for the between-terms vacation and so could share in the glory of it all.

It was a cold, rainy morning when we prepared for the great business expedition and our preparations were in proportion to our excitement. It was so long since I had been downtown that I was nearly overcome with stage fright and a painful self-consciousness. Luckily, since I so seldom went out of the house in cold weather, my winter clothes had survived better than any others, and I was able to scrape up a fairly respectable-looking wool skirt and a jacket with pockets. The pockets were very important, indeed, for carrying home the loot. Tientung wrapped me in scarves and shawls till I could hardly breathe, and Mingteh checked all the papers over and over before heading to town on the bus alone to hire a taxi. It was a problem to move me about. Although Mingteh could have wheeled me in my chair the rather long distance from our house to the bus station and parked the chair with his good friend at the gatehouse, it would be well-nigh impossible to hoist me up the very high steps of the bus, and once we got to town there would be no way of foreseeing how I was to get home. I was very lame and walked painfully at best, but what worried the children was their anxiety about certain heart symptoms of recent development.

Tientung was darting about the room. "Here's your bag, Lu, with all the papers in it, and there's the camphor." She thrust on me a small phial of Chinese medicine. "Now if you feel the least bit heart-y, promise you'll let me know." Her earnest brown eyes entreated me, and I promised—with no intention of fulfillment. "We'd rather let the whole thing go than have you get sick or overtired," she went on.

"Don't worry," I assured her, "I'm feeling fine and we'll have no difficulty at all. Isn't that the taxi hooting?" It was. Mingteh had persuaded the driver to bring it up to the top of the hill and in a few minutes I was being wheeled up and helped in. The pleasures of the taxi ride quite went to my head; I was actually dizzy for a few minutes, overcome with the excitement of seeing the trees whizz by. But when we got out of the campus onto the road to town, I forgot my dizziness and all my tension about having to see officials and be seen and only enjoyed the sights of the crowded markets, the buses and bikes and the people, people, people just living. Crossing the Pearl River on the humpbacked bridge, I saw boats again, and a gull strayed in from the not-so-distant sea. So delighted was I that only as we approached the bank did I realize how agonized the children both were at the prospect of having to talk to the clerks there. They were both entirely ignorant of banking procedures and had been thoroughly imbued with a kind of sense of sin about money. They seemed to fear that to have more than their comrades might transform them into that symbol of all evil, capitalists. Besides this haunting moral discomfort about having unearned money, they were terrified that I might do something wrong, for which I would be reproved publicly and thereby lose face.

"Don't fash," I rallied them as the taxi swooped through the bicycles and stopped at the door of the Bank of China. "I never saw a bank yet that didn't treat depositors politely. You know it's government policy to encourage overseas Chinese to send in foreign exchange, and someone inside China must receive it and deposit it in the bank."

"I know," answered Tientung as they carefully pulled me out and set me up on the sidewalk, stick in one hand, and Mingteh holding my arm, "but I'm so used to thinking in terms of five fen at a time that I feel somehow immoral to have anything more."

"Yes," agreed Mingteh, "everyone I know in the commune in the country would think two hundred yuan a big sum for the whole year's income."

Once inside the hushed precincts of the bank, however, none of their fears were realized. As I had foreseen, the clerks were all courtesy in opening savings accounts in the names of the two children, and no one turned a hair at our request for 1,000 yuan in ten-yuan notes. I had hesitated about this myself, visualizing the mass of paper involved, but I knew it would be difficult to use larger denominations in our local market. Now I was glad that Tientung had brought along her extra knapsack, as we divided clumps of bills and stuffed them into my capacious pockets.

"Now," said I as we staggered out onto the wet, windy streets and headed for the taxi stand at the corner, "shall we do any shopping before we go home?"

"No," they cried in chorus, "let's go home, quick!" So, grinning weakly at each other and furtively patting our bulging pockets, we said no more till we were safely home and in and up the stairs with the big door bolted. Ho Jie was at market and for the moment we were alone with the loot.

Suddenly Mingteh's stern face relaxed. Tientung cried, *"Wah!"* and with one accord we all dug the money out of our pockets and bags and threw it all over the room. For a couple of minutes we yelled and whooped as bills showered on our heads, and then suddenly sobered down into our normal anxiety as the children got down on their knees and picked up the treasure.

"Gosh, I'm glad Ho Jie didn't catch us acting so crazy," said Tientung. "Now here's a question—how shall we share this good luck with her? What's the best way?" Mingteh was counting out the cash and clipping it into neat bundles.

"We'll stow this in several different places," he remarked, getting out his keys. "Certainly we must see that Ho Jie gets some good out of this, too."

"Couldn't I just tell her I got some money from home and give her an extra month's wages?" I was delighted that the children anticipated my own wish to share our luck but I was a little puzzled to understand why they made so much of it.

"No, that wouldn't be the right way to do it," replied my diplomat from Gansu. "She will know naturally that we are using more money —you've simply got to get some new clothes for summer for one thing—and she will think you are crazy if you just start handing it out. In fact, she might be offended. It would almost be like . . . tipping her." Tientung hesitated to use such a really dirty bourgeois word.

I took this in and reflected in a flash on the century of American mistakes in the name of benevolence.

"But we plan to send some of Daddy's back pay home to his family when we get it," I demurred, hoping for clarification.

"That's entirely different, Lu, don't you see? When you do that, you'll be acting for Daddy inside the family. No, the thing to do is to buy her something she wants and wouldn't spend money on herself, something she almost needs but not quite. I have it. A new mosquito net, of the best-quality cotton. There's a high-priced kind that doesn't take ration tickets. She'd never use her tickets for a new one while the old one hangs together and she wouldn't want to spend that much extra for the unticketed one."

"I think I see," I murmured, feeling for the nth time how little I understood. "Will you buy it?"

"Sure, I'll go this afternoon and we'll wrap it up like a present and give it to her this evening."

After supper Mingteh ceremoniously handed over to a giggling Ho Jie a red-wrapped parcel containing the "high-class" net, good enough for a wedding present. Her joy knew no bounds. She spread it out and admired the quality, estimated the price, and carefully folded up the red paper while scolding Mingteh for the extravagance of the wrapping.

Then she carefully rewrapped it and stashed it away in the bottom of her safest box—and spent all her leisure time for the next two days sternly supervising Tientung's patching of her old one. She was perfectly happy in the knowledge of her concealed resources, and Tientung, meekly patching under her severe inspection, winked me the message that she, too, was satisfied with the solution found.

Tientung had to go back to her job in Gansu at once, so she could not help me solve the problem of buying the much-needed clothes. Twice before we had made abortive efforts to find some replacement for my worn-out things. The first time, Tientung had succeeded in buying a length of unrationed material for a skirt; she took the cloth, and an old one for a pattern to copy, to a tailor in the city and asked him to make it up. But this was during one of the more radical phases of the Cultural Revolution and the poor man, after much debate with his fellow workers, decided that it was too dangerous a thing to undertake the manufacture of a foreign-style garment—they might well be severely criticized for such an act. However, he did make a really courageous gesture, seeing how worn-out the old one was and recognizing that it might be a case of genuine need: he would make one for me if the University authorities would write an order, all stamped and sealed, to clear him of responsibility for catering to foreign taste! This so alarmed Tientung that she brought the cloth back and between us we hand-sewed a strange-looking little number that I had lived in ever since. A second attempt by Mingteh was equally unsuccessful. At my request he had tackled the cloth store, with who knows what inner trepidation, and had come back with a piece of gray gabardine, which the clerk had assured him would be just the thing to make into a garment for his aged mother. His aged mother was not too enchanted with it, but made an all-out effort to create a shirt. I cannibalized the most suitable of the worn-out ones to make a pattern, and cut and sewed, but it was a disaster. Something went very wrong and the sleeves covered my fingertips, the collar stood out from my neck like a ruff, and I could only breathe freely when it was unbuttoned.

The solution to my problems eventually was a political one, as all solutions must be when politics are in command. Although I felt rather foolish doing so, I asked the "leadership" for help in "solving this practical problem of my daily life," because "solving . . ." is officially one of the duties of the Party leadership, a duty dating historically back to the period when the Communist-led Liberation Army would enter a rural area and liberate the peasants from the local despots. At such times, the PLA's first action, once order was restored, was to demonstrate the difference between their army and the *Kuomintang* (KMT) by actively helping the peasants get firewood, salt, oil, rice, and cloth—instead of looting them.

After discussion it was determined that it would be correct to deputize an obliging young woman teacher to accompany me to a famous cloth store in the old city, a place where foreign diplomats' wives and delegates to the (Canton) Trade Fair could shop. There was unrationed material to be bought there, and a tailor accustomed to making Western-style clothes, indeed, assigned to that particular international duty. Since this errand was now under the aegis of the Leadership, and not a private affair, I was granted the use of a car from the University car pool, a dizzy privilege.

The young woman, whom we called "Sister L," and I set forth on a shopping expedition of such proportions that I trembled. We lavishly invested in washable silk for two skirts and Dacron for two shirts, and with her helpful advice and interpreting, ordered the construction of two summer costumes that would make me look as much like everyone else as possible, while accommodating to my special size and shape. No one would even need to know the indulgence that lay beneath in the shape of two nice white silk slips. Sister L, being an overseas Chinese with more sophisticated experience, was able to sympathize with my needs, and also knew how to explain what a petticoat was to the incredulous tailor. I wondered unworthily what the diplomats' wives wore.

Naturally enough, as soon as I had a new skirt and blouse to wear, I began to think of where to wear them. The prospect of meeting people on the road became less fearsome, and I stopped finding excuses to avoid being seen.

Spring 1971

"KEEP YOUR FEET up, Lu." Mingteh was pushing my heavy wheelchair, with his heavy mother in it, up the broken sidewalk of our hill, headed for the smoother road that led to the FLD Library. On one side was the overgrown hedge of palmetto, lolling over and occupying half the narrow walk, its sharp, fan-shaped leaves brushing my arm; on the other was a steep drop-off where the torrential rains had eroded the slope. I hoped Mingteh was strong enough to cope and tried to avoid looking anywhere but straight ahead.

Straight ahead at the top of the rise a solitary tall, stout man was sweeping the road with a bundle of twigs for a broom, but most of his attention was upon our progress. The broom wagged to and fro, raising a good deal of dust, but his eyes were fixed on us. With a shock I realized that it was the former head of the University, obviously now reforming his ideology by this public labor. He was a man of advanced years, with scholarly capacities, but most notable for the extraordinary dexterity with which he managed the conflicting elements of the University for longer than any other incumbent who had ever held the office. There was no recognition in his poker face as our eyes met, although he knew who I was and I knew who he was. The etiquette of such moments was the frozen stare—one must never show acquaintance with one under political discipline—but I was not equal to the occasion. I gave what I hoped would be perceived as a friendly and neighborly nod of greeting, as if it were the most natural thing in the world to meet the University president sweeping the roads. Actually, I didn't feel that sweeping the roads was work to be ashamed of, for anyone. What hurt was the knowledge that he had been sent to do it in order to humiliate him publicly, not for any real misdemeanor, but as a play in the struggle of politics; the knowledge that those in power really looked with contempt upon manual labor themselves, although they claimed to be the political defenders of those who live by manual

John Lo and Ruth Earnshaw Lo
at their wedding, Shanghai,
August 5, 1937

The Los, John, Mingteh, Ruth,
Tientung, en route to Wuhan, 1947

Tientung, Ruth, Mingteh, in Wuchang, 1952

20th wedding anniversary, Canton, 1957

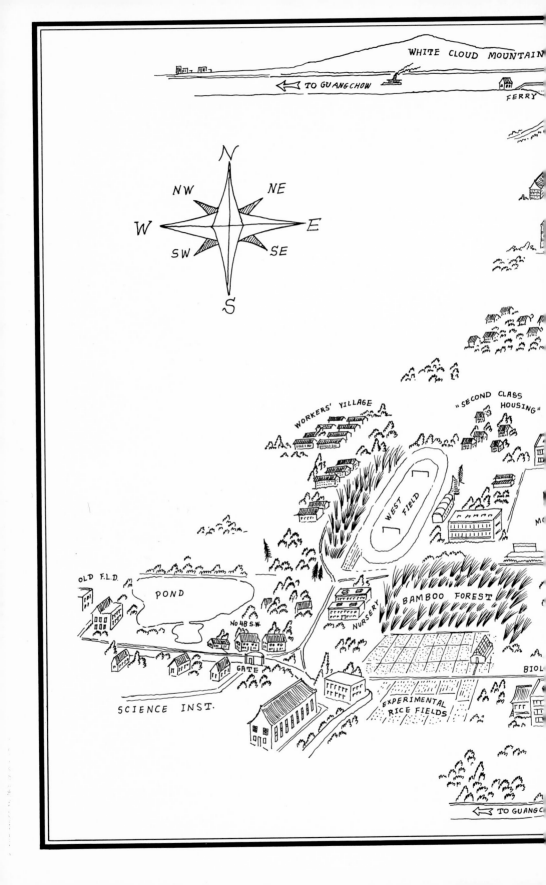

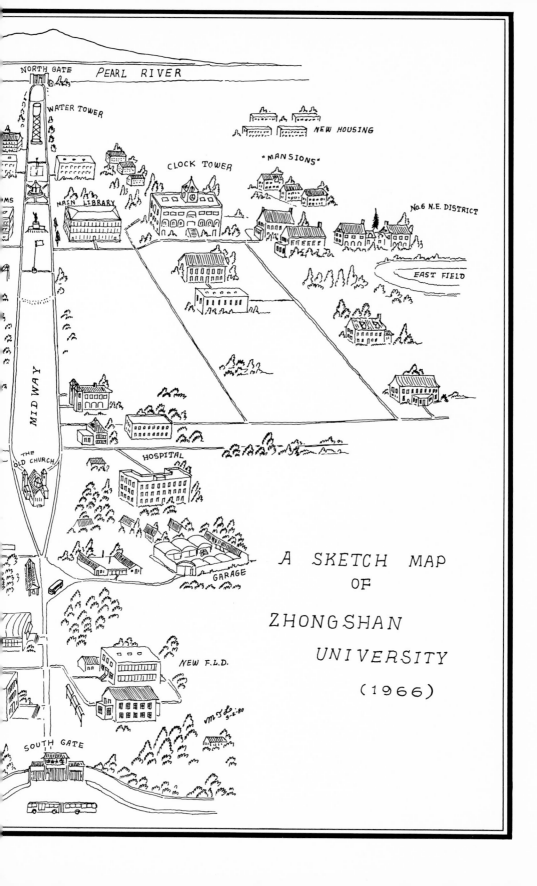

NORTH GATE
PEARL RIVER
WATER TOWER
NEW HOUSING
CLOCK TOWER
"MANSIONS"
MAIN LIBRARY
No.6 N.E. DISTRICT
MS
EAST FIELD
MIDWAY
THE OLD CHURCH
HOSPITAL
GARAGE
NEW F.L.D.
SOUTH GATE

A SKETCH MAP
OF
ZHONGSHAN
UNIVERSITY
(1966)

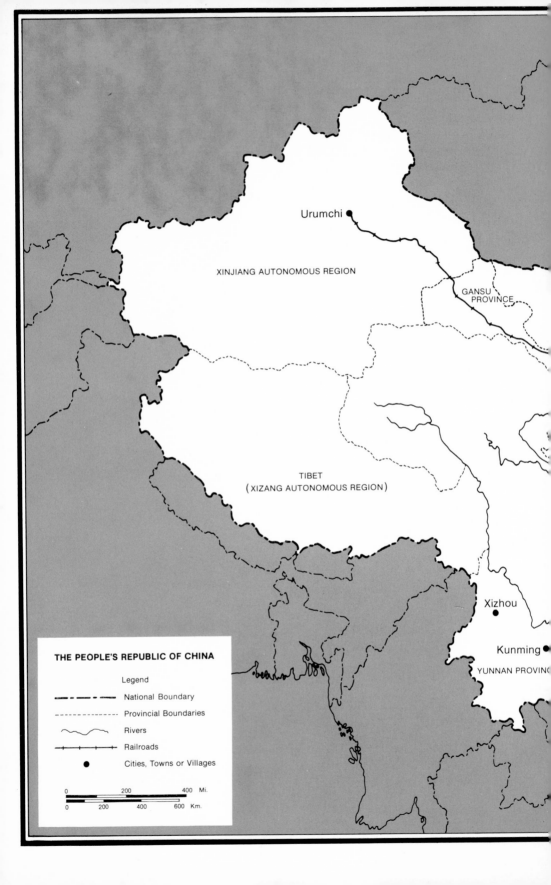

THE PEOPLE'S REPUBLIC OF CHINA

Legend

National Boundary

Provincial Boundaries

Rivers

Railroads

● Cities, Towns or Villages

0   200   400 Mi.

0   200   400   600 Km.

Urumchi ●

XINJIANG AUTONOMOUS REGION

GANSU
PROVINCE

TIBET
(XIZANG AUTONOMOUS REGION)

Xizhou
●

Kunming ●

YUNNAN PROVINC

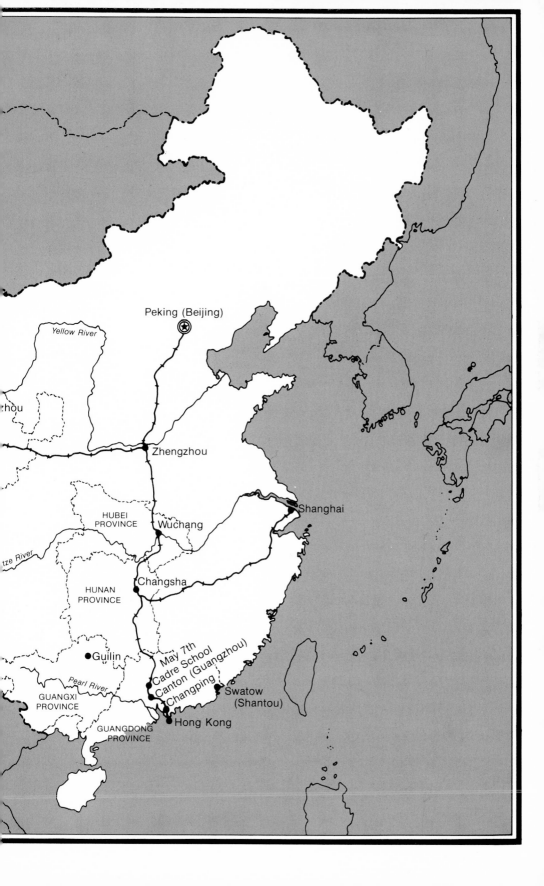

Mingteh at the Chang Ping Commune, 1965

Ruth with Buttons and Tiger
on the balcony of #48, Canton, 1966
Tientung in Peking for the Mass Reception, 1966
Ruth and Timmy Willy at #6, Canton, 1970
The Los' house, #6, Canton, 1978
(*Katharine Kinderman photo*)

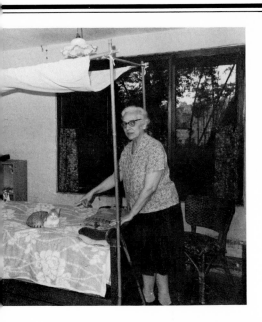

Mingteh, Manman, Ruth,
Canton, 1976
(Left) Ruth and Timmy Willy,
1972 (*Richard Hadden photo*)

Ruth and Dorothy Douglas, Dong Fang Hotel, Canton, 1975
Mingteh and Ruth, Canton, 1978

Official document sent by the Zhongshan University Party Committee to the family of Dr. Lo Chuanfang stating that his designation as a Rightist was incorrect. The penciled words at the top of the page are a request to the Branch Committee to pass the document on to the family. The characters in parentheses are the numbers one, two and three, representing space for filling in additional information.

请转给 张/如

错划右派分子改正通知书

〔79〕中改字第 0041 号

根据中共中央〔1978〕55号文件指示，我们对 骆传芳 同志 1958 年 4 月被划为右派分子进行了复查，认为属于错划，决定给予改正，恢复政治名誉。并作如下安置处理：

（一）

（乙）

（丙）

中共中山大学委员会

一九七九年

此件发给本人、其所属单位及有关亲属各一份，存档两份。

---

please give to family

Notice about Wrongfully Designated Rightists

(79) Zhong Rectify No. 0041

According to Directive No. 55, 1978, of the Central Committee of the Chinese Communist Party, we have carried out a reinvestigation on the designating of Comrade Lo Chuanfang as a Rightist in April 1958, and consider the case to be one of wrong designation. It has been decided to rectify this case, reinstate his political name, and . . . [The last eight characters were crossed out by authorities. The phrase refers only to cases when the former Rightist was still living.]

**Committee of Chinese
Communist Party**
Zhongshan University

March 21, 1979

A copy of this notice is to be given to the person concerned, to the unit where he works and to his family. Two copies are to be kept in the files.

labor. I was caught in the tangle of contradictions between real politics and real ideals, and could only reach out across the social space with a small symbolic gesture that I hoped would make the day less bitter to a man I respected.

Mingteh and I were on our way to accomplish a really heady errand. My new Department Leadership had told me that I could again take out books and magazines from what was left of the FLD Library. The prospect of something fresh to read after four years of literary famine made us both tremble with eagerness. It would be my first appearance at the Department for years, and I did not know who would be there, or in what political condition, or what the atmosphere would be.

After four years of Cultural Revolution, academic work was getting started again. The whole Foreign Languages Department, including, of course, the English Speciality, to which I had been assigned ever since 1953, had arbitrarily been pulled out of the University and transplanted to the Foreign Languages Institute, a lower-level institution academically, located near White Cloud Mountain, in the suburbs of Canton. I was told that I was to stay on at Zhong Da because there was no suitable housing for me at White Cloud Mountain. I doubted this, but had no choice. I was then assigned to work with a group of teachers responsible for teaching reading skills in English to students majoring in the sciences. In former times this work was somewhat despised by the "speciality" teachers as being "technical" and not "literary," and, in fact, to be transferred from "speciality" teaching to what may be translated as "Outside English" had been a punishment for Rightists in the late fifties. I knew little about the work I was to do and less about those who would be my colleagues. Still, it made me feel more like a whole person to be asked to go back to work at anything, and I faced the new situation with considerable interest.

Alighting at the door of the building now assigned to our work group, I waited for Mingteh to fold up and secure my chair with a bicycle lock and then went in. This building had been built before Liberation to house the president of the Canton Theological Seminary, and it was an impressive mansion, with high ceilings for coolness, big windows for light and air, and massive iron-studded doors for security. Now it had been subdivided and partitioned for the use of the Outside English faculty, with a makeshift library set up in what must have been the drawing room, a makeshift language laboratory upstairs in the master bedroom overlooking, at a little distance, the bus station, whose noise made it impossible to make a recording or listen to one. Bedrooms and sun parlors and studies had been converted into uncomfortable and inconvenient classrooms and offices. In the large basement dwelt Hing Jie, the longtime cleaning woman and general factotum of the Department. Now she erupted from her den and literally fell on my neck. "Ah, Lok Tai, you are well again! How good it is to see you! And Lok Sam . . ." She paused and wiped her eyes. "But Lok Ming-duk is with you, isn't he? A son is a great comfort." She turned rather fiercely on Mingteh and read him a brief but effective lecture in Cantonese on the duties of a son to his widowed mother. He grinned somewhat sheepishly, but accepted her remarks. They had been the best of friends since his primary school days.

Our noisy welcome on the steps had given ample warning to all within of our approach, and when I limped into the small library office, everyone was prepared to act with appropriate correctness. No one looked up from his work, but everyone saw me. I went to the desk and addressed the librarian. "May I go into the stacks and select some books for teaching materials?"

"Yes, of course." We had not met socially for nearly five years, but there was no sign of that. The last I had heard of her, dear little soul, was that her home had been totally looted and her invalid husband left alone to fend for himself while she went to Cadre School. Mingteh, as poker-faced as the former University president we had just encountered, went to the newspaper rack and retired into the pages of the *Jen Min Jih Pao,* the official, and hence blameless, Peking newspaper. Back in the stacks, I felt almost dizzy at the sight of so many choices, although the shelves were sadly depleted. When the Department went to White Cloud Mountain, most of the books went with them. However, there were rows of duplicate Everyman classics, all of Dickens, Thackeray, some Arnold Bennett and Stevenson, and shelf upon shelf of unwanted copies of the *Advanced English* textbook used in the Soviet Union by students of English, and at one time adopted by the FLD Speciality as its Bible.

Seeing those familiar maroon-covered volumes filled me with mixed emotions. Obviously they had been left behind by the Departing Speciality as being of no use to them. My experience with them had been instructive.

When John and I had joined the Speciality faculty in 1953, we found all our colleagues there engaged in studying and extolling the marvelous new English texts used in the advanced schools of our "big brother," the Soviet Union. At that time everything Russian was good, and the correct attitude, had I but known it, was one of reverent awe. But in 1953 I was still very innocent and inexperienced politically, and when I was asked my opinion of the texts, I frankly gave it: they were probably very good for Russian speakers, but needed a lot of adaptation to be usable in China. In this opinion I think I was by no means alone. Most of my colleagues were experienced and competent language teachers, by no means devoid of common sense. But in the atmosphere of that year, anything but sycophantic praise of all things Russian was tantamount to rejecting everything good and reasonable (i.e., socialist) in the world.

The obligatory Russophile attitude of that period even led some of my colleagues to such extremes as staying up all night to translate into Chinese the pronunciation exercises of the text, originally designed to help Russian speakers cope with the English pronunciation system. We found it necessary, first, to teach our Chinese students to make Russian mistakes, in order to correct them according to the sacred book. I found with amusement and amazement that my native American pronunciation was not considered as "correct" as the pseudo British-English taught in the Russian book.

My criticism of the Russian texts sealed my doom at Zhong Da for some time, and I received black looks as the Woman Who Had Criticized the Soviet Textbook. But the Russian texts, raised to preeminence by political considerations, presently fell into disfavor for the same reasons: revisionism was discovered and everything Russian became an abomination and the books were retired (but thriftily kept on the back shelves, just in case?). The young colleague (now in the Cadre School tagged as a monster) who had supported the Russian book most vociferously and found my American accent so painful came very quietly to see me one evening, possibly sent by the Party leadership, to say that my criticism was not without reason on technical grounds, but—warming to her task—the most difficult part of the apology having been accomplished, she sternly advised me that I "should be more careful hereafter to consider the political effects upon others of my actions."

But to return to my first post–Cultural Revolution visit to the library, as I stood hesitating between the exciting prospect of rereading *Middlemarch* or *Oliver Twist,* one of the young teachers brushed past me, and I realized that she had squeezed my hand, though she didn't look at me. I worked my way down the shelves to a gap in the ranks of moldy books and, looking through into the next stack, caught the beaming glance of another former student. He, too, said nothing. At the end of the row, feeling somewhat tired from being on my feet so long, I looked about for a chair. Suddenly, out of nowhere, a stool was pushed forward. A stir in the outer room told me someone important had entered. Following protocol, I continued my earnest inspection of the shelves. Then a vigorous, friendly hand fell upon my shoulder and I was being greeted warmly by the new Leadership, a youngish woman Party member who had come in along with a PLA man from the University's leading group.

"Ah, Xia Lao-shih, I'm glad to see you are able to come out," she said, and I believed her. "We're all looking forward to your lecture on phonetics next week."

The PLA man said something to her.

"Would you like to have some of the students come and push you over in your chair?" she asked. "We know you have a problem with walking."

"Thank you very much. That would be very helpful," I replied, wondering who would be honored by this official duty. To appear in public pushing a foreign teacher in a wheelchair in the atmosphere of the aftermath of the Cultural Revolution was going to be a political duty not easy to perform.

Subsequent visits to the library to get teaching materials for newly organized classes revealed more and more interesting fare concealed in out-of-the-way nooks, and I was soon privileged to take home armloads of back numbers of the *Saturday Review,* the *New York Times Book Review,* and—marvelous—the *New Yorker,* as well as such nourishment as the *Guardian* and the *Daily Worker.* Mingteh and I sat up late nights, gulping down news of the outside world, studying the advertisements, comparing our impressions.

It was from this reading that we first began to get a concept of all that had been going on in the turmoil of the sixties in the United States. As teachers of English, John and I had always been among those allowed to read such foreign publications as authority admitted; students were limited to different degrees at different times. But from the inception of the Cultural Revolution onward, although books and journals continued to pile up in some "classified" part of the library, we had no access to them. The only news of affairs in America was what filtered through in the officially published Chinese papers and what we heard on our "illegal" radio.

For the first time now we learned of the Freedom Riders, the demands of the students in the universities, the riots and demonstrations, the development of the women's liberation movement. Although we had heard a limited amount about the war in Vietnam, we had no idea that there was a powerful movement in the United States resisting it. Mingteh eagerly devoured every bit of information about space research and electronics, and I found a new dimension of interest in the heretofore unheard-of struggle to preserve the natural environment. Communications science, linguistics, biology in its new social and philosophical applications, a world of intellectual excitement suddenly opened up for us.

The new and sometimes absurd new words filled me with delight, and I collected gaudy examples of the language of a new world. I had not heard living American spoken by living Americans since 1951; my language was frozen as of that year. The implications and usage of "cool," "square," "zap," "with it," "way out," and countless other expressions were as obscure to me as if they were in a foreign tongue. Not quite foreign. More like reading Shakespeare or Chaucer without looking at the notes. I read with wry satisfaction many instances of the current use of "like" in place of the classic "as if" and recalled how the Department Speciality politicos (now monsters) had spent weary hours criticizing John's qualifications as a teacher because he had observed this phenomenon in his wider reading and mentioned it in class as an instance of language change. To the rigid dogmatists,

English had no right to change, and "modern" meant nineteenth century.

When I read about the struggle of the Freedom Riders and the enormous progress toward civil rights, I was moved to tears. Tears of joy at every victory, and tears of frustration when I saw how the old stereotype of "racist America" was perpetuated in the English language textbooks used in China in the smug story of "Little Tom," a persecuted black child, and in horrible, sensational accounts of racist violence. The blacks were always pictured as born losers, and their glorious achievements in liberating themselves were ignored.

The America I rediscovered in this orgy of reading was not the America I had seen in 1947 in many respects. I could easily see that there was much confusion, disorder, and social dislocation and disease. But the overwhelming impression was of the tremendous vitality and vigor with which people were coping with the crop of problems springing from the changes since World War II. There was racial strife and the blacks were not fairly treated—but there was awareness of the problem, and strong forces, black and white, uniting to change the situation. The environment was being polluted by industrial expansion, but there were concerned citizens able to speak out on their own initiative and make their concern known effectively. Students in America, like those in China, were discontented, and like their Chinese counterparts their demands ranged from the really fundamental to the palpably absurd, but they were not being used by the politicians to kill each other. Reading about gourmet cuisines when I was slightly hungry made me feel less than happy. But the same page that carried the announcements of marvelous new cookbooks and esoteric remarks about cheese and wine announced campaigns for contributions to the world's hungry.

The America we saw reflected in the pages of these magazines was full of contradictions. It was not ideal. But it was alive.

I counted the chairs and calculated the available space on Ming-teh's bed: the two high-backed wicker chairs, two smaller ones (one had to be near a wall because of a weakness in the right hind leg), two extremely uncomfortable wooden desk chairs, Ho Jie's bamboo stool from the kitchen, room for four thin people on the bed, and my wheelchair. On the round dining room table I had spread out several dictionaries, some piles of mimeographed lesson sheets, and several current copies of English-language Chinese magazines, which I had taken from the recently reopened library. These last were bait for conversation. Anyone could safely talk about any topic taken up in *China Reconstructs, China Pictorial,* or *Peking Review.*

I was now prepared to meet a class for the first time in some five years. There was not then, in 1971, a new enrollment of first-year students, because there was not an acceptably revolutionary way to select them, but there were remnants of the classes admitted before 1966 and a good many newly appointed young teachers, who, when faced with the prospect of teaching, realized how totally unprepared they were for their technical work. It was the duty now of the older teachers to help them make up their deficiencies and to work with them in preparing new teaching materials.

Hearing voices below, I opened the window and tossed down the front door key so that my trusted colleague on the sidewalk could open the door and bring in the hopeful learners. Going up and down was getting to be a real problem, and I was still afraid to live behind an unlocked door. The students had readily agreed to come to my house for lessons, to save me from walking and themselves from chair-pushing.

In they trooped, half a dozen young men and three girls, plus the Leadership, the Party member colleague who was responsible for organizing the work and managing me. I tried to make this task as easy for him as I could, because I really respected and liked him. All the students in this first class were actually newly appointed teachers, my academic colleagues. It was probably easier for them to accept teaching from me than from any of the other older teachers, since they had never confronted me in a factional struggle: they had a personal history of political conflict with most of the others, which would make for a difficult classroom situation to say the least. Many old teachers simply refused to teach at all, saying that they felt they were not qualified; certainly they had all had to listen to enough criticism to shake their confidence and destroy any teaching relationship.

Perhaps never in the history of education has the establishment of rapport between teacher and class been so fraught with problems as in China after the Cultural Revolution. Traditionally, students in China have held their teachers in the most profound respect and often affection. In spite of all the hardships and difficulties of the war years, John and I had always found this special relationship ample compensation for all the troubles we shared. Even after Liberation this was the case; although they criticized John in public, they often made it clear that their basic feelings for him were unchanged. But now, after four years of revolutionary practice in downgrading the "bourgeois intelligentsia," how would these young people handle the conflict between their early cultural training to respect teachers and the things they had been doing to teachers—urged on by Chairman Mao—as a patriotic duty? How could teachers face them after their experience of harassment, treachery, and violence? Could I rise to the demands of the high calling of a teacher when my class included someone who had accused my daughter of concealing hand grenades? How could I correct the grammar of someone whose voice kept ringing in my ears saying, "Let me do whatever your son would do if he was here"?

There is no denying that we were all a little tense as I greeted the class and there was a welcome flurry over the peculiarities of the seating arrangements. When everyone was settled, we began. Once upon a time the first meeting of a class would be the occasion for the teacher to state clearly the objectives of the course, the requirements for the students, references and texts to be used. Now this was reversed. It was for the representatives of the students to tell the teacher what they wished to be taught and what they were prepared to do. It was like a collective bargaining session between union and management, and not without surprises for me. Not the least of these was the slightly patronizing word of commendation to me for being willing to teach at all, and for my having asked for student opinion, rather than "dictating from on high."

Formalities over, though, we very soon got on reasonable terms, based on our mutual recognition of their need and my concern. It was like fresh air in a stuffy room to be back at the old job of listening to their stumbling speech, analyzing their linguistic problems, and tactfully leading them to find their solutions.

Besides meeting with these young people as students, I now began
to spend a good deal of time working with them as colleagues, in the
preparation of new textbooks for the course they would have to offer
in the spring term.

One of the fruits of the Cultural Revolution was the total discred-
iting of all previously used textbooks and teaching methods. Whatever we did from now on had to be different or it would be condemned by the radical students as being reactionary, if not
downright counter-revolutionary. Some of the ideas for change that
came up were eminently sensible and could be adopted without
difficulty: for example, introducing commonly used technical terms
for each subject field at the very beginning in teaching pronunciation. It gave the chemistry students a pleasant sense of achievement
to learn to say "chemistry" when they were being taught the English
/k/ phoneme even if it did cause some later confusion in spelling.
They felt that it was somehow revolutionary to practice saying the
names of farm tools, such as "hoe," "tractor," "shovel," even though
there were predictable troubles ahead when they would discover that
the pictures in the English dictionary did not match their mental
images of the things named. (A Chinese hoe does not look like an
American one, and the tractors used in Chinese communes, tailored
to fit Chinese needs, were not precisely the ones in the book.) And
I hope never again to have to slug it out with a determined peasant
student as to the difference between shovels and spades.

Ideological problems arose between students and teachers over
such points as the correctness of naming an individual as the discov-
erer of some scientific truth. "All real progress is the result of the
collective labor of the working masses, and it is bourgeois to credit
individuals with discoveries or inventions," they would announce.
"Columbus would never have discovered America without the collective labor of the sailors." This indisputable fact made me writhe,
accustomed as I was to bourgeois historical works, and aware of the
general acceptance of such ideas as that Mendel's law was the result
of Mendel's research, that the name of Darwin was quite well known
in connection with the theory of evolution, or that the periodic table
of elements was often referred to as "Mendeleev's Table." The only

heroes to be memorialized now were to be the anonymous working masses, and the teacher was in trouble who attempted to put forward the notion that people in other countries learned a different version of history. The very knowledge that there was such a thing seemed to support revisionism.

Even teaching the English alphabet in its accepted order of *abc* was questioned by some who maintained that it would be easier to memorize the names of all the letters in groups which rhymed (*bcdegptvz*). Happily the Party Leadership listened to my despairing appeal for reason in this, and the English alphabet was restored to its conventional arrangement as being necessary if one were to use an English dictionary.

The leaders of our working group at this time were extraordinarily gifted. They recognized that it would be possible to improve the teaching materials and methods if a more scientific linguistic base were used, instead of the old literary approach. And they managed somehow to bring together members of the conflicting factions and mold them into a comparatively harmonious and efficient team. The more experienced teachers were encouraged to offer lectures on linguistics, grammar, teaching and study methods, and this made us feel good. Our work was needed and we were respected. And the younger teachers were encouraged to improve their language skills with our help, and to learn more theory.

It was a real pleasure to work on the lectures, going over books that John and I had studied together, meeting his neat handwritten notes in every margin, learning from his comments and cross-references. I felt that I was really working with him still, and it was a great comfort.

It had appeared that the Cultural Revolution had killed culture in the People's Republic, but it was alive. Toward the end of 1970 it was stirring again, in a somewhat guarded way; all over China, just as in our little language-teaching enclave at Zhong Da, dedicated teachers were licking their wounds and, against what would appear to be all the suggestions of self-preserving common sense, were again going into classrooms, meeting with students, and trying to put together some kind of acceptable educational system.

Even in the still more volatile field of the performing arts, there were signs of an effort to encourage study. The first such sign that came to our attention occurred when I received a letter from a young girl whom we had known as "Damei" ("Biggest Little Sister") in Wuchang. She had been a kindergarten classmate of Mingteh's and knew all the same people we did. Now she was working as a pianist in a revolutionary opera troupe stationed in Changsha. She dutifully inquired after the health of all the family and reported Wuchang news, then announced that she was being sent to Canton for a period of special study of the Yellow River Concerto. She hoped to come and pay her respects the next weekend. I showed the letter to Mingteh, and we tried to recall the young lady. Getting out the family picture album, we found to our pleasure that a picture had survived showing a lineup of chubby children, photographed together on some ceremonial occasion. Surely that scowling three-year-old with the orange in her fist must be Damei.

"Well, it'll be good to see someone from Wuchang," I said. "We haven't been in close touch with people there for so long. I hope Damei will really come and stay with us." And she did. And much ensued therefrom.

On a cold, rainy Saturday evening she blew in with the wind, and I welcomed her as a substitute for my Tientung, with a hot bath and the best supper Ho Jie could procure. As we sat at table that night, I saw a strikingly beautiful girl, rather taller than average in China, with cheeks flushed from that treat, a hot bath, her black hair spread around her shoulders to dry, animated, full of laughter, and Mingteh, for once relaxed and laughing, exchanging gossip in the familiar dialect of home. How delightful it was to hear them chattering in John's native speech, to be able to understand what was going on! I realized anew how strong was the bond of being *tung-xiang-ti*— "people from the same place." Damei had a heavy program of practice and study and she was very conscientious about doing her work. But by the time her study period was over and she returned to Changsha I had a strong suspicion that in the future our lives were going to be closer than in the past.

I was right.

Summer 1972

AS A MATTER of fact, this visit of Damei's was by no means surprising. Her family and ours had long been intimate in our Wuchang days, and it was most natural that her mother should want her to get in touch with me when she came to the strange city of Canton. I was "Aunt Ruth" to her, by family tradition, although she probably didn't remember me personally.

When I had joined the Lo family, as Third Daughter-in-Law, in 1937, I had been given into the hands of Damei's mother, to be tutored in the ways of Chinese family life. Grace, as she was called then, her Christian name, was younger than I, just a schoolgirl, but she entered into her task of teaching me with unbounded enthusiasm. She taught me to speak the Wuchang dialect used in John's family and coached me in etiquette. From her I learned that I must always use two hands in offering the ceremonial cup of tea to my mother-in-law or to a guest, that I must walk with departing visitors not only to the front door, but out onto the porch and down the road a bit, and, by precept more than example, that I should not talk or laugh aloud in the presence of my elders. At sixteen, Grace was pretty as a flower, round of face, dimpled, and laughing, singing as much as she talked, animated and volatile. Damei, her daughter, was just like her.

They were alike in many ways, but their experience was very different. Grace, at sixteen in 1937, had always lived the sheltered life of a beloved young daughter in a secure home, surrounded by parents, uncles, aunts, cousins, older brothers and sisters. Damei, at twenty-two in 1971, like Mingteh, had lived through a revolution, and like Mingteh, although she was full of the gaiety of youth upon occasion, she had experienced the destruction of the society that had a place set aside for such children of the educated as themselves. They had grown up in a world inexplicably hostile to them and their kind. Like her mother, Damei was gifted musically, and that talent had made possible some higher education for her. Like Mingteh, though, she had gone with her classmates to take part in manual labor in the countryside, and even more than Mingteh had known terror and danger during the Cultural Revolution. They had much in common.

Although Damei was not a Lo, she had spent some of her childhood's early years in the Los' big old house on Tan Hua Ling (Street), where Mingteh was a frequent visitor and playmate. The home on the terraced hillside was the center of a busy family life for several generations and for all manner of kin. At Mid-Autumn Festival, at Chinese New Year, at Christmas, and on everyone's birthday there would be great gatherings of the clan and all its connections.

When John and I were sent to work in Canton in 1953, it was a real sorrow to him to leave this family home and family life. All the family scattered at about this time, as its members were assigned work in different places. The old house was left in the care of Fourth Brother and his wife, my "Fourth Sister-in-Law."

And now, in 1972, after nearly twenty years, Fourth Sister-in-Law and I were enjoying a reunion. It was really Mingteh's doing.

All during the Cultural Revolution, I had drawn my professorial pay, although John's had been reduced. Now, as the University struggled back to normal life and most of the teachers were liberated, the back pay that had been withheld was returned. Everywhere on campus one could see families installing bamboo bars in their ground-floor windows, a sign that there was more cash in the house than usual. Those who had suffered from the looting just before the Workers' Propaganda Teams entered to take over now blossomed out in new Mao uniforms, and there were new bicycles and radios bought as investments.

When John's share was delivered to us, I said to Mingteh, "You know I've felt Daddy would like us to send some of it to Wuchang to help his younger brothers and sisters. But I'm afraid it would get them into trouble if they had a big money order to collect. You know how it can be in Wuchang." He nodded soberly. He had heard a good deal from Damei, more even than I knew. He never questioned the necessity of sharing our resources with the family.

"Here's an idea," he urged. "Why don't we invite Fourth Aunt [to me Fourth Sister-in-Law] to come here to Canton for a visit? You know she has relations here and would like to see them, too. [That is, she could visit them without rousing political suspicions, as she might in visiting me, a foreigner.] She could take back some money in cash to share with all the family."

"Good! We'll do it. You write to her." He did. But the answer when it came was negative, though wistful. She was utterly involved with the care of Yuan-yuan, the third of a series of grandsons left in her lap by her daughters, who were all employed full time, serving the people in various professional capacities.

"That's too bad," Mingteh fumed. "Fourth Aunt is too good to everybody but herself! I'll just tell her to bring the baby along." And so it came about that a thin, tired, but radiant Fourth Sister-in-Law and her beloved, inseparable, but exhausting little two-year-old companion came to Canton and spent three happy weeks with us.

At first she couldn't rest. She was so used to being in continuous motion from daylight to dark—washing, cooking, shopping, cleaning—that she hardly knew what to do in a situation where meals were not her responsibility and there was nothing to do but amuse Yuan-yuan. And even that took little energy, because he spent most of his waking hours pushing himself up and down the hall in my delightful wheelchair, a plaything of vast potential. When I saw that what she really wanted was something to do, I got out my scrap bag and boxes of what I had considered hopelessly worn-out clothing, and together we went over what to her experienced eye was a treasure of *cloth*. As we sorted and snipped and put this into the pile of material for diapers, that into the heap for little boys' jackets, and the buttons and trimming into a basket, we caught up on the events of the missing years.

It developed that the family house in Wuchang had been a very dubious gift when it had been made over to Fourth Brother.

In 1953 the ownership of a twelve-room house and a piece of urban land was not important politically. There was no way to get rid of it, so the only thing to do was to share it with as many tenants as possible for as long as possible. It was not in the nature of that eminently Christian man, Fourth Brother, to be a harsh or extortion-ate landlord, so there was no immediate difficulty. Housing was scarce in Wuchang, and people were glad to rent the space, even though it was not very convenient for anyone.

However, during the Cultural Revolution the blow fell one morn-ing, when a delegation of Red Guards visited the place and told Fourth Sister-in-Law that they must vacate by evening of that very day. They were implementing the same policy that had brought us the company of Joe Doakes in our home in Zhong Da in Canton, but characteristically, the movement was carried on with more vio-lence in Wuhan (Wuchang) than in the South. Wuchang had been famous throughout its long history for its violent politics, whereas Canton is known for a capacity to compromise and adjust.

Confronted by shouting Red Guards, who made no distinction at that moment between the owner of a single-family house and a landlord (by definition an exploiter of the peasantry), Fourth Sister-in-Law was obliged to find a place to go and to move into it within a few hours.

"How on earth did you do it?" I asked when she told me the tale.

"I just prayed," she answered, "and the good Lord sent Grace's husband over to our place just at the moment I needed help and he found our elder cousin and the neighbors told us about a couple of empty rooms in a building down the street a way, near the market. We took what furniture we needed most and sold or just gave away what we couldn't use. By the time your Fourth Brother came home from work that night, we were all settled!" She smiled as she recalled his amazement. "The family had helped, of course."

"What kind of place did you find?" I asked, trying to remember the street and its various social gradations.

"We got two rooms in a courtyard," she told us. "There is a water tap in common, so I don't have to carry from the well, but for washing clothes we all go down to the place at the market where there is more room. There are cement troughs there, so it is more convenient. It was hard to go the first time, though!"

I could imagine. But like so many situations I had seen in China, the superficial appearance and the reality were confusingly far apart. Viewed from one angle, it could appear that Fourth Sister-in-Law, formerly the mistress of a mansion, had been forced by popular demand to give up her luxurious life and join the masses in a slum; no longer the daughter-in-law deputy for an honored *Lao Tai-tai,* managing the domestic affairs of a respected family, but surrounded by women who had been taught to consider themselves her class enemies, obliged to squat by the common washing trough to scrub her husband's work clothes, her baby grandson strapped to her aching back, because his mother had to leave for work before dawn and could not take him with her.

But Fourth Sister-in-Law was a realist and not prone to self-pity or to dramatizing herself. She saw it in her own way.

"Actually it was a liberation for me," she said. "Managing that big house was a headache from morning to night. It was different when Mother Lo was there. She always knew what needed to be done and we worked well together. [I recalled Mother Lo had always said that Fourth Sister-in-Law was a model Chinese daughter-in-law.] You know, I always did a lot of social work before, visiting the sick and so on, but in recent years, what with the house and the babies, bless 'em, on my hands, I've hardly had time to keep on with it. But now, with just two little rooms to keep clean and no tenants to placate, I can join in the *Jia-shu* activities and do a lot more. I still can visit the sick and I'm closer to people." She beamed with satisfaction.

I pictured the street in my mind: a cobbled roadway laid centuries before cars would appear to make it seem narrow, with a walkway of worn stone slabs down the middle; drainage ditches, rich with the effluvia of past dynasties, on either side; whitewashed walls, with plaster flaking off to disclose mudbricks, lining the roadsides; little flights of stone steps leading into gatehouses opening into crowded courtyards, where poles strung with washing dripped in the hot humid air; children spilling over the high wooden thresholds onto the stone flagging; exasperated, tired women quarreling in shrill voices; and the smell of frying sesame oil, a permanent element of life. I thought of Father Lo's long breeze-swept verandas, scarlet pillars, and hanging plants perfuming the air, the little birds in cages swung high out of reach of the cat, the polished floors, the flower-patterned Kiukiang porcelain drums holding pots of jasmine in pairs by every door. I remembered the endless procession of people that Mother Lo and Fourth Sister-in-Law unobtrusively helped: medicine for this one, a job for that one's son, a place in school for someone's daughter, friendly concern and counsel for another. Where were they now? Fourth Sister-in-Law was explaining.

"I'm closer to people now. I'm busy on the Street Committee, and we are working on a lot of things together. We want to start a tailoring cooperative for the neighborhood women so they can do productive work. I'd like so much to join in that." She sighed.

"Why don't you?" I encouraged. "You have a real flair for dressmaking." I glanced at the shirt and slacks she was wearing, made by her own hands to be sure, and in the almost statutory cut of the day: baggy blue cotton slacks, long-sleeved blouse, worn outside the pants, and a blue cloth jacket, adorned on the lapel by a large red Chairman Mao badge. Although not differing in material or basic cut from those everyone wore, there was a touch of style about them. They fitted perfectly on her slender, childlike figure; the modestly colored print blouse was fresh and crisp; and the collar flared becomingly to frame her thin little face. Although her straight black hair was combed sternly back, as befitted a grandmother, and was held in place behind her ears by proletarian bobby pins, the calm forehead, perfect brows, and dancing eyes still showed what had captivated Fourth Brother years ago.

"As soon as Yuan-yuan can go to the nursery school, I'm going to get a job. I dearly love the grand-babies, of course, but I'm *tired* of being a grandmother. Our women's group is planning to put on a performance of *Red Lantern* [one of the model operas of the Cultural Revolution] and can you believe it?" Her thin cheeks turned pink with pleasure and laughter. "They've asked me to take the lead! I haven't sung or danced since my first baby, but I still can!" To my amazement, she struck a pose as in the Chinese opera, her work-worn hands suddenly delicately expressive, as she began to sing a familiar aria, moving with agile grace from one conventional pose to another.

"Why, Sister, you're as good as a professional!" I applauded. And little Yuan-yuan, who had been watching with shining-eyed approval, shouted, *"Hao! Hao!"* (Good, good.)

"I take him with me to the rehearsals, of course," she explained, dropping down beside him and unnecessarily wiping his little nose with a hand once again grandmotherly. "I can't go anywhere without him."

When Fourth Sister-in-Law returned to Wuchang, she took with her not only bags of potential clothing for the grand-babies, cash in a discreetly concealed money belt, but also our warm and pressing invitation to "Aunt Grace" to come and spend her vacation from school with us when Tientung should be back from Gansu. Grace's visit was one of deep significance. While it meant a very great deal to me to renew the friendship begun so long ago in my honeymoon days, it was clear to me that it was also going to mean a lot to Mingteh.

Damei's first visit to Canton to study had been followed by other visits, and Mingteh was becoming very familiar with the schedule of trains running between Canton and Changsha, where Damei was still working as pianist for the opera troupe. Grace's visit to me would give all the interested parties an opportunity to discuss future possibilities.

Grace ran up the stairs as lightly as she had as a girl, and we fell on each other's necks and wept. Wept for the losses we had both known, made more bitter by the separation from those who shared our sorrows, wept for joy that we could see each other again and strengthen old family ties.

We looked at each other and sought the people we had been. The Grace I had remembered was young and vibrant. Even in the blue cotton school uniform she was slim and elegant, her abundant black hair fashionably curled. The woman I saw now was only a little changed, her hair powdered over with gray, no longer curled (that was bourgeois in 1972), figure a little fuller (six children), face tanned from working in the fields at Cadre School, the strong, expressive musician's hands callused and brown. Only about the eyes there were fine lines now, and while the laughter still bubbled up, in repose there was sadness around the mouth. Closer inspection suggested that the roundness of the face might be more the effect of high blood pressure than healthy plumpness. The Grace of former times would never have welcomed the suggestion of a nap while there was one sight unseen or shop uninspected.

I did not ask her how I had changed. Courtesy would have forbidden a true answer, and I could see only too well as we looked over old family photographs. My once brown curls were white, the blue eyes behind the plastic-rimmed glasses looked tired; never slender, I was now definitely stout, and the deterioration of my lame leg made the walking stick a constant companion. Only when enthroned in my wheelchair, which I could move about by hand with ease, did I feel comfortable and in command. And in recent months I had been forced to admit that there was sometimes a frightening breathlessness, an all-gone feeling on frequent sleepless nights, and a chronic cough. But in the excitement of having companionship I forgot my bad health and felt young again.

There was news of years to catch up on. By 1953 Grace had six children, the smallest one in arms, the eldest in sixth grade. Qualified music teachers were in great demand, and she was among the first of her generation to come out of the nursery and take up professional work. Thus she was considered "progressive," but there were many conflicts and contradictions that made her life stormy. Raised in a Christian home, a student in the Christian mission schools with foreign teachers, and with many friends and connections abroad, she was not easy for the new order to assimilate.

Grace, too, set the sad things of the past aside and concentrated on enjoying her first real holiday in years. It was no problem for her to find things to do! The pleasure of shopping in Canton after the grim restrictions of Wuchang gave her infinite satisfaction, as she hunted for just the right present for each of the girls at home, the prettiest blouse, the most suitable pullover for the boys. She herself was wearing the usual uniform of the teacher when she arrived, but in one shopping trip transformed herself. Though Canton had its ultra-revolutionary phases, because it was so close to Hong Kong and the Western world, it was never, for such long periods of time, as puritanical about dress as Wuhan and other inland cities were. Grace might have to put away her pretty blouse when she went home, but in the meantime she would enjoy it to the full!

With Tientung home for her vacation, coming and going on expeditions to town, and Ho Jie outdoing herself to prove that Cantonese cooking was superior to Hubeinese, we should have been a very happy family. But through all our feminine holiday atmosphere, Mingteh moved like a dark shadow of gloom. He would make brave attempts to rise to the occasion and make polite conversation, only to sink into black silence beyond our reach. When his "Aunt Grace" first appeared, he had commented revealingly, "When Damei is fifty, I expect she'll be just as beautiful and charming as her mother." The only times he came to life were when the mailbox held a letter from Changsha. The trouble was, Damei wouldn't say yes and wouldn't say no.

All too soon the summer holiday ended and our party scattered. Grace went back to Wuhan. In spite of my needing her so badly, Tientung had to go back to Gansu. I thought our good times were at an end until Mingteh received a telegram that made him explode with excitement. Damei was coming! Only for the weekend, but she was coming. Surely she wouldn't come just to say no. Nor did she. On September 11, two solemnly happy young people waited upon me ceremoniously early in the morning to announce that they were engaged, wondering aloud at my lack of surprise.

It was all to be kept a tremendous secret for the time being, of course, but the family should know. There would be difficulties to overcome, that *they* knew. Damei was assigned a job in Changsha, and Mingteh one in Canton. All their superiors at work had warned them, and given them horrible examples, of the hopeless folly of marrying outside one's own work unit.

"You'll have to wait for years to get together," said Damei's Leadership. "Marry someone in Changsha. We'll introduce . . ."

"It's apt to be a long time before you can arrange a transfer," Mingteh's friends had advised when he hinted of the possibility. "It's all but impossible to move someone from out of town into Canton. You'd have to try to move to Changsha, and you'll never get as good a job there."

It was all too true. We knew of friends who had married in spite of being assigned to work in different places and who after ten years were still separated, seeing each other only over Spring Festival holidays once a year. The job assignments to different places loomed as an insuperable obstacle.

Marrying was "solving your personal problem" and came a long way down the list of priorities. To change jobs in order to get married to a particular girl instead of finding a more conveniently located one was "bourgeois sentimentality" at best. It could only be accomplished with a great deal of struggle, petitioning to bureaucrats, waiting—and tears.

Under no circumstances could they hope to marry until Damei turned twenty-five and Mingteh twenty-eight: the marriage law in effect in 1972 made that explicit. They would have to wait until next summer, the summer of 1973, before the wedding. Meantime they could begin working on the problem of transfer, write daily letters, exchange photographs; and Mingteh could continue his close study of the trains between Changsha and Canton, seizing every long weekend for a quick trip. The prospects for the future were not uncertain—they were very certainly poor. But the young couple had the present happiness of their resolution to join their lives if and when they could.

1972

SISTER L AND I were sitting on the edge of Mingteh's bed discussing Technical Questions. We had become firm friends over the problem of my wardrobe, and I enjoyed her subsequent little visits very much. But whenever she came to see me, Sister L came with a carefully prepared Technical Question to justify her daring, though authorized, contact. Sometimes these were about matters of English grammar, sometimes about my wardrobe, but there was always a mentionable reason for her presence. Earlier on in the Cultural Revolution, even with Technical Questions, such visits would have been unthinkable.

But there was a new atmosphere in the land in the spring and summer of 1972. The Shanghai Communiqué, with its promise of developing relations between the United States and the People's Republic of China, clearly marked the beginning of change. The period of total isolation had been ended, and an interest in foreign ways could no longer be attributed to political backwardness or to a sinful hankering after bourgeois life-styles. If Premier Chou Enlai and Chairman Mao had had contact with foreigners, been seen on the TV shaking hands and conversing, then a modest friendly gesture by a young woman to an old one need not be misinterpreted.

Overseas Chinese had often been in great difficulties during the Cultural Revolution because, having lived abroad, their life-styles were not 100 percent Chinese. Often their speech reflected that their childhood education had been bilingual. They didn't use the local slang with perfect ease. Many of them were accustomed to bilingual home life, in both language and culture. They enjoyed the foods that they had known in their foreign homelands, and inevitably they had the more sophisticated world view of the traveled. (Tientung, in Gansu, had usually been taken to be an overseas Chinese, and although such were scarce in that remote inland province, people expected her to be a bit different from the local girls and were surprised and pleased with her for taking kindly to northwestern ways.) During the Cultural Revolution, the overseas Chinese sometimes exaggerated their Chinese cultural traits in self-defense. I sometimes felt that Sister L found some relaxation from the stern discipline of the times in the international atmosphere of our home. By no stretch of the imagination could our life-style have been called American, but it was certainly not Cantonese, or even Hubeinese, either. It was just our own, and we were what we were, not trying to be anything else.

On this fine October day we were interrupted in our discussions by one of our Department leaders, Little Li, who brought with him a stranger, a youngish cadre, uniformed and extremely polite.

"Mrs. Lo," said my friend from the Department, using the English I had taught him years before, "this comrade has come from the Foreign Affairs Bureau to talk to you about some American visitors who have asked to see you." He beamed reassuringly.

I blinked. This was news indeed. What Americans were there in China who might know me? The last time I had been summoned to meet a foreign visitor had been fourteen years earlier, in 1958, when an Australian tourist had looked me up, introduced by a mutual friend from long years before that. Well, in 1972, I thought, almost anything could happen.

Speaking in Chinese, as protocol required, and interpreted by my former student, the official gave me what seemed to be routine instructions "for guidance of persons in contact with foreign visitors." This visit was arranged by the highest authority—he glowed —and it was necessary, of course, to treat the visitors with all due respect. As it was obvious that most private persons (like me) would not be equipped to entertain such exalted guests at a meal, it was suggested that the University would be glad to provide tea and appropriate teacups or other refreshment that I might request. And, of course—he smiled, in what was probably meant to be a disarming, folksy way—I would want to clean the house and make everything tidy. The guest would come next day in the afternoon, and Comrade Li—he bowed to his colleague, my former student—would check on the preparations. And with bows and smiles and a swift critical look around the room they noted that there was the necessary portrait of Chairman Mao, although it was not the usual Tien An Men poster but one showing the Chairman in the pre-Yenan days, and that my only other picture was one of the famous "international friend," Dr. Bethune. Satisfied, they departed.

"Oh, Mrs. Lo, how exciting, who is it?" Sister L was thrilled to be in on such an historical event. "Let me help you clean up."

"I don't know a thing about it," I answered. "And never mind about the cleaning up, thank you just the same." My natural feelings were rising through the paralysis of the official atmosphere. "I'll be damned if I'll clean house just because some unknown persons want to see the only Yankee in Canton." Sister L's eyes nearly popped to hear such a sentiment in such "language."

My Department friend now returned and began to explain further. "You must have seen in the paper [flattering but unjustified implication as to my scholarship] that the famous American musicians, the Had-duns, have been in Peking as the personal guests of our Premier Chou Enlai," he said. "They have asked to see you." I remembered that Mingteh had mentioned this unprecedented cultural event, mostly because Damei was interested in anything to do with piano music, and the "Had-duns" were pianists. But I had been out of touch with American cultural life for so long that the name meant nothing to me. Still, if they had heard of me from some mutual though unguessed friend, I was perfectly willing to see them. But not to wash the floor. I made that clear to my friend. Knowing me from of old, he made no further attempt on that front, but proceeded: "I'll ask leave for Mingteh to stay home from work tomorrow to help you entertain [read, wash the floor], and I'll send over some cakes and fruit and tea and cigarettes . . ." His strategy developed as he spoke.

"Thank you, that is not necessary." I was adamant. If the food Mingteh and I had offered to John's relatives when they visited was not good enough for Premier Chou's guests, they could lump it. Not that I had anything against either Premier Chou—whom John and I had admired and respected sincerely for many years—or his as yet unknown visitors from outer space. Visitors could take us as they found us, and I would not play games.

When Mingteh came home for lunch, he had already been briefed about the visit and was vastly amused at the effect upon his colleagues at the electronics parts factory where he now worked as a technician. "Everybody's dying of curiosity, Lu," he said. "Can't you think who the visitors may be?" I tried and tried, but all was blank.

"Whoever they are, they are going to see Life in the Raw," he promised. "It is my day to sweep under the bed, though, visitors or none." (Floor washing and heavy work generally fell to him now. Ho Jie had developed high blood pressure.) Since I knew for a fact that Timmy Willy, the current cat, had left a fish head under the bed, I made no further objection. While the cement floor dried, we collaborated on tying some green plastic tape around the arms of the two matching wicker chairs, partly to remedy some of Timmy Willy's claw-sharpening effects, partly because they felt so sticky. I had scrubbed them with soap one time and they had never really dried out. Ho Jie viewed our slight preparations with suppressed curiosity, but said little. This was official business on a high level and she wanted no part in it.

Early the next morning when I looked out the window, I noted someone loitering at the end of the garden, as well as someone else strolling on the front roadway a little downhill from our door. When I mentioned it to Mingteh, he said, "Oh yes, official visitors, special protection." I shuddered inwardly.

Toward noon my Department friend came again, ostensibly to see that Ho Jie understood about the basket of teacups, enough for an army, and the thermos bottles of high-class tea, which a servant from the guesthouse was bringing us. He looked anxiously about, was relieved that the fish head was gone, and approved the brightened chairs (the cushions had been turned over) and the unusual table-cloth covering the scarred wooden dining table. An arrangement of bright orange berries and bamboo branches made an unconventional but pleasingly festive touch, and the bowl of autumn pears and bananas, though too modest for exalted guests, brought us a grudg-ing "e for effort" response. I felt sorry for his embarrassment and confided that I intended to offer the guests some moon cakes—it was the season of Moon Festival. Earlier in the Cultural Revolution they had been banned as being one of the Four Olds, but now they were back in style. The Cantonese in particular welcomed back their favorite pastries, delicious, indigestible tarts stuffed with dates, bean-paste, or spiced ham. This year we had a good supply and could share them with our unexpected guests.

As courtesy demanded, Mingteh went downstairs after lunch to haunt the front door, in order to welcome the guests as they approached. I sat in my wheelchair awaiting events. Who on earth were these American pianists, who had electrified the Chinese cultural world with their program of Western music, "From Bach to Rock and Back"—the first such concert since the Cultural Revolution began?

Voices below. I limped to the head of the stairs and looked over the rail. Hastening up the steps toward me was the totally unexpected but indescribably welcome figure of my old friend Frances Roots. Fran, my first American friend in Wuchang in 1937, was the daughter of Bishop Roots, for many years the Episcopal bishop of the mission diocese of Hankow. He had been the intimate friend of Chou Enlai and had played an important part in Chinese foreign relations. He was also an old friend of John's and all his family. The Roots family was connected to mine with innumerable ties of friendship over the years. The last one I had seen had been Mrs. Logan Roots, who was Tientung's godmother. She and Logan and their children had left China in 1951. Since that time I had had no direct word from them, but I knew that we had not been forgotten. And indeed, we were not! When Frances and her husband, Richard Hadden, were invited by Premier Chou Enlai himself to come to the PRC as his guests, they had immediately resolved to find me if I was still alive. They had heard that I was not. When they asked their host if they might see me, he had arranged it at once. They had just flown down from Peking that morning and had been brought to my house.

Their interpreter-guide politely bowed himself out, saying, "There is clearly no need for an interpreter to help old friends communicate," and Mingteh and I were left unchaperoned with our first contact with the outside world since 1958.

I had never dreamed that our visitors were going to be real friends with whom we might talk confidently, so I had not consulted with Mingteh about what we should say to them. Experience had taught me to rely on his political judgment as being better than my own. Naturally somewhat impulsive, I tended to trust everyone who acted friendly, but he was wiser and often had occasion to remind me, "Don't say things to anyone that you wouldn't say to everyone." He had seen too many things happen to people as a result of impulsive remarks picked up and quoted out of context in the political struggle for survival. So, happy though I was to see friends who would not consciously cause us difficulty by misquotation, I realized that, lacking our intensive education in political infighting, they might easily misinterpret or misquote something and cause disaster. I followed my canny son's lead and said nothing that would disturb the tranquillity of the newly improved Sino-American relationship.

Indeed, I would not willingly have said one word that I thought would in any way jeopardize the success of Premier Chou's policy. Keeping the Chinese people isolated from the modern world had done them no good. It had fostered ignorance, dogmatism, and chauvinism, and led to a situation in which the excesses and outrages of the Cultural Revolution were inevitable. Though well aware of the suffering caused by the systematic degradation of China's scholars, this was not the time to air their problems. To prevent any recurrence of those excesses, it was essential to keep doors open now. I knew that John would see it that way, and so I passed lightly over events that would have brought tears to the eyes of his friends.

So they heard about financial security, the free medical care, the low rent of our officially presentable apartment, and saw my airy bedroom behind Mingteh's cleverly contrived partitioning, where Timmy Willy lolled at his ease, the very picture of domestic bliss and a relaxed life. They saw and heard about the wheelchair, but nothing was said about the ailing heart and crippling arthritis that had made it necessary because the "revisionists" had threatened Canton with air raids; they heard about Mingteh's and Damei's recent engagement, but not about the difficulties caused by their work assignments in different cities. We told them about Tientung's adventures, pioneering in the loess hills of Gansu, but not about the factional infighting that made her choose to go so far from home, and which now, after four years, still kept her in the Northwest, in spite of all our efforts to bring her back to stay.

And we heard about their wonderful tour of Chinese cities, their concerts of Western music, and their reunion with Frances's father's dear friend Premier Chou. All too soon the interpreter-guide was back to carry them off to the official farewell banquet before they left for Hong Kong and home.

The captains and the kings having departed, Mingteh and I sat looking at each other across the emptied teacups. I was exhausted. And all he could say for a long time was *"Wah!"* But after finishing off the moon cakes and draining the thermos flask of high-class tea, he began to rally.

"That was the greatest surprise of my life," I told Mingteh. "To think that the famous American pianists were our old friends from Hankow! How I wish Tientung had been here to share in the fun! Would it be safe for me to write her about it, do you think?"

"I think so," he replied. "After all, they were the personal guests of the Premier. We certainly were in good company."

We sat silent for a few minutes, while Timmy Willy licked the last crumbs from the cake plate. Then we both spoke at once.

"Wouldn't this be a lucky time to try again to get Tientung transferred back to Canton?" I ventured.

And "Mother, I'll just send a telegram to Tientung tomorrow morning to let her know how ill you really are!" Mingteh grinned.

December 1972–January 1973

MINGTEH'S URGENT TELEGRAM to Tientung to come home at once to take care of her aged mother did indeed arrive at a fortunate moment, and in the shortest possible time she was back with us, with permission to stay to nurse me for an undefined period of time. "That means *always,*" she declared and unpacked her bags and bundles and settled in. "We'll get you well first and then see what to do next, but I'm *here!*" Her brown eyes flashed. She looked so rosy and strong, fresh from the bracing Northwest. I realized with a sense of shock how thin and pale her tall brother looked beside her.

And so it was that on a cold December day she went along with Big Li, a Department colleague, and me to my now routine hospital visit.

The interview had gone as it always did, and I was sitting back, listening dreamily as Tientung explained and explained my difficulties in sleeping, my coughs and dizziness, all so tiresome to me and probably to the doctors, too. The dreaminess deepened into darkness. Where was I? I opened my heavy eyelids to find myself lying on the examination couch, doctors leaning anxiously over me, Tientung holding my hand, Big Li covering me with his worn padded coat. I felt very comfortable, only a little cold, but extraordinarily remote. I thought slowly, "I must have fainted or something. Now I ought to say something. Let them know I'm all right. I wonder what time it is? Shouldn't we be going home?" Dimly I focused my attention on what seemed the most important point, what time it was—how long had this been going on? I looked at Tientung and to our mutual dismay the words burst forth, *"Quelle heure est-il?"*

I could see from her puzzled expression that I had cued in on the wrong language. Baffled, I reviewed bits of sentences in my mind, but nothing came out. "Oh well," I thought, "it doesn't matter. Tientung is here. She will cope," and I closed my eyes and smiled at her.

A stout and resourceful little soul in any emergency, she coped. While I drifted off into a troubled doze, she and Big Li and the doctors concluded that the best thing to do with me was to keep me in hospital for observation. As that got to me, I tried to sit up to object. I had seen that hospital before and I was in no way going to stay there. But I found to my confusion that I couldn't sit up, nor could I say anything in any language at all. I looked appealingly at my daughter and, reading my thoughts, she explained, "Doctor says that there is a special ward for foreign patients at the Number One Hospital, where you can get the care you need. That's where people from Shameen go." (Shameen was the island where the diplomatic corps lived.) I shook my head. I didn't think I belonged in that high social category!

"But there's another possibility," she went on. "There's a ward here in Number Two Hospital where they hospitalize the foreign seamen and workers on the ships. It's not quite as high-class as the diplomatic ward, but it is here and it's cheaper."

I thought. "Here, cheaper, seamen." I nodded. I would rather take my chances with the seamen!

Next thing I knew I was lying on a stretcher in an anteroom full of blankets and brooms. I wondered if that was where they kept the Chinese doctor between calls. People drifted in and out, a nurse brought me a pill and a drink of hot water. Big Li, shivering rather —I still had his overcoat wrapped round me—looked in and handed me a bun in a brown paper bag; Tientung kept reappearing with things for me to sign. Doctors came in and listened to me with icy stethoscopes. I had a dim impression of a slow elevator ride, of trundling through corridors full of people, and then through a series of rapidly unlocked doors, into the sudden quiet of a two-bed ward in an obviously "secure" area. After an eternity of confusion I found myself being tucked into a bed—a bed with a mattress, not boards, in a green-walled room apparently at the top of the nine-story building.

Doctors and nurses kept coming in and sticking me with injections and plying me with pills. Tientung hovered around me as I was relentlessly sponged down and submerged in a gigantic pair of flannel pajamas. The seamen must be enormous, I thought, as I fell asleep again.

Waking, I found a smiling little woman setting down a well-loaded tray beside me and Tientung standing by. "Now here's your dinner, Lu," she admonished. "Eat it up!"

"Where's yours?" I was thankful that the words came out in English.

"Right here. I'm going to stay with you, never you worry." She helped me sit up and moved the tray nearer. The contents smelled delicious. I looked more closely. I couldn't believe my eyes. A big glass of milk, steaming soup, chicken, potatoes, vegetables, bread and butter, fruit, cake—all in the quantity presumably required by seamen. It was obvious that foreign guests, including seamen, ate from a different table then than their Chinese hosts. I hadn't seen so much good food for years. I needed no urging, and when I saw that Tientung was equally well provided for, we set to like starving seamen, or, rather, very hungry teachers, let us say.

Visitors to China say, with justice, that Chinese cooking is the best in the world, and that the cuisine of Canton is the best in China. (This is denied by the defenders of Peking or Szechuanese cuisine.) But no matter how skilled the cook, it is necessary to have some raw materials, and bit by bit, during the long years of revolutionary turmoil, the available raw materials had become increasingly scanty. More and more of the time our meals consisted of rice and a vegetable, stir-fried in a minimum of peanut oil. As eggs became more and more scarce and expensive, we ate them less and less. Milk was not available at all without a medical prescription most of the time, and not worth getting even then. Meat was rationed (roughly twenty English ounces per person a month), sugar was down to about five English ounces a month for each in Canton (in the North there was often a ration of sugar only for Spring Festival). Bread was poor in quality, inconvenient to buy, and took more grain ration tickets than the same amount of rice. Transportation disorders had disrupted the normal distribution of fruit, and while it was not rationed, it was expensive. The situation was not one of famine; rice was still available, but a balanced diet was nearly impossible to achieve. The effect of this was easily seen: the reduced resistance to disease, the lack of energy, the sallow faces of the people in the crowded clinic and in the hospital showed that a general malnutrition accompanied every set of symptoms.

When Mingteh came back to the city from the commune, he was in better health than the college students. The food in the country was not what the foreign visitors reveled in, but the hard outdoor work made it possible for the young people to bolt their three or four big bowls of rice at a meal. Eaten in that quantity, new rice (only available in the country communes) provides enough protein to maintain health, even if there is not much meat. But the city workers, especially the "intellectuals" doing indoor work, couldn't eat enough rice to keep up the balance needed for health. Tientung, in the Northwest, where the peasants lived on millet, corn bread, potatoes, and occasionally mutton, would come home to Canton looking rosy and plump. After a few weeks at home she, too, would be pale and tired.

Every day in the Seamen's Ward began with the arrival of Elder Sister Pan to wash the cement floors. She was a little, plump, peasant woman, proud of her strength and bubbling over with satisfaction at her present position in life. For she was a member of the real ruling class, in her own opinion at least, and her work of cleaning the hospital floors was serving the people, a task set by the Party. She wore a rather large Chairman Mao badge on her smock, and very soon found occasion to tell Tientung proudly that it had been given to her for being a model worker. People always told Tientung their life story. Her genuine interest in every human being who crossed her path seemed to draw out the most extraordinary confidences from the most reserved people. Not that Elder Sister Pan was particularly reserved—she was too ebulliently happy for that. She had been decorated at a big meeting, she said, because she had invented a new way of washing the floors, using two mops at a time instead of one, thereby doing her work quicker and better. The other workers, even the top-class foreign-trained doctors, had been told to learn from her. And, indeed, there was much to be learned from her simple, whole-souled devotion to a task some would have been too proud to do. Besides washing the floor, Elder Sister Pan daily brought in a thermos bottle full of the hottest and most delicious coffee I have ever tasted. I told her one morning how good it was, and she blushed with pleasure.

"I'm glad you like it," she beamed. "I know that Americans love their coffee, and I go to the kitchen at four every morning to cook it for you specially."

Hospital life everywhere, it seems, is full of the same weary contradictions: you are supposed to sleep, so you are awakened and washed; you are supposed to eat, so you are dosed with horrible-tasting medicines that spoil your appetite; you are supposed to relax, so you are confined in an environment full of strange noises and distressing sounds. The Seamen's Ward was quieter than the crowded rooms on the lower floors, where the Chinese patients lived surrounded by ministering relatives in a state of noise and bustle that would have been unendurable to me even in the best of health.

I saw a bit of it one morning when I was being wheeled out for a test of some kind. It was the hour for face washing, and all the attendant relatives (there weren't enough nurses to go round to give this kind of care) were dashing about with washbasins of steaming hot water. Patients who could do so were shuffling about, going to the WC, and bedpans were very much in evidence. Everyone was talking at the top of his voice, and the public-address system was blaring out inspiriting patriotic songs. Pale faces, bandaged limbs, half-clad emaciated forms hobbling painfully through the crowded passageway, glimpsed through the clouds of steam, made a scene from the Inferno. Yet, exhausting though the clamor was to my ears, to most of the patients it was probably supportive. The attendant relatives represented the loving care of the family, the insistent public address announced to them in every strident note, "Chairman Mao and the Party care for *you.*"

At least among the seamen we had less music. But the music we had, during a scheduled recreation hour every afternoon, was unforgettable. My next-door neighbor, whom I saw only when he peeked through the crack of the door for a glimpse of Tientung, had brought in with him a portable gramophone and a single recording of the Beatles singing "Let It Be." It was the first time I had heard this phenomenon of the sixties, and I enjoyed it thoroughly, if only as a change from "The Helmsman." The nurses explained apologetically that one must make allowances for comrades from foreign countries, and that it seemed good for his spirits to listen to his native music. I hope it was.

When first I entered this medical enclave, I was too exhausted and dim to object. I felt only a tremendous relief at having given up the struggle to keep going. I knew that Tientung was there, and that I could depend on her absolutely. Our roles were reversed. It was delicious to let go, eat the fantastic meals, obediently take my pills and horrid teas, and let the doctors investigate my complaints. At night, even if I still could not sleep, I could lie in comfort on a *soft* warm bed and hear Tientung breathing close by. I knew that for the time being we were both on a safe island in time and space and that Mingteh was holding the fort at home.

But as time passed by and the doctors went on and on, poking and testing, I began to wonder. Why was I here? What was the matter with me? Would I ever get out? As we all realized presently, my physical symptoms were caused by the strain and anxiety of the years of the Cultural Revolution, climaxed by the shock of John's death. Every night for months, instead of sleeping, I relived the agony of his last hours. Confined to the house by our difficulties with Joe Doakes, and later by my increasing lameness, I had been alone too much. I was suffering from nervous and physical exhaustion. I had a moment of panic one day when attendants brought a Polish ship's officer into the ward. He glanced sharply at me as he was escorted past my always open door, and I could hear him asking in careful Chinese where they were taking him, who I was, why I was here, why didn't they inform his consulate, and so on. I remembered the series of locked doors we had passed coming in, the unobtrusive guards near the elevator. Was I being protected or was I a prisoner? Was Tientung a prisoner, too?

It was Christmas. I wondered if anyone else knew. Elder Sister Pan bustled in, beaming as ever. "I know this is your festival day," she smiled, "so I've made you an extra bottle of coffee. You might have visitors!"

Morning rounds, the usual parade of doctors, the head foreign-trained specialist, the young Red Guard–type interns, the Chinese herbalist, and, trailing behind, in a position indicating to experienced eyes that he was probably not wholly liberated as yet, a very sad, thin, nervous man with dark circles under his eyes to whom all spoke curtly when they did not markedly exclude him. As the procession passed the door, he was the last to go by. He looked in, caught my eye, and smiled one quick, fleeting, confiding smile, raised both hands in a little gesture that might have been a greeting—or a blessing—and then hurried on to keep his penitential position in the parade. I knew beyond doubt that it was Christmas for him, too, still, in some as yet unreformed corner of his heart.

But now it was my turn to be checked for the day. In came the usual parade, but augmented this time by a tall, very handsome stranger in PLA uniform, attended by several hospital cadres in their very best uniforms. Tientung had risen when they entered and stood behind the group as they surrounded my bed. I could see her signaling to me with reassuring grins and winks that were almost too much for my composure.

The tall officer beamed on me and shook hands and made a formal speech in a dialect not one word of which I could comprehend, but the general meaning was obviously friendly. I could recognize high brass when I saw it, even when it was being polite to me, and I responded as well as I could. All the staff seemed to be very impressed, and the politeness was so thick in the air that I grew breathless. Turning suddenly on the doctors, the officer rapped out what sounded like severe warnings, gesturing toward me, then softened somewhat as he made ceremonious farewells. The doctors yessed him out of the room, and I was left with Tientung, scarlet with suppressed mirth at the whole scene.

"You've made it, Lu!" she chortled. "That was a high, oh, a very high guy indeed. Sent to inquire about your health from—oh, boy! If some folks could see you now!" She was just barely able to recover her poise as the head doctor came in again and handed me, with smiles and bows, a great bundle of letters and murmured something to the effect that these should make a good Christmas for me. What a treasure! Letters from half a dozen dear friends in America who had been silent for years. Or at least, if they had written, I had never got their letters. How did they know I was ill? Where had the letters been? Never mind. The great thing was that I was in touch with them again, they still cared, and someone somewhere in China cared enough, too, to see that I got the letters.

Spring Festival, sometimes called Chinese New Year in the West, comes toward the end of January or in early February and is the turning point of the year. Everyone takes a holiday, for as many days as he can. Everyone tries to go home. Buses and trains are packed to the point of suffocation. Everything winds down just before the holiday begins, and the administrator who wants to keep good relations with his work-staff for the coming year must be prepared to overlook a good deal as the old year wanes.

In the hospital there was an atmosphere approaching anarchy. As regular nurses and attendants took off for their holiday, new faces appeared. One evening when I was scheduled for "moxibustion treatment," a strange middle-aged woman brought the usual herb cigar and lighted incense stick. In moxibustion, a roll of compressed dried herbs is lighted in the glow of the incense stick and then slowly rotated just above the surface of the skin at various strategic spots. It made me feel slightly warm and, when I got over my apprehensions about being burned, pleasantly relaxed. Why, I don't know. As usual, tonight's nurse proceeded to tell her life story to Tientung as she skillfully toasted selected areas of ankle and wrist.

"These young nurses don't really know how to give this treatment," she began scornfully when I had complimented her upon the effect she was producing. "They haven't really been *trained.* Now I was finishing nurses' training at . . . [a once famous missionary hospital] at the time of Liberation. We didn't learn anything about Chinese medicine there, that's sure!" She cackled mirthlessly. "The foreign doctors said it was all nonsense, but I grew up in the country, where they didn't have anything else, and I always thought there was a lot to it. My grandmother was a midwife and she taught me how to do this treatment before ever I went to that foreign nurses' school. Talk about nonsense! They taught us plenty of nonsense at training school." She sniffed and obviously wanted to spit, but that was something the school had trained out of her, clearly. "Now Chairman Mao teaches us that Chinese medicine is good, and it is lucky for me that I can do both kinds of treatment, Western and Chinese."

"Which do you think is better?" I asked, perhaps unfairly, but I wondered how she reconciled these contradictions in her mind.

"It's better to walk on two legs," she answered, giving the correct reply in the words of a popular slogan, "but these young girls nowadays have had no *training.*"

"Aren't you going home for the Festival?" asked Tientung, tucking me up as the treatment concluded.

"No, no." The rather jaunty air melted away, and the lively face became an impassive mask. "I'm on duty over the holidays." Her former self seemed to peek through briefly, then she looked down. "I have to finish writing my self-criticism."

Tientung nodded silently in understanding and did her the special courtesy of walking with her to the door. But as she went out, she turned and said over her shoulder once more, "These young girls have no discipline."

The young nurses, who presumably had criticized her for her foreign training, may or may not have had "discipline"; the ones who cared for me certainly were beyond reproach in their kindness and consideration. But there was a definite breakdown of discipline going on somewhere, I thought, as the New Year Eve approached. By this time as many of the Chinese patients as could with safety be discharged had left. No one wanted to greet the New Year in the unlucky situation of a hospital bed. Among the foreign seamen, of course, Chinese New Year meant nothing, but something of the holiday atmosphere penetrated even here. My next-door neighbor had played his Beatle record unceasingly all morning, and now he was being visited in quite irregular fashion, off-hours, by two fellow workers from his ship. Their talk, in Spanish as far as I could make out, grew louder and merrier, and I suspected that an absentminded guard at the doors had overlooked a bottle. Presently the clamor was sufficient to bring the remaining doctor on duty, and the visitors were politely but firmly ushered out. Tientung could come out from behind the door where she usually hid at such times to avoid notice.

Our ninth-floor room had a big south-facing window, now opened to admit the sun and air. A square of watery sunlight on the floor looked cheerful. I was about to comment to Tientung on the improvement with the departure of the visitors when to my unspeakable shock I saw the shadow of a man on the floor in front of the window. As I looked, it jumped up in the air, landed again on its feet, then stood with arms outstretched. Slowly I turned my head toward the window, to see a slight pajama-clad figure standing on the broad cornice that ran around the outside of the building. He held up a bottle in his hand and grinned happily in, then, waving his unoccupied hand, began weaving along the ledge with a kind of dance step, occasionally leaping straight up in the air and landing still on the ledge. The instant he moved out of sight, Tientung ran for the door to get help and, heart or no heart, I jumped out of my bed and pulled down the window. In a minute Tientung was back, and the sounds we heard from the corridor told us that the runaway had been sighted and was being coaxed and coerced back into the building.

"Don't you think my rest cure is just about completed?" I asked Tientung.

"I certainly do," she agreed. "But to get you out I have to get all sorts of papers signed, and probably the doctor in charge will have gone by now. But don't worry. If you think you'll be okay for a couple of hours—I don't think they'll let anything more happen for a while, anyway—I'll organize it!" She was already beginning to pack up her own things as she spoke. "You eat your lunch and get as much rest as you can and I'll be back to take you home by three o'clock—'Tho' Hell should bar the way'!" And she was off.

When the nurse came with my lunch, nothing was said about the dancing sailor on the window ledge, but I was told, "This afternoon we are having a Big Cleanup and someone will be washing the windows on the outside. We hope it won't disturb you."

I was familiar with the tactics and strategy of the Big Cleanup. Periodically, every primary unit small group everywhere, in schools, shops, factories, offices, would devote one of the statutory political study periods to cleaning up the premises where they worked. No one, in principle, would be excused from this socialist labor, although irreverent members of the masses sometimes murmured that it was remarkable how some comrades always had urgent meetings to attend at such times. But woe to anyone whose political record was less than shining with virtue if he scanted his efforts. Those hoping to gain points in the continuous struggle for political approval would vie with each other to clean the latrines or do whatever was dirtiest and most unpleasant. It was not a very efficient way to deal with sanitation, but the socializing was rather fun. The Number One in every organization, whether a chief clerk or the governor of a province, was expected to join with the lowest of the masses and do his share. This was very good for the souls of the innumerable Number Ones, who otherwise might be tempted to pull rank and let others do the dirty and unhonored manual labor. In the hospital this would mean, of course, that doctors, surgeons, nurses, interns, and all, down to the washers of the dead in the morgue, would work together in a vast cleaning down of the whole hospital and its grounds.

Although there was routine attention to sanitation in the hospital, the annual New Year cleaning was on a scale and of a vigor beyond anything else in the year. For the youngsters, who had grown up in the tradition of mass participation in such jobs, it was a time for a bit of skylarking, but for the older specialists, accustomed to a well-nigh feudal respect from all beneath them, it was a real test of their political stand. Many eyes would be upon them, to see how willingly they shared in the dirty work. Model Workers, like Elder Sister Pan, would be the leaders of work teams including the top brass of the institution, and the latter would have to obey orders.

There was a clashing of pails and a swishing of brooms and a lively burst of chatter as the cleaning squad descended on the Seamen's Ward, but clearly they had been told to make as little disturbance as possible. And there really could not be too much more cleaning needed in an area served regularly by such a model as Elder Sister Pan. Their stay in our room was short and cheerful. The washstand, already immaculate, was polished again; the lighting fixtures were dusted by at least three different workers; all the woodwork was wet-mopped over and over, and the floor given one more do than was needed, chiefly to mop up the footprints of the cleaners as they passed on down the ward. I wondered that someone bothered to open the window without cleaning the glass but held my peace.

It was quiet in the ward now. The squad had moved on. I heard a sound outside the window and naturally, after the morning's scare, was instantly alert. Then I recalled that the windows were still to be washed and waited to see who would be doing this rather unpleasant task. The ledge was a good four feet wide, to be sure, and, as the sailor had demonstrated, could be traversed safely. But nine floors is a long way up, and I for one would not have liked to be out there. Neither did the window washer who now appeared. First I saw a hand carefully pushing a bucket of water across the width of the window, then a leg slid along, and then a face looked in, as the owner, clinging for dear life to the window frame, came upon the unexpectedly open window. It was the sad face of the man with circles under his eyes, whom I had noticed at the time of the Christmas inspection. He was looking sadder than ever, and his paleness and tense grip on the window frame showed plainly that he was suffering agonies of terror at the height.

"Come in," I called. "I'm afraid I can't close the window for you."

Without a word he carefully lowered himself into the room, his eyes thanking me. Visibly trembling, he sank onto a chair and wiped his face. The door into the ward corridor opened with a whine and he jumped to his feet, reached for his bucket and rag, pulled down the window, and began polishing the glass. A stern young face looked in the door and some curt words were spoken. I understood the window washer's reply ". . . nearly finished . . . doing the inside now . . ."

Again the whining door, and now cheerful voices. Tientung and Sister L and Elder Sister Pan, pushing a wheelchair, hurried in.

"Get ready, Lu! You're going home!" cried Tientung, and Sister L began stuffing things into the bag she had brought.

Elder Sister Pan glanced sharply at the window washer, who had been mechanically polishing the same square for some time. She went up to him and, with surprising gentleness, took the rag from his hand.

"That'll do, Old Wang," she said. (Not "Comrade"—that was reserved for the politically liberated—but the kindly country-style "Old" that could mean anything from formal deference to a superior to the affectionate respect of the younger for the elder.) "I'll finish in here so Professor Xia can get ready to leave."

With a swift and eloquent look of farewell, he went out the door, and Elder Sister Pan picked up his forgotten bucket and hurried after.

Soon I was rolling through empty corridors, descending in the freight elevator, headed for the side door where a car awaited to take us back to Zhong Da. The outside air was cool and damp, full of the innumerable smells of Canton: acrid coal smoke from cooking fires, frying, a river smell with the salt tide coming in, even in this city street, a whiff of flowers—but no Lysol. A bit shaky and a bit dizzy, I leaned back and watched the streets flow by; the lights coming on in houses and shops, now the chain of lights over the bridge, the traffic procession of bicycles and buses, people hurrying to get home before dark on this last evening of the old year. How good it was of Sister L to leave her dinner preparations to help bring me home! How glorious to be back, I thought, as we entered the great gates of the University, caught up in the general festive mood of home-coming shared with the uncounted millions of China.

Summer 1973

I PRESSED MY nose against the screen and tried to look straight down the outside wall of the house to locate the windows in the flat below. I measured the wall of our three rooms with my walking stick and tried to recall how the downstairs rooms had looked on that one occasion when I had been in them, the night before we moved into the upstairs of Number 6. My chief impression had been that there were windows and glass doors everywhere; there was one very large living room, with a kind of sun porch with huge French windows on one side, and a large square dining room, then a pantry with its built-in cupboards, and the large kitchen, then an afterthought type of bathroom and a courtyard with a water tap and a cement washing trough. Although I couldn't believe the downstairs was really bigger than the upstairs, I concluded that Tientung's daring plan was not wholly impossible.

This was, to move downstairs. If we could move down, two great ends would be accomplished. I would be able to go outdoors more easily (I had not been out once during the five months since my return from the hospital, because of the stairs); and by boldly reorganizing the available space, we could create what would be four more or less independent living units. As the date for Mingteh's and Damei's wedding approached, it became more and more obvious that there was no way for four "families" to coexist in the space now assigned us.

Even before the Cultural Revolution, Chinese family life had always been very collective. The need for privacy so urgent to the Westerner was not a generally shared cultural trait in China—although in our family, John and I saw eye to eye on that point, as on so many others. We could happily share a bed, but not a desk or bookcase. We took it for granted that our children, too, needed private space, and they had grown up with the great luxury of rooms of their own. When Mingteh went to live in the commune in quarters shared with a dozen other lads, it had been a difficult adjustment for him to make. Normally, when a son married, he would bring his bride to his parents' home, but Mingteh wanted terribly to have a separate home of his own. Tientung, having left her job in Gansu to take care of me in my illness, had to continue to live at home in the role of nurse. She had taken over Ho Jie's small room, and Ho Jie had my study alcove, while I lived behind a paper partition in the biggest room, surrounded by all the books and paraphernalia of my work. Mingteh slept in one corner of The Room, as we called our common dining room–sitting room (which was sometimes also my classroom). It was clearly no place to bring a bride.

But a bride was coming and something had to be done, and fast. Although after the wedding and the wedding trip, the young couple would have to be separated—Damei to go back to her job in Chang-sha—they had to have something she could think of as home, a place they shared with no one else. Damei in Changsha should be able to feel that she was only temporarily "away from home," and they would both work hopefully toward the goal of permanent reunion.

All their lives Tientung and Mingteh had been staunch allies. The politically caused isolation of our family had naturally thrown them together a great deal and they understood and cared for each other very deeply. In childhood days, if Tientung wanted to go to the movies to see the Russian ballet over and over again, a sleepy, bored, but loyal Mingteh would escort her; when Mingteh tore his clothes in a scrimmage, Tientung mended them and averted Ho Jie's wrath. Now, if Mingteh wanted a home for his bride, Tientung was resolved to see to it that he got it.

Hence the daring plan. With my measurements, observations, and recollections for a guide, she laid out a scheme for partitioning the downstairs that would most ingeniously make possible a cubicle for Ho Jie in the south-facing sun porch, a large half of the living room for Mingteh and Damei, a sun porch cubicle for me with an attached study-cum-dining-room for common use, a partitioned-off room for her, with a communications line cut off down one side to connect the kitchen-bathroom end with the living quarters. Thanks to the peculiar construction of the house, it was possible for each "family" to have a private door to come and go by without crossing anyone else's territory. When I saw her plan, I was amazed and somewhat dubious.

"How can all this be done," I exclaimed. "You know the Housing Bureau!"

"Of course," she agreed. "But they can't refuse to let you move down, because of your health. And what we do on our own, we do on our own. If they agree to give us 'a few bricks and some cement,' I know that the masons and other construction workers will be glad to show Mingteh and me what to do. We already know all about whitewashing, and Mingteh can do anything, especially for Damei," she finished.

And so it proved . . . permission granted . . . the move began. With the changes completed, Mingteh could set up his bridal bed, with its huge mosquito net canopy, the gleaming new dresser, and his father's old desk in the room that was to be his own home for his own "family." It was really a very pleasant big room with tall windows on two sides and a no longer functioning fireplace, which gave it a very cozy American look, if no heat. Tientung and I sewed frantically at the hems on the golden-brown window curtains (no cloth tickets required) and she got them in place just in time. When Damei arrived, her "home" was complete—red paper "double happiness" character posters on the wall, a new red quilt cover, and (a Western touch) flowers made it look reasonably like a bridal chamber.

The rest of the rooms were still empty, and somewhat redolent of the newly applied whitewash, for we did not intend to move down until after the honeymoon. The "wedding feast" would be prepared in Ho Jie's familiar kitchen upstairs and served in the new home. Tientung and I thought it would be too shattering for Ho Jie to have to cope with such an event in the uproar of moving.

The "wedding feast" possible in 1973 was only a shadow of what would have been the norm for the wedding of an only son in bygone days. And what we could do in our present situation was not even up to the standard of a peasant's wedding in the commune, where old ways quietly persisted in spite of political education against feudal customs. Mingteh had purposely refrained from letting his peasant friends know about this marriage because he couldn't entertain them on the scale they would have expected. When they learned of the event later, they would forgive his reticence, knowing that his father had recently died and his mother was an invalid.

In 1973 no one really knew what to expect for a wedding, anyway. I was aware of some of the usual pre-Liberation Chinese family customs, but I knew that everything had to be different now. Weddings in China are the business of the bridegroom's family, not the bride's. Since I was thoroughly disqualified by my ignorance and my illness, all the arrangements had to be made by Tientung.

So she saw to it that the wedding presents were wrapped in red paper (red for celebration, white for mourning in China—always) and planned with Ho Jie a succession of worthy meals.

As soon as Damei arrived and was welcomed, Mingteh whisked her off to the police station. This unlikely spot was the scene of the only legally required part of the wedding, the issuance of a stamped and sealed pink paper by the local authorities, registering the marriage. The requirements for getting this paper were fairly simple. The bride must be over twenty-five, and the groom over twenty-eight; they must have the permission of their primary work units; the bride must satisfy the authorities that she was not being forced into marriage by anyone, but entered into that contract of her own free will. This was a provision of the New Marriage Law promulgated soon after Liberation to protect women from forced marriages. In some places, where the Cultural Revolution did not interfere with usual procedures, a medical certificate might be asked for. Identity was established by presenting work cards (issued by each one's primary work unit) and the ever important *hukou*. There was no more ceremony than in sending a telegram or buying a stamp. After waiting in line for a couple of hours, while other couples got their pink papers, Mingteh and Damei procured theirs and came home, in a fog of mixed feelings. Damei looked shy and confused when I greeted her as Mrs. Lo: her maiden name would be used all her life, as there is no title of Mrs. in the PRC and married women do not take their husband's family name now, although there is still a strong feeling that a bride leaves her father's family and belongs to her husband's.

No parade in a covered sedan chair accompanied by shouting children; no firecrackers to announce her arrival; no red silk costume; no masklike face carefully painted by envious girlfriends; no terrifying ordeal of bowing to the ancestors together, to the parents. . . . No wedding bells. No wedding ring. No flowers. No white veil. No bridal procession. No throng of well-wishing family friends to hear—and by hearing—support the wedding vows. No wedding vows at all. No wedding cake. No hilarious departure in a cloud of flung rice—the thought of this waste of edible grain brought me down to earth with a thud.

At least the *hukou* guaranteed them their share of the essential food; their pink paper entitled them to demand—if not get—housing together. Armed with this evidence of legality, Damei could get free transportation for one twelve-day "home visit" a year. A new family, very hygienic, very economic, very socially acceptable, had been recognized by Authority.

I knew that Authority had done all it could to dissuade this pair from joining for life. The Leadership in such cultural units as the opera troupe where Damei played the piano liked to have a hand in the arranging of suitable marriages for their members. Why should they encourage a marriage that would inevitably pull a talented (and very beautiful) girl out of their work unit? It was more or less tactfully suggested to Damei that Mingteh had "complicated foreign relations"—hence would never be a good risk politically.

There was now no longer the authority of the family, only their influence, the natural concern of parents, no longer backed up by economic dependence or religious sanctions. From the viewpoint of Damei's parents, marriage to Mingteh meant security for their girl; from my viewpoint, Mingteh's marriage to Damei meant that he was taking a wife whose background was familiar to him and to me, and that I was getting a daughter-in-law with whom I might hope to communicate linguistically, and most of all that at long last my son was doing what he wanted, not what circumstances forced upon him. He had looked over the field, found the girl he wanted, and carried her off in the face of official resistance.

Thirty-six years earlier, in the summer of 1937, Mingteh's father and I had celebrated our wedding in Shanghai. It was not a casual or impulsive step for us, either, but a lifetime commitment, entered into after much sober thought and with much joyous hope.

We had planned to be married in church in Shanghai on the twelfth of August, as a kind of symbolic union of cultures. The twelfth of August, that year, was the day when, according to Chinese legend, the Heavenly Herd-boy and the Spinning Maid in the sky were united after long separation, a pleasingly poetic reason for choosing that day. But we reckoned without international affairs.

On the fourth of August, John came early to his brother's home, where I was a guest, to say, "Would you mind if we get married tomorrow, instead? There is talk of a Japanese attack on Shanghai and I have been able to get tickets on an upriver boat. It leaves tomorrow at midnight. It'll be a rather busy day, but can you manage?" This was the kind of understatement I was going to get used to over the years.

Shanghai was tensely waiting to be attacked; a typhoon was lashing the coast; everyone we knew was frantically trying to find a way to a safer place. But somehow during that day we managed to buy a diamond engagement ring for me (this was very important to John), an innerspring mattress (we couldn't get one in Wuhan), and a wedding cake; find a classmate of John's in Holy Orders who could perform the Episcopal ceremony at Second Brother's house; find my American friend Marian Fitch, who was to be my bridesmaid; arrange for a wedding dinner at the YMCA; buy a bridal bouquet; and get my hair done (this was important to me).

John's loyal family members, in spite of their fears of impending battle, managed to provide the atmosphere of bridal joy, doing everything they could think of to make the American bride happy.

After the ceremony the wedding party made their way to the YMCA where the "wedding feast" was held. We were seated at the table after a dinner I could not taste; the waiter handed me the knife to cut into the towering wedding cake. While I hesitated, someone ran in and spoke urgently to John at the head of the table. He stood up and announced calmly, "I'm afraid we'll have to go now. The boat is said to be going out into the harbor to avoid being mobbed. We'll take the cake with us." And in minutes I found myself, still clutching my wedding bouquet, white gown and all, in the center of a flying wedge formed by the wedding guests, plunging through a shouting, teeming crowd of refugees all trying to get on board the last boat upriver. Ahead I could see the classmate-clergyman (fortunately also a soccer star in school days), clerical robes flying in the typhoon, cleaving through the mob. Beside me walked John, carefully carrying the wedding cake and managing to make haste without appearing to hurry. Thrusting our tickets and appropriate cumshaw into the hands of the armed guard at the end of the gangplank, the best man ushered us on board and into the holy hush of a British riverboat first-class dining saloon. Doors banged on the shouting outside, some orders were given, the roll and crash of the gangplank coming up, and we were on our way. Still stunned, the members of the wedding party who had succeeded in getting on board sat around a green baize-covered table and ate the cake.

That was the wedding I was remembering while I waited for the three family guests who were to make up the company for the wedding feast of our son.

Ho Jie, aided by her sister and with Tientung doing a rather large share of the peeling and chopping essential to Chinese cookery, was preparing as fine a dinner as revolutionary conditions permitted. With eight persons to sit at the dinner table, there must be eight dishes and a superior soup. There must be chicken, pork, fish, salt things and sweet things, side dishes of pickled eggs, and spicy condiments. Alas, there could be no *kwei yu,* the special Yangtse River carp essential to a feast in Wuchang, but in Canton there had to be, and there was, an equally prestigious dish involving dried squid. Ho Jie declared it was necessary to have a kind of pork-taro "sandwich," rich and succulent, requiring a special kind of taro not to be found on the market; but—triumph—her nephew had grown some in his backyard and saved it for this occasion, so it would be possible to fulfill the festive requirements.

Our guests, to represent the family in welcoming the bride, were two Cantonese ladies, the sisters of my Fourth Sister-in-Law, and the tenuously connected "cousin" who had proved so great a help in smuggling Tientung and Mingteh out to Shanghai during the fighting in 1968. (In 1937 when John and I finally reached Wuchang after our river adventure, to supplement the Christian ceremony in Shanghai, the family celebrated all over again. When we rode up to the gate, right from the boat, we were greeted with salvos of fire-crackers; the whole house had been repainted, whitewashed, and decorated with brilliantly colored flowers and scrolls; and every member of the family within reach, plus uncounted classmates and colleagues, all were gathered to a great feast that overflowed the guest room into the family dining room and onto the veranda. Third Son was bringing home a bride and the occasion must be marked.)

Although low key as celebrations go, Mingteh's wedding was a tremendous change from the generally penitential atmosphere of anxiety of the Cultural Revolution and was enjoyed accordingly. The only flaw in the possible enjoyment was that I was unable to attend the feast. Still a shaky convalescent, I had developed a fever that laid me low. However, the great merits of Tientung's architectural ar-rangements were proved by the convenient connection of my sleep-ing cubicle on the sun porch with the commonly shared dining-room-cum-study. Lying on my bed behind the door, I could share in the festivities in spirit, while avoiding the confrontation with the octopus soup, which I secretly dreaded.

Following this official welcoming feast, the young couple spent several days visiting and being visited. They called formally upon a few older people, friends of their fathers' and parents of their friends, leaving little packets of candy behind as a way of announcing their marriage. These calls were returned and wedding presents brought: towels, dishes, pictures, thermos bottles—so much needed for the boiled drinking water—were offered and gratefully accepted.

In old China, at a set date after the wedding at the groom's home, the bride would be expected to go to visit her mother. Al-though no one was making any effort to follow this protocol con-sciously, it seemed just the right thing now for Mingteh and Damei to go to Wuhan to visit her family and enjoy the celebra-tion of her wedding with her sisters and brothers. Following a hectic but enjoyable round of feasting there, they went on to Changsha, where it began all over again and Mingteh was offi-cially welcomed into Damei's professional "family." This was even more cheering and by the time Mingteh had to come back to Canton to work, bride and groom both felt they had had a really bang-up wedding in three installments.

Now the honeymoon was over. Damei, in Changsha, was officially recognized as a married woman by being granted a tiny room to herself. Mingteh exerted all his considerable ingenuity to make it comfortable for his bride, putting in wiring for lights, scrubbing and cleaning, scrounging furniture. There wasn't room for much, but this would be their home together over the October First holiday, over New Year, over May Day, over any three-day weekend when Mingteh would be able to buy a ticket and go to see her. Over Spring Festival, she was entitled to somewhat elastic visiting privileges at Canton.

Back at Canton, Mingteh settled into his solitary bridal chamber to write letters, count days . . . and study English.

I had never really believed that once the young couple were married there would be too long a delay in Damei's being transferred. I could imagine the authorities trying to discourage a marriage that would inevitably disrupt their work force, but I couldn't think it possible that a newlywed couple would have to accept the program of part-time family life that now developed. Mingteh and Damei, more realistic, and aware of the experience of others, grimly settled in to a regime of letter writing and weekend and holiday reunions.

This was not my idea of married life, but I comforted myself on their behalf with the fond, but delusive, belief that if and when my longed-for grandchild should make his/her approach obvious, the disciplinary separation would come to an end, and, for the sake of the baby's welfare, the family could hope to be reunited. How wrong I was.

In August 1974 my granddaughter, Manman, was born, and everyone rejoiced and welcomed her. But remorselessly the statutory fifty-six days of maternity leave sped away, and in spite of all our pleas, there was nothing for it but for Damei to board that northbound train once more, taking the baby along. A peasant woman from a commune would be privately hired—as I hired Ho Jie—to sit with the baby and help with the washing while Damei was at rehearsals or performing; that was what everyone else did, and we were lucky to be able to afford a helper. No one seemed to see it as I did.

That is, no one but Mingteh. This total blockade of his personal life confirmed his determination to emigrate.

IT IS DISCONCERTING to be asked if you are really dead or not.

Three of my former students, now gray-haired teachers and veterans of the Cultural Revolution, were sitting on the edges of chairs in my small living room, paying a most unexpected ceremonial call one day. I assured them that not only was I not dead, but I was taking a renewed interest in life.

Why, I asked, did they have this appreciated but unnecessary concern for my well-being? I couldn't set aside the thought that when I had so desperately needed friends in 1969, they had all been silent and invisible. Small thanks to them that I was now struggling onto my feet.

"We heard through the former Department leader [last seen tagged as a monster, now reported to be teetering on the brink of restoration to power] that you were seriously ill and not even expected to live." They finally got it out, with some embarrassment.

"That was probably wishful thinking," I replied. "I have no such plans."

With the usual politenesses they retired, presumably to report to whoever had sent them. It was scarcely credible that they should take such an initiative upon themselves without a "hint" from someone.

After their departure I sat for a long time in my wheelchair, staring out the window at the water buffalo grazing on the former tennis courts, and I faced some unpleasant facts.

I had not precisely planned to die, that at least was true.

I remembered that when the new program of work began in the Department in 1970, and the "Outside English" teachers began coming to the house to work with me, one of them had confided that some of the young instructors were afraid that after John's death I might attempt suicide.

I was surprised at the violence of my rejection of such a course. And it had almost frightened my young visitor when I said firmly, "Impossible. I am a Christian! I could never take my own life." At that time, in the atmosphere of the Cultural Revolution, such a declaration must have sounded insane.

But now I had to admit to myself that while not planning to die, I certainly had not been planning to live. I had been temporizing. I'll hang on until Mingteh gets out of the commune. I'll pull through until Tientung gets back from Gansu and gets a suitable job. I'll wait until Mingteh gets married. I'll hold out until Damei is transferred and the family united. I'll wait until the baby is born. . . . I accepted my role as an invalid. I could see Tientung growing pale and careworn under the burden of double duty as an English teacher in the newly organized FLD and housekeeper-nurse, and I accepted that, too. I accepted being phased out. No. It wasn't good enough.

I had often thought that one of the greatest weaknesses in China was the people's toleration of what ought to be intolerable. Now, insidiously, this passive endurance had grown upon me.

It was intolerable—or should be—that Mingteh and his wife and baby should have to dwell apart. It was intolerable—or should be—that Tientung should have no options about her life and work, but must accept spending her days working under the authority of those who had, in effect, blighted her father's career and contributed to his premature death—and who now openly looked forward to my demise. It was intolerable that I should consent to spend my few remaining years sitting in my wheelchair in a tiny cubicle watching the leaves patter down from the flame-of-the-forest tree in even the prettiest garden in the world.

What could be done?

A familiar figure in a green uniform, the mailman, was coming down the street. Would there be a letter from Changsha? That was all-important. Or was it? No. Would there be a letter for me?

Possibly there might be. There might be a letter, there might be a parcel notice from the customs office, there might be a new American magazine. Ever since the delivery of the great bundle of "delayed" letters when I was at the hospital, there had been an ever-increasing flow of mail from friends in America. I felt in my heart that I would never again see the faces of these faithful friends, but I was grateful for their concern and tried hard to respond, even though typing one page was two mornings' work, preceded by many hours of thought during sleepless nights, deciding what I dared say. I took great care that my letters, like a sun dial, should record only sunny hours. Now, while waiting for the knock of the man in green, I thought with fresh insight about my overseas friends. They were scattered all over the United States. They didn't know each other, except by chance, through their acquaintance with me. They were (at least in Mingteh's eyes) my "old lady friends," professional women mostly, nearing retirement, or, if retired, enjoying new freedom for travel and service and study, busy heads of families, concerned with grandchildren, active in their communities, with one interest in common—the welfare of one old lady in a wheelchair in Canton. They didn't think that I was dead. They assumed that I was alive, alive as much as they were.

The expected knock came, and a cheerful announcement, "Parcel for you, Professor Xia!"

Glorious! As soon as Mingteh got home for lunch, I would dispatch him on his bicycle, armed with his seal, my seal, the *hukou* book, and his work card, to the postal station where parcels were kept to be called for. This was a surprisingly busy spot, mainly because so many Cantonese have relatives in Hong Kong and overseas. To it, even during the Cultural Revolution, came a considerable stream of parcels every day. The Chinese postal service requires that parcels be wrapped in cloth and sewed up securely, but my American packages came done up in brown paper. It was easy for the clerk to find them in the mounds of bundles.

Opening parcels was thrilling. It was best to keep such things inconspicuous, so they would be brought to my room and examined behind closed doors. First the dirty outside paper would be removed and the lavish lengths of nylon string carefully rolled into balls. Then the inner clean brown paper would be folded and set aside, to be doled out to Ho Jie to line the chickens' basket, washed, and reused until it melted away. Then each item would be unwrapped and gloated over: the envelopes of life-giving milk powder, each guarded against Canton's humidity with a pliofilm bag, itself a treasure to be scrupulously saved for reuse; the packets of instant soup, with their appetizing colored pictures of such incredible viands as oxtails, glowing tomatoes, green peas. We never ceased to wonder at the luxury of being able to have vegetables that belong in different seasons all at the same time. When you don't have refrigeration and there is no nationwide food distribution, naturally you eat what is in season until it is out and then start on the next item on the calendar. Then there might be a little glass of dried chipped beef—save that glass —and we'll save the beef for Sunday dinner, with a scrambled duck's egg. Protein! The cheese powder—possibly not so nourishing as the real cheese, which would have turned moldy en route, but so delicious in varying the taste of the monotonous dishes. The amazing high-protein drinks, the delectable dates, prunes, and raisins, to be rationed out as desserts for days. And the surprises! What pleasure there was in finding a little notebook of colored paper, a box of crayons, balloons for a neighbor's children, little rolls of candy, colorful Christmas wrapping paper and ribbons, and above all, the wealth of marvelous unbreakable containers, with nice tight lids, mouse-proof, roach-proof, and damp-proof. Ho Jie would deal them out judgmatically to appropriate friends to encourage the flow of supplies of local eggs, vegetables, and chicken. Never anything so crass as an exchange: just a "thought you might like this funny foreign thing" today, and a "here are a few eggs" tomorrow.

The invisible treasure in each parcel, however, that could never be taxed by the customs office, was the assurance each package brought that, on the other side of the propaganda barrier, beyond time and distance, there were friends who still trusted and cared.

Books and magazines had been coming through since the days in the seamen's ward. Piaget—how John would have enjoyed these; Tolkien—Tientung found a new world; Herriot—now why did the first volume get in and the second get confiscated? Collins's account of the moon landing—with new meaning coming out of each rereading; mathematics, electronics, physics—Mingteh, "Oh this is just what I needed"; *Jonathan Livingston Seagull*—"But that's being criticized, how did that make it?"; the Brontë poems—Tientung,

"Oh!"; Adelle Davis—"Vitamins? Food?"; Highet, *"Man's Uncon-querable Mind"?* Yes.

Magazines—*Audubon's* revelation of America's beauty, its immi-nent danger of destruction, and the rallying to defend it; *The National Geographic* with its mind-stretching journeys, but most espe-cially its reports in depth of America's states and cities. *Arizona Highways*—pictures to be lovingly cut out and pasted up on blank whitewashed walls to serve as windows on a wider world. From these we all began to build up our images of the land I had left and to which we were now all dreaming of returning, some day, some how.

One day there was a rude shock when I opened a newly delivered magazine. Slipped between the pages was a printed leaflet, in Chi-nese, factional political propaganda. One glance was enough to show me that it would be exceedingly dangerous to be found with such a thing in the house. Whoever could have put it there? The maga-zine envelope was sealed as usual. The sender could not conceivably have enclosed such a thing. None of my "old lady friends" could have dreamed of it. Trembling all over, I hastily hid the magazine and its enclosure in the bottom drawer of my dresser, pulled some old clothes over it, and sat down on the bed to wait for Mingteh to come home. I didn't dare leave the room. When my son came in, I drew him into my cubicle, locked the door, and showed him the horrid thing. He took a very grave view of it.

"This could be just a random use of the mail to send in subver-sive propaganda from Hong Kong," he said. "Or it could be a kind of provocation or test, to see what *we* would do with it. In any event, the best thing to do is for me to take it at once to the Leadership and explain how it came. We cannot be held respon-sible for what is sent to us. Anyone could send anybody anything after all."

I recalled with a cold feeling down my spine a chilling little story I had read years before in the *Reader's Digest,* called "Address Unknown," in which a victim of Nazi persecution revenged himself upon an enemy by sending him incriminating letters, which, discov-ered by the Gestapo, led to his richly deserved liquidation. Sheer terror gripped me.

"Don't fash"—Mingteh's usual admonition. "I'll get rid of it at once."

And he was off on his bicycle to the Clock Tower, to hand it in to the cadre responsible for such problems among the masses. All the time he was gone, I had visions of his being stopped on the road and searched, of his accidentally losing the thing on the way, or of his being detained for questioning. I was even more terrified than when it had been in the house in my drawer and I the only one involved.

In a short time, though, Mingteh was back, all reassuring smiles. "I gave it to Comrade Liu and explained how it had come just this morning," he told me as we sat down to our belated lunch. "He said that we did the correct thing in handing it in, and that if anything like that came again, to do the same. We are not held responsible for what comes to us in the mail. Everything that is delivered here has already been inspected and it is not our fault if something gets through. What would be wrong would be to keep it and show it to people."

I was thankful that the problem was solved for the moment, but thereafter, every time I opened a parcel or book or magazine I had a moment of cold fear until I had made sure no such scorpion was lurking within.

It would have been silly after this experience not to recognize that all mail, coming in and going out, passed through various hands and could be inspected by persons of various political opinions. I could see why my Chinese friends had stopped corresponding with friends abroad. It was altogether too risky. Yet to me this contact with my friends in America was rapidly becoming a psychological necessity. I had a growing conviction that I must keep up the lines of communication in case sometime in the future Mingteh and Tientung might want to claim their American heritage.

I had to admit that I myself was feeling increasingly insecure. After the Shanghai Communiqué and the visit from the Haddens, I had allowed myself a degree of optimism about the future in China. Our future and China's future. Now I had to face the fact that all my years of experience in China made clear: whatever the situation at the moment, it was bound to change, and often into its diametrical opposite. If today the foreigner was a "foreign friend of the

Chinese people," welcomed with the most seductive hospitality in the world, tomorrow, often due to circumstances not only beyond his control but beyond his possible knowledge, he could be the subject of subtle hostility, social isolation, or even the victim of mob violence.

Yet within this changing social climate, sometimes warm and delightful, sometimes terrifying and alien, there was always a persisting network of personal relationships, the quality of which often determined how the social climate would affect one's fortunes at any time.

Resolutely putting aside my hopes and wishes, I tried to look as objectively as I could at the possibilities for my children. At times, clearly, my being there with them was a help and a protection; as long as I lived, I would give them a degree of financial security—a considerable point with Mingteh's problem in maintaining two homes. But equally, at any time, no matter how exemplary their own behavior, they could never get out from under the shadow of their foreign connections and of their father's political "hat."

And apparently I, too, was in the shadow. Although my health was slowly improving and I was eager to get back to work, in spite of the restoration of the English Speciality, I was no longer needed. An authentic Englishman had arrived on the scene to strengthen the faculty of the FLD; but even he was not allowed free contact with either students or teachers. There was, again, a growing tension in the atmosphere that reminded me of June 1966. The liberal trend that had begun in 1972 was now reversing. The wind was blowing from the opposite direction.

First evidence of political changes in the offing came at the local level with the rehabilitation of the leading Party members, the same persons who had been instrumental in putting John "on the wall" and then had been enthusiastically labeled as monsters in 1966. Accused of all manner of misdoings, mobbed by the Red Guards, deprived of prestige and position, paraded with wooden "monster" tags round their necks, forced to spend weeks, months, years, at meaningless manual labor, writing and rewriting self-criticisms, the two leading members of the FLD were now emerging again.

Considered objectively, they had never been in a position of sufficient power to do anything meriting the severity of the punishments that befell them. True, they had been personally unpopular in some quarters because of their arrogance and misuse of what power they had to gain petty material advantages. But their original rise to authority through political maneuvering, their crashing downfall in the fury of the Cultural Revolution, and now their gradual return to positions of leadership, as national political tides ebbed and flowed, had little to do with justice or personal deserts. They were no better and no worse than thousands of petty bureaucrats who carried on the administration of the nation's affairs.

There was little new in the situation. What had aroused hopes in 1966 was that some of the "rebels" had for a time been spokesmen for the great silent unorganized majority. Such uprisings against oppressive authority had occurred many times before in China's long history, and undoubtedly would occur again and yet again, until or unless some way could be found to get rid of a few rats without burning down the barn.

There was no denying it, the future would see more storms. And people like us would always be "expendable."

And then one day the man in green brought a letter from Mingteh's godmother, Ruth Abells Douglas, my roommate at the University of Chicago back in 1931. She announced that "if it is convenient for me," she hoped to come to pay me a visit. The next letter, she had achieved permission to come. The next, a date, the last week in April 1975. Now there was a new incentive, a new hope. I began to come alive.

I carefully pulled the curtains to cover the windows in Mingteh's room and prepared to iron my good shirt and Tientung's and Mingteh's better coats. A vigilant passerby might observe the ironing and make trouble over this bourgeois use of electricity, but I was determined that we should not appear too dilapidated when we went to meet Ruth Douglas at the station the next day.

The preceding few weeks had been a frenzy of preparations within the household. While I had been recalcitrant about cleaning house to welcome the unknown Americans who had turned out to be the Haddens, I had other feelings about welcoming Ruth. Not that she would have cared the less for me for having a dirty house. We shared living quarters too long in student days in Chicago and were on too intimate a footing for false pride. I wanted to present a positive picture of ourselves and our lives. In spite of myself I kept thinking of that possible over-the-shoulder reader at the post office.

The children and I had decided that we would be entirely truthful in everything we said, but that we would not be in the position of spreading "negative impressions" of our socialist paradise through our privileged contact with a foreign visitor. We wanted the contact to continue.

This was a rather special visit, we discovered. Ruth was coming, not as a tourist under the Travel Service guidance night and day, but as a person-to-person visitor, possibly the first American to do so for many, many years. Official visitors, journalists, Ping-pong players, overseas Chinese, even reformed Kuomintang generals had been allowed to travel about, but possibly never since the Cultural Revolution sealed everything up tight had a private citizen, an American woman, come to pay a social visit to an old friend. Of course, the Foreign Affairs and Travel Service had to be involved in arranging her entrance and her stay at the Dong Fang Hotel, but she was free to spend as much time with me at home, unchaperoned, as she wished. As a final and special concession, she was allowed to bring with her, her daughter, Dorothy, a graduate student in biology, to help on the journey and to get a glimpse of Canton, the only place they were to visit.

While I was ironing her uniform, Tientung came in looking grim. "I'm on the wall," she announced, taking the iron out of my hand and continuing the task.

"Where?"

"In front of the Clock Tower. Someone has put up a whole lot of wall posters about the old FLD, and they've raised the whole business about my being admitted 'by the back door' again. Since I've just recently been appointed to teach in the Department, it gets me off to a nice start, to criticize all that again."

"It seems like very careful timing," I mused. "With Ruth coming here tomorrow. She'll have every chance to see that poster on the way to the house. She can't read Chinese, I know, but she could recognize your name. What if she wanted to photograph a typical *da zi bao?*"

I couldn't figure out what or whose interest might be served by putting the spotlight of *da zi bao* criticism on Tientung (and thus on our family) at this moment. It all was very complex. I only knew that it made me uncomfortable. And this alone might be sufficient reason for the whole thing. I resolved not to let it spoil our pleasure in the visit.

Tientung seemed to have come to the same conclusion. "I'll go see someone," she said. Which she did, and to such effect that when Mingteh passed the bulletin board a little later in the afternoon on his way back to work at the factory, he observed that a whole new set of posters had been pasted over the ones about Tientung. While this solved the immediate problem, it reinforced our decision to be ultra-careful of what we said. We felt very much under observation.

It was almost time for the college car to come to take Tientung and Mingteh to the station to meet Ruth and Dorothy. I was still lying in bed. Early in the morning, before breakfast, the clinic nurse had come unexpectedly to take a blood sample for a checkup, and I was feeling sick and weak, all my brave resolution drained away. "You kids go," I said to Tientung defensively. "I just don't think I can make it. You'll easily recognize her—"

"Lu, you get out of that bed and get dressed," interrupted Tientung. "If Ruth can come all the way from Vermont to see you, you can get to the station to meet her. You *owe* it to her. Now budge!"

Strengthened by shame, I obediently donned the "garments of gladness" we had repaired the day before, the navy blue silk skirt, the blue Dacron blouse, the invisible but infinitely supportive petticoat. Lined up at the front door, we inspected each other. Mingteh was looking a foot taller than usual in his neatly pressed blue uniform, his curly hair well brushed down in front, but as usual erupting in back; Tientung in the uniform, baggy but neatly creased slacks, and a modest touch of lavender visible at the neck of the ironed blue coat, black hair in shining decorous waves. A surge of pride in my handsome and indomitable children gave stiffness to my spine, and

I climbed into my wheelchair to be rolled up the hill to the waiting car pool limousine.

Sitting in the car in the station park with Tientung while Mingteh went to check arrival times, I got my first shocking glimpse of modern Westerners as they began swarming out of the station from the incoming Hong Kong train. The only people I had seen for a decade, aside from the Haddens, were Zhong Da students and some few teachers; the students now, being all worker-peasant-soldiers, and the teachers all leaning toward the protective coloration pattern of blue and faded Mao uniforms. I couldn't believe my eyes as I took in blue jeans, the long hair, the beards, the high heels, the short skirts (1975). Frances Roots Hadden, being China-born herself, had naturally and gracefully adapted her costume to the local taste, and although her clothes were brighter in color than was usual in 1972 in the PRC, she had given me no preliminary experience to prepare me for what I now saw.

"This is nothing," comforted Tientung, who not infrequently had to work with Travel Service guides, coaching them in English, and who therefore had seen these wonderful sights before. "I just wonder what Ruth will look like."

So did I. But before I could worry very much, there they came across the plaza, Mingteh triumphantly leading two "foreign American females"—Ruth, looking at that distance to my suddenly misty eyes just like the tall, beautiful young woman I had seen holding that same Mingteh in her arms at the font when he was baptized in 1945. Behind her marched an even taller young woman, her daughter, Dorothy, with her long dark hair flying about her shoulders, dressed in blue jeans and pullover.

"Gosh, ain't she modern!" breathed Tientung, jumping out of the car to run and meet them. But if Dorothy was satisfactorily modern, Ruth was equally satisfactory in her Quaker black, white, and gray, elegant, modish, but the irreproachable picture of a *lady* in the eyes of the admiring Travel Service guides following with the Douglases' so correctly limited luggage.

After first greetings we checked our two visitors in at the Dong Fang Hotel and settled down to a week's conversation, only interrupting ourselves from time to time to agree with Tientung and

Dorothy and the guides as they worked out a timetable for such sightseeing as the guests wanted to fit in around the daily home visits.

Feeding our dear guests was a problem. Because they were something above and beyond the tourist category, we were entitled to some special rations, but we ran into bureaucratic Clock Tower snags in collecting the necessary tickets, and in the end it was "family connections" who saw to it that the cuisine of Canton was kept up to standard. This was a source of mixed feelings to all of us. We wanted our guests to have the best, of course, but it was hard to hold our tongues when they enjoyed the beautiful dishes Ho Jie prepared —pork and chicken and fish and various vegetables such as the "masses" had not seen in years—and praised the healthful quality of Chinese foods in the jargon of the Natural Foods movement. I thought of Tientung's years of living on millet porridge in Gansu, of Mingteh and his young comrades in the commune, living on rice and pickles contributed by charitable villagers, of my own breakdown on the meatless, milkless diet of years. Well, at least for this week we were all eating well!

When, at the end of that glorious week, our guests departed for fabulous Vermont, our general plans were all agreed upon. Basking in the glory of such privileged visitors, Damei had been able to bring my granddaughter, Manman, home for ten days to meet the company, and while at seven months she was not in position to grasp all that had been decided that was to affect her future, the young lady seemed to approve her father's words: "I want my daughter to grow up in the kind of world, Lu, that makes people be like your friends."

1976

IT WAS INDEED the end of an era in our family when Ho Jie retired. For more than fifteen years she had managed our household affairs, liberating me for the work of a college professor, endearing herself to us all by her loyalty and resourcefulness, as well as her cooking. Now a combination of circumstances had brought us to the realization that it was time to implement the plan that her niece, Ah Zun, and nephew, Ah Cho, had long been advocating—that she should go to live with Ah Zun and "take a rest." For several years her high blood pressure had given us all great concern; in fact, Mingteh and Tientung had been taking care of two old lady invalids for some time. At Ah Zun's, Ho Jie could take life easy and enjoy the honors of old age as she had always planned it. Our household was about to change focus, and it would be beyond her strength to cope.

We all felt sad to see that short, stout figure going up the hill with Ah Zun and Ah Cho carrying her bedding roll (augmented at the last moment by the impulsive gift of the diamond patchwork quilt), the suitcase with a lock (where the never-used but much appreciated mosquito net was secured), and the innumerable baskets and bundles of salvage that meant so much to her thrifty soul. We knew that we would be seeing her again, often, we hoped, but it was the end of an era.

In spite of every effort, Mingteh had not yet been able to get Damei transferred to Canton, nor would the local authorities hear of his moving, with me, permanently, to Changsha. It had been hard enough for the young couple to be separated with only their own feelings to consider, but now that baby Manman was involved, the situation was becoming desperate. Any illusion that I had clung to that the arrival of the baby would soften bureaucratic hearts had long since vanished. Why should anyone fret about a baby's preference for being with her mother—or a mother's emo-

THE END OF AN ERA

tional attachment to her baby—when it was perfectly simple to leave the infant with an old country woman in a foster home? The child would be fed, clothed, and sheltered. What more could one ask?

Mingteh asked a great deal more. He wanted a home, with his wife and their child within it, not a lifetime of riding the trains for a few stolen hours of "home life." He wanted to raise his child as a person in a home of her own.

The baby's first year had been, perforce, spent with Damei, living at the hostel of the opera troupe in Changsha. An old peasant woman had been hired to baby-sit when Damei was at work, and until baby was weaned there was no serious problem. But hygiene and bottle feeding were a closed book to old "PoPo," and new arrangements for Manman's care had to be made. Now the severe Changsha winter was approaching. There was no heat in the hostel, and no convenient way to cook the baby's food. She was beginning to want to run about, and it was going to be beyond "PoPo" 's strength to keep up with her, keep her warm and dry, and feed her properly. If Damei had to go to the countryside with the troupe, Manman would be in a potentially dangerous situation. This, of course, Mingteh could not endure!

It was decided that Manman was to stay in Canton with Mingteh and me, for the cold months at least, and I was to supervise an amah who could do the actual baby care, washing, feeding, and so on, tasks beyond my strength. Mingteh would take care of the child over the weekends, and Damei would "serve the people" in Changsha.

Inquiry among Mingteh's numerous friends brought to our attention a baby amah qualified by experience if not by any professional training, who would come to live at our house, take care of the baby, and cook our simple meals. She had performed a similar task for another university family when both parents had been sent to Cadre School, leaving a young family otherwise stranded. Ah Po, as she was called, was reputed to be something of a specialist with babies of Manman's age—and photographs of those whom she had nursed through the toddling and spoon-feeding period were impressive evidence of her skill. We waited anxiously for her to move in and make the transfer of Manman to her care under Damei's supervision.

At last Ah Po arrived. She was a little woman with a shrewd, ever-smiling face, neatly, even modishly, dressed in Chinese traditional tunic and trousers, not in the modern uniform. Her gray hair was cut rather short and combed back very smoothly, held in place by a kind of round comb, which she had decorated by binding it with pink plastic string. In her pierced ears were small gold earrings, and her bare feet were squeezed into black plastic sandals, which she removed as soon as she went on duty. She had tactfully provided a squeaking rubber dolly to use in making friends with her new charge, and she seemed to be knowledgeable about babies. But I knew that I was going to miss our Ho Jie's honest, round, smiling face.

Ah Po was definitely a town mouse, and she had learned quite different lessons from the Cultural Revolution than Ho Jie had. Whereas Ho Jie worried lest she commit the sin of bourgeois lifestyle if she (or I) wore a new or too stylish garment, Ah Po gloried in being as fashionable as she could contrive to be. Her well-plucked eyebrows were raised a trifle on the first washday when she saw the patched and mended and faded garments Damei and I hung out. Where Ho Jie had approved and encouraged thrift to the point of parsimony, I felt that Ah Po slightly despised anyone who, with a professor's income (everyone knew everyone's salary in the University, of course), did not wear more stylish or better quality clothes. Ah Po liked the idea that the Cultural Revolution had raised up the proletariat (meaning Ah Po) into the class of those who wore jewelry, silk gowns, and perfume, and spent their abundant leisure going to movies and the opera. Ho Jie saw the revolution as bringing down the *tai-tai*'s and making them work as hard as she did. And by preference, Ho Jie worked very hard indeed. When her scheduled day's work was done, she would cultivate whatever bit of land she could latch onto; Ah Po watched the clock and when her statutory rest hour came after lunch, she would promptly hand over the baby to whoever was at home and spend her two-hour siesta time sleeping soundly behind her mosquito net or reading Mingteh's newspaper or a worn and tattered paperbacked Chinese novel. Proletarians, in Ah Po's opinion, had regular working hours, and regular weekends off. If the baby cried off schedule, it was Mingteh's problem or mine. Ho Jie had simply joined the family. Ah Po came as an employee.

Living in a large family in crowded quarters has its trying aspects, but mutual respect and human affection ameliorate a good deal. Living on terms of total intimacy with an employee is a different thing. Ho Jie's life was governed by a concept of duties and responsibilities, both hers and mine. Ah Po was concerned with her rights and Mingteh's responsibilities as paymaster.

Our whole family structure puzzled Ah Po, and, I fear, troubled her, too. In her experience, a family was chiefly an economic unit, and discussions, usually acrimonious, about money were the chief content of all encounters. To get and maintain economic advantage over other members, each person carried on a continual campaign of intrigues and alliances. It bewildered her to find that Mingteh and Damei declined her efforts to make trouble for each other, and my firm refusal to discuss family affairs with her was clearly very disappointing. Over the years Ho Jie had been with us she naturally came to know all about us, but she never discussed what she knew.

Our family structure at the time puzzled me a little, too. From a Chinese point of view there were two ways for it to develop. One was for Mingteh to assume the role of head of the family, as a married man and father, and for me, as an invalid old mother, to retire into my generously provided figurative chimney corner, take life easy, gossip with the amah, spoil the baby, drink Chinese herbal teas, and die at an appropriate time (not too long delayed). My daughter might wait on me, but could have no other role in Mingteh's house. The other and possibly more modern development (though not without its prototype in the feudal family) would be for me to assume the role of the powerful matriarch, because of my superior financial power, handling all the funds, keeping both my children—and daughter-in-law—in a state of submission and obedience for financial advantage. If my health permitted, I could even continue professionally, and be active in the power struggle of the University.

But we were struggling, more or less consciously, for a third way of life. I wanted to see my son and daughter and my daughter-in-law all achieve genuine independence with their own families, and I wanted independence for myself, too. There was a delicate balance to be achieved among economic realities, psychological maturing, comparative physical strength, political problems, and historical emotional ties. It was gradually becoming very clear that we could not operate as a Chinese family without crippling either the younger or the older generation. In the political, social, and economic situation in China, we could not operate as a new-style American family. With every passing day of the autumn of 1975, the spring and summer of 1976, it became more obvious to us all that we would have to find some way of returning to America.

But with every passing day of that time, it looked more and more difficult to make a move.

Only by going to America could Mingteh, Damei, and Manman hope to be united; only thus could Tientung get sorted out from the political problems stemming from being her father's daughter at Zhong Da. Only thus could I hope to achieve the combination of independence and continued affectionate family life that I wanted.

The political skies were darkening, and we were not alone, by any means, in feeling constant apprehension. There was no reliable news. In the University the situation was filled with contradictions. On one hand, the "monsters" who had been overthrown for being too conservative were now being rehabilitated and restored to the very same positions they had occupied before the Cultural Revolution. On the other hand, academic politics seemed to be more radical every day. Life became a continuous guessing game—what would be the safe thing at any given moment? The next moment the very opposite might be required. The safest thing was to say nothing and avoid notice.

Whereas in 1972 contact with foreign culture was approved on high, in 1975–76 the tide had turned, and the newly come foreign English teachers at the University were practically kept in quarantine, and their colleagues in the FLD dared not talk to them without permission from the thin and round-faced young woman cadre, now returned from White Cloud Mountain filled with zeal. No longer did the young teachers from the "Outside English" team dare to come to visit me, even with the most nonpolitical "Technical Questions," and I passed weeks, months, in almost total isolation.

How could one apply for permission to go to America and still avoid notice? That was a knotty problem. In fact, how did one go about applying for permission to leave? It appeared that no one knew, and it appeared most untimely to go about asking. There were so many things we didn't know about: about passports, visas, health certificates, foreign exchange, costs of travel and maintenance en route. Answering these questions was to keep us all busy for a year. And all the time we learned, Mingteh continued his unremitting struggle to get his little family united.

Damei showed me where the padded long coat for cold weather was kept, and where the sweaters for different kinds of days, the little pile of coverall smocks, the shirts, the socks, the little cloth-soled shoes, the padded open-door pants—and the diapers. The bamboo crib was set up, and the mosquito net hung (even in midwinter we were plagued by mosquitoes), the supply of toys, some old ones for familiarity, some new ones for diversion, laid out on the dresser. The last instructions had been given to Ah Po; Damei's bags were packed and ready. Manman seemed to have accepted that Ah Po was the person who carried her about when Mama was not there, and she had no objection to raise when a walk was suggested. And Damei, holding back her tears as long as her baby was in sight, shouldered her bags and set off to her solitary tour of duty in Changsha. Her husband could not even go with her to the railroad station—he had to stay to give his moral support to Manman. Mingteh and Damei had planned with loving care to make the transition as painless as possible, but babies know more than they can say. How can you explain to a person with just fourteen months of experience in this world that mothers are needed to play in the orchestra so that model operas can go on?

"She'll just cry for a while and then she'll forget," said Ah Po confidently, bouncing the wailing baby in her arms. "Chk, chk, we'll go to market and buy lots and lots of candy for Manman!" Secured in her bamboo stroller, Manman was not convinced, and the heartrending wails of "Mama" echoed down the hill, as the now not-so-confident nurse and her charge sought diversion.

I watched them out of sight, cursing my physical weakness and all the circumstances that caused such grief in such an innocent—unnecessary grief, for no reasonable reason—and I, who loved Manman so, unable to pick her up and love her back to smiles and confidence. Not till Mingteh got home from work and took her in his arms did the heartbroken wailing cease, as she fell asleep to her favorite tune of "Scarborough Fair."

To some extent Ah Po was correct; Manman did get used to her new nurse and in time became very fond of her. But her real life was lived in the hours when her father was at home to play with her, teach her to walk, and tirelessly pace the floor singing to her. They comforted each other. Both were missing Mama.

January 1976

I woke to see Mingteh and Tientung standing by my cot peering through the mosquito net to see if I was conscious. The person inside a mosquito net can see the room outside it better than someone outside can see in; in the moment before our eyes really met I could see the children's faces, and I was shocked. Tientung's cheeks were tearstained, and Mingteh looked pale and grim. What could have happened? Too early for mail or a telegram from Changsha. I sat up and pulled the net aside.

"Mother," Mingteh began. I knew then this was the most serious kind of thing. "Mother, we've just heard that Premier Chou Enlai has died."

"How? When?" This was the worst thing that could happen to China.

"Mingteh picked it up on the morning news and called me in to hear."

I let the flap of the net fall back into place and lay down again. "We thought we'd better let you know before you heard it on the Zhong Da news and maybe didn't understand it all." Tientung put her hand inside and patted my shoulder. "Until we are told officially, we don't know, of course. Just stay in as usual and keep quiet."

I agreed. I had a positive genius for going out for little walks on the impulse of the moment, and inevitably, the moments I chose turned out to be moments of historical crisis, with shooting in the streets, demonstrations against foreign imperialism, or parading of monsters. It had become a byword in the family that if Lu wanted to go out, something awful would probably happen. This had an inhibiting effect on me, but I had to concede that the inhibition was necessary.

The two turned away to get breakfast and I could hear them conferring tensely in Cantonese.

Knowing what the content of the morning news would be, I was able to understand a fair proportion of the announcement, but I was surprised at how brief, how terse, it was. I felt a personal sense of loss that surprised me. I had certainly never even met the late Premier, but I had always felt that he represented sanity, continuity, and integrity, as well as the idealism of such revolutionaries as sought justice rather than power for its own sake. All during the storms of the Cultural Revolution it had been Premier Chou's steadying influence that had saved situations and calmed down the excited youths. Himself, by origin, a member of China's highest intellectual class, he commanded the trust and respect of that class, even during their darkest hours when they were degraded and humiliated. He was the very type of the "good prime minister" of the traditional opera, loyal, wise, protecting the helpless. With him gone, the prospects for us in the Ninth Category (intellectuals) were dark indeed.

In the middle of the morning little groups of students began visiting our back garden, where four old pines towered above the tropical flowering trees and ghostly eucalyptus. Some of the girls already wore little white rosettes in their hair, a traditional token of mourning. Some of the young men had ragged strips of black cloth safety-pinned to their jackets. In each group there would be one or two apparently selected for special agility, who would throw off coat and shoes and, barefooted, climb up the rough pine tree trunks thirty or forty feet nearly straight up to where the first bristly evergreen branches began. The climber would take a knife from his belt and sever the branches, tossing them down to be collected in the baskets the girls had brought along. They worked silently for the most part, and I saw more than one girl wiping her eyes surreptitiously. Team after team came and went, and I could not leave the window. As each team stripped away the lower branches, each one that followed had to climb higher until their danger became almost unbearable to watch. I hoped there would be no human sacrifice in the effort to memorialize their hero, but in their mood of the moment they would not have cared. China, the middle way? Nothing in excess?

I knew that the pine branches would be woven into wreaths with white rosettes or used as the background for characters expressing the mourning of the students at the inevitable memorial meeting. Pines, evergreens, are the symbol of immortality in China. I was glad that our garden could supply something needed on this occasion.

China is strong on ceremonies of all kinds, and funerals are very great and important occasions. On the family level they reinforce the hierarchies of seniority and face, strengthening unity and sharpening conflicts. Every degree of grief is assigned its form of expression, from the role of the prostrated chief mourner, who must be physically supported in the funeral procession, through those who must wail continuously, with formal stylized gestures, to those who stroll at the end of the procession with little white armbands or black ribbons pinned on with the ubiquitous safety pin. The Cultural Revolution had swept away the formalities of ancestor worship connected with funerals, and had made most of the conventions taboo for one reason or another, but it had never in the least diminished the Chinese feeling that a funeral must be celebrated fittingly. New conventions had speedily sprung up to replace old ones.

Now that the chief mourners of anyone dying were the comrades of the primary work units, the heart of the ceremony was the big meeting, followed by a funeral procession. At the big meeting, an enlarged portrait of the deceased would be on display, surrounded by green wreaths and black and white banners with slogans and tributes. There would be an abundance of speeches and at some point in the procedure everyone, in correct order of protocol, would file by the coffin, if it were present, or by the life-size portrait, and bow. During the factional fighting, when someone had been killed in the street battles that occurred so frequently, a funeral procession was often an occasion that incited still more killings. The political significance of every funeral was exploited to the utmost.

There was intense suspense, among the students at least, as to the funeral ceremonies for Premier Chou Enlai, because every little detail of protocol was a clue to the future political developments within China. Who would stand where, what slogans would be displayed and by whom, what official assessment of the late Premier's life would be made, and by whom? Would the masses be admitted to view his body in state? Where would he be buried?

It was a shock when it was learned that, according to Premier Chou's own expressed wishes, his body had been cremated immediately and his ashes scattered from a plane, so that dead, as alive, he would belong to all of China and never form a rallying point for conflicting factions. No opportunistic "friends" would exploit his burying place, and no vengeful enemy could desecrate it. There was no official tomb, only the unavoidable memorial meetings, the publication in the papers of the lists of mourners, the messages of condolence from foreign powers, then sudden silence. Locally planned meetings to honor the great man were canceled "on orders from Peking." No further explanations were given.

Premier Chou's extraordinary revolutionary action in ordering that his ashes be scattered made a deep impression upon me, both as revealing his great understanding of his country's culture and politics, and as pointing the way to the solution of a troubling dilemma. This was the question of the suitable disposal of John's ashes.

The small carved wooden box containing them had been placed in a columbarium at the city funeral hall, where it stood, one among hundreds of similar boxes, waiting until there should be sufficient civil order for the families of the bereaved to know what to do with them. No one knew what would be acceptable in post–Cultural Revolution society. (On some occasions during the Cultural Revolution tombs had been violated, graves plowed under. In Shanghai, the Christian cemetery where Father and Mother Lo were buried had been bulldozed out of existence.) In Canton, at the end of the year, unclaimed caskets were removed to make room for more, and if living relatives made no other provisions, were buried in a common grave somewhere north of the city. Although none of us felt that the small wooden box was more than a symbol of John's sojourn with us, we could not bear the thought of that symbol's being treated disrespectfully. So at the end of the statutory time, Mingteh had brought it home, and I had kept it near me. We never discussed it, and I really never thought much about it, except to wonder what we should do with it if we should all leave the country. Now, Premier Chou's actions suggested a solution.

When I told Mingteh and Tientung my idea, they both immediately approved. Their father had been born in Wuchang, on the south bank of the Yangtze River; it was home to him. It was to Wuchang he brought me as a bride. All during the years of the

Japanese invasion, when we were refugees in far western Yunnan, we had dreamed of our return to Wuchang, hoping to live on the old campus where he had grown up. When we were reassigned after Liberation to work in Canton, he was always homesick for the old place, and in his last days with me had often spoken of our going back some day. I suggested that Mingteh take the little casket back to Wuchang and find some way of depositing it in the middle of the great river. Like Premier Chou Enlai's, John's ashes would rest in no ordinary grave.

We wrote to John's brother and sister in Wuchang about our plans and they, too, agreed that it would be the most fitting thing to do. So when Mingteh had a few days' holiday in midsummer, he set out for our old home, carrying the small box in his knapsack. Before he went I copied out a few lines from the Episcopal burial service and gave them to him.

"There is no magic in ritual," I told him. "It makes no difference to your father whether any particular words are said over his ashes. But it may make some difference to you if you have these ideas in your mind when you go on this errand. It may also help your aunt and Uncle Jamie to be reminded of these things."

I hope it helped.

The picture Mingteh brought back showed me the sorrowing faces of John's brother and sister standing with Mingteh as he held the small casket in the shadows of the big Yangtze River Bridge. A ceremonial photograph had to be taken. Mingteh told me how he and his father's kin had gone immediately from the train to the bridge and taken the picture, then gotten on a small launch they had arranged for. Well out in the mainstream of the river, they had carefully weighted the little box and together slipped it into the swift-flowing brown water to sink and finally rest deep down on the riverbed. This great river would be John's lasting monument and now he would be safe.

September 1976

The stillness of the hot September afternoon was torn by the deep-toned trumpets blaring the message of the death of the Leader. Over

and over they insisted on the terror of their news, on the terror of
a realm without a ruler, on the terror of death. Then silence. Even
the cicadas stopped their shrilling while all of China waited for the
words. Again the despairing horns. A riderless horse was careering
madly through a desert over a fading caravan trace marked by
bleaching bones. It was all so old. It had happened so many times
before.

Now the wooden voice came from the loudspeaker confirming
what everyone knew and had long been expecting—Chairman Mao
had died.

Along with whatever personal grief the multitudes might be feeling at the passing of the Chief, at the end of an era, for everyone
there was anxiety and insecurity—who would catch that riderless
horse? Here there was no ritual shout, "The king is dead, long live
the king"; here there was no second-in-command with the people's
mandate to carry on the government. The Good Prime Minister was
dead. The Grand Old Soldier, Chu Teh, too, had died. The very
earth itself had trembled and shaken and snatched away half a
million lives on the eve of the death of the successor to the ancient
Sons of Heaven. What now?

What now indeed? First there must be the appropriate ceremonies, and while these long-planned rituals are carried out by those
who seem to exist to maintain protocol, those who exist to maintain
power can do what is necessary. Step by step the voices over the air
instructed the masses: the thirty days' mourning, the wearing of
black mourning ribbons, the decorous behavior on the streets, the
holding of memorial meetings at all levels, the nationwide observance of silence at the climax of the national ceremonies in Peking.
The papers carried columns of messages from foreign governments,
from personages, from persons. There was a great lying in state, a
viewing of the old man's body by hierarchies of delegates, a grand
memorial meeting attended by all the great of the land, and finally
the embalmed remains were to go on view in a crystal coffin in a
tremendous tomb in Tien An Men Square. This last seemed to me
like a touch of the Russian taste for the macabre, but it was more
likely that it was the modern expression of the age-old Chinese
predilection for the bizarre in confronting death. The Ming tombs,

the lady with the jade suit, the porcelain cavalry troops unearthed at Sian, the North China Plain with its infinity of grave mounds now leveled into commune fields; all over the Middle Kingdom there are traces, some spectacular, some pitiful, of various Chinese ways of dealing with death.

The pine trees in our garden had been stripped of their evergreen branches by the students mourning spontaneously for Premier Chou Enlai. There was not much greenery left for Chairman Mao's memorial meeting, but no matter, everything had been arranged well beforehand, and the ceremonies went off with the greatest precision. And for once in human memory, every man, woman, and child in China kept silent for five minutes, to memorialize the author of The Little Red Book whose words they had been echoing for a lifetime.

Like everyone in China, we waited in suspense for what might come next. Who or what would fill the space at Tien An Men? The answer came faster than we had expected.

Big Li was standing at my door, beaming kindly on me as always. He wore a ragged black mourning ribbon pinned to his jacket, and it seemed to me that faded garment fitted even more loosely than ever. He looked thin and tired, and I knew that he, like everyone else, had been attending a good many meetings—and like everyone else was worried about the future of the nation. "I've come to tell you news," he announced, and I knew that he had probably been delegated to do so for mixed reasons of kindness and policy. And thus I heard officially the now well-known story of the downfall of the Gang of Four. The riderless horse had been bridled and was moving along at least in the direction of charted roads. He had turned his back on the howling desert—at least for the time being anyway.

"Now it is the time to do it," said Mingteh, when in December there was reason to hope that things would remain stable. "We'll petition for permission to leave. Damei and I have done absolutely everything we can think of to get our family united—and we won't stop trying. But we'll get going on our plans to go back to America. This is a time of change. Mother and I will petition our primary units at once."

"Right. And you can count on me to do everything I can to help you," spoke up Tientung. "This is not the time for me to go, but I think it is right for you and Damei and the baby. You can't live this way, hopelessly, any longer. At least you can do something," she continued from the shadows while Mingteh prowled restlessly up and down the small room. "It's taken us nearly a year to find out even the first things about procedure. The Department probably wouldn't like to let me go—they're so shorthanded, and the enrollment will be bigger next term. If I apply with you, I might delay everything, and"—she hesitated—"I have a hunch this is not the time for me to go. There is something more for me to do."

Every time Damei had had to leave her precious daughter behind and go off to Changsha alone, my heart had bled for her. But only now did I begin to share really deeply the pain of such separation as I accepted Tientung's decision to speed our departure by withholding her own bid for freedom.

The next morning, December 18, 1976, Mingteh delivered our two letters, one to each primary unit.

We had no idea it would take seven months before we should get a reply.

Now a new era began. It was on St. Valentine's Day. I heard a knock at the front door and there stood Damei! The mysterious forces that ruled our lives had unexpectedly granted the longed-for transfer to Canton, and the family could be united. It was almost too good to believe that now we were only waiting for the response to our petition to leave.

With Damei at home, we could part with Ah Po, and manage everything for ourselves. Like all our contemporaries we would be dependent on the nursery, the canteen, and our own efforts in the struggle to survive.

Our day began in the dark at half past five, when Damei and Mingteh began tiptoeing about, fixing the fire, boiling the water, and washing the clothes that had soaked overnight. I would hear Mingteh quietly trundle his bicycle out of the courtyard as he went off to get the day's supply of drinking water. (Zhong Da's supply came from the polluted Pearl River, and everyone had to carry clean water from a Canton city supply source.) Presently I would be aware that Manman was waking up, and voices from the other side of the paper partitions would give me a clue as to what the day's disasters were going to be:

"*Wah!* the fire's out!"

"Here, let me fix it, you go dress Manman."

"She isn't wide awake yet."

"Let her sleep a little longer. Say, these pants aren't dry. Where's her other pair?"

"Where *are* my keys?"

"Manman wants her blue shoes. Are they dry?"

"One isn't. Where are her pink ones?"

"Oh, dear, this is the last egg. Can you get some on your way home?"

"Where's the ration book? No, not that one, the other one."

"Which one?"

"The one for eggs, of course."

"You don't need ration tickets for them. Or do you?"

"Where *are* those keys?"

"Oh oh, it's raining. Quick, help me get the bedding inside."

"Where's the bicycle pump? I've got a flat tire."

"I'll fix it."

"Daddy, I don't wanna go to school today. I wanna go to work with you at the factory."

"Hey, where's the *hukou* book? Mrs. Wei's here to write in the new ration."

"Did anybody feed the chickens?"

"All right, Manman, don't cry. Daddy'll take you to the factory for a little while."

"This kitchen light bulb's burned out. Is there a candle in the cupboard?"

"Here's the last one. Take the Commodities Ration Book with you and try to get a new bulb. Don't forget to take the old one to exchange!"

"I may not have time. Yesterday I had to stand in line for a whole hour, and all I got was a head of lettuce."

"Yes, Manman, you can take Fat Bear with you. Hey, where are Fat Bear's overalls?"

The courtyard door bangs as three hurried, harried people depart, Damei with the market basket tied to the back of her bicycle,

Mingteh with Manman perched in the wicker baby-seat on his handle bars, now screaming loudly that she *won't* go to school, that she *will* go help Daddy at the factory. (If she wins this round, it means she will spend a quite happy and illegal morning at the workshop, playing around Daddy's bench, probably enjoying the company of two or three other little girls of her age, also rebels from scholastic custody. The problem will come at noon and naptime.)

With the departure of the younger ones to work, I would take over as cook. It was hard work and I was not too good at it, but it gave me genuine satisfaction to feel that I was sharing in the life of my generation. I knew that on the other side of the kitchen wall in the adjoining house was another old lady, like me, fanning those wretched coal cylinders, washing the carefully measured-out rice, and cleaning the day's vegetables. I could hear her chopping hers as I would be chopping mine. Sometimes I would find myself whistling at my work, and sometimes she would tap on the wall in a companionable way.

My whistling is of the absentminded kind, more pleasing to the whistler than to a critical ear. I wander from one old tune to another, guided by unconscious association. My hands would be busy with the cabbage leaves, my conscious thoughts concentrated on controlling that stove. I usually started with a few bars of the Internationale, which concluded every news broadcast at that time. Then I would slip into John's favorite, "Swing Low, Sweet Chariot." "Don't Fence Me In" (for my father), then "Go Down, Moses" ("let my people go"). Then, one unlucky day, "Yankee Doodle." There was a rapid series of knocks on the wall. I desisted in alarm.

At noon, when Tientung came home, she said, "Old Mrs. Wang stopped me on the road home to tell me to give you a hint to be more careful what you whistled!"

I remembered when the children had sung "Oh, Susanna" in 1972, and realized that the wind had indeed developed considerable force in the opposite direction.

WORKING ON A flower bed, his back to the road, a rather thickset man was squatting in the shade. He wore a white T-shirt and sun-bleached khaki pants, the usual black plastic sandals of Canton on his bare feet. There was nothing in his appearance at the moment to indicate his rank. I looked a question over my shoulder to Mingteh, who was still panting slightly from the effort of rolling my heavy chair up the hill in the hot July sun.

"That's him, I think," he breathed, and made a polite kind of coughing sound to let the man know we were in his presence.

We were there on a fairly desperate errand. Desperate in the sense that we were nearly in despair over the fate of my petition to leave China to return to the United States. As was required, I had handed in to the authorities of my primary unit in the FLD a letter (translated carefully and with much thought by Mingteh and Tientung into polite Chinese) asking permission to go back to my native America, because of my advanced years (sixty-seven), failing health, and wish to see my childhood home once more before I died.

This was strictly in accord with normal behavior for my age and general situation. Technically speaking, I was entitled to retire at sixty with a retirement pension for the rest of my days, although full professors were seldom, if ever, really retired. They were in such short supply in the work force that they were generally kept on the active payroll, but not expected to do a full load of work. Of course, the more one could do, the better. But all my efforts to make a more substantial contribution to the work of the Department had been declined, and it seemed perfectly clear to me that since I had so uncooperatively refused to die, nothing else I might do could be acceptable to those now restored to the leadership of the English Speciality.

All the known policy since 1972 favored my request. Mingteh had filed a similar petition with his primary unit at the electronics factory, asking to be allowed to accompany me on my return to America, as I (presumably) was too feeble to make it alone. For an only son of a widowed mother to have such a duty was normal, indeed positively praiseworthy.

Both our petitions had gone in on December 18, 1976. Why had I had no response? Every day heightened our anxiety as we waited, imagining all manner of dreadful consequences resulting from what now looked like a rash and most inadvisable act. At that time, the end of 1976 and first half of 1977, the full implications of the program of the Gang of Four were by no means clear to everyone; all this was before there was any normal relationship between the U.S. and the PRC. Our anxiety was not unreasonable, considering our experience.

Now it had taken all Mingteh's determination to make the trip to the top of the hill that Sunday morning, to ask the current Number One of the Revolutionary Committee what had become of my petition.

Another polite cough got no response. Mingteh ventured to speak. "Comrade Lai, I have brought my mother, Professor Xia, here to speak to you this morning."

Possible curiosity caused the great man to look over his shoulder, but it was not sufficiently urgent to make him get up or greet me. He simply stared.

Mingteh persisted. "Professor Xia has sent in a petition to the FLD asking permission to return to the United States, but after six months there has been no reply. Can you advise us . . . ?"

The Great Man rose and, still standing in the shade, looking over my head, while we remained in the sun, grunted: "That kind of affair is not as important as other problems in the University. We have no time to bother about it. Just wait a while and by and by you'll hear." Then he turned back to his preoccupation with his flower bed. It was, after all, Sunday morning, his statutory rest day.

We were dismissed. In spite of the heat of the sun, I felt cold all over. With some difficulty Mingteh negotiated the chair back down the path and trundled me home. I was speechless. I had never before met, personally, the full force of bureaucracy as it is experienced by the "little people," undefended by any political influence. I had never before met anyone in China who failed to offer at least token courtesy to white hair.

Naturally enough, although this rebuff added to our anxiety, it did nothing to diminish our resolution. I marveled at Mingteh's determination and refusal to be discouraged as I spent sleepless nights debating the wisdom of our effort.

Then one summer morning Tientung dashed in at lunchtime to intimate mysteriously that I might just possibly have visitors that afternoon. This was a signal that I'd better be up and dressed, but she would only look mysterious and excited when I pressed for more information. When the expected knock summoned me to the front door, I was, therefore, slightly prepared, but not really ready for what I saw. The group on the doorstep included several Clock Tower cadres, some familiar, some unknown, but notably The Great Man from the hill, and, as his interpreter, the Rehabilitated Monster, the lady Number Two in the FLD. With what I thought, myself, to be admirable composure and really Christian forbearance, I greeted them and asked them to come in and be seated. They did.

The Great Man spoke at some length, to my confusion, and then the restored monster interpreted the message: that my petition had been considered by the University authorities, and it had been decided to grant it and send it on to the next office concerned. There was a good deal more in The Great Man's speech about my age (my hundredth birthday was in sight), my general failing health (my bones ached), and the Principled Implementation of Policy toward older teachers and overseas Chinese. But there was no explanation of the long delay, or why the affirmative action now.

I asked no questions, merely thanked them politely for the information.

One of the accompanying officials said something to The Great Man, who looked exceedingly uncomfortable. He spoke again, and again was interpreted, to the general effect of "hoping that I would feel free to express any criticism that I might have in mind as I was preparing to leave." (This is a routine procedure; even tourists are asked to criticize, and their remarks are treasured up in the interpreters' little notebooks and passed up the line, where, it is to be hoped, they may be the base for reform.)

After the routine answer of having no criticism to put forth, I allowed myself the relief of expressing the hope that the rest of my departure proceeding would move more expeditiously. This brought on (after interpretation) a great deal of what sounded like a well-rehearsed speech. I realized with astonishment that this was something like the self-criticism required by the Party after a Big Mistake.

The visitors finally left, with quantities of polite smiles, expressions of regret at my departure, assurances of cooperation and aid in the business of getting off.

Tientung, whom I suspected of hiding in the courtyard with the chickens until the coast should be clear, now appeared, bubbling with laughter.

"Oh, this is too good, too good!" she cried. "This is *it!* What do you think did it?"

"I don't know," I answered. "All I know is that I'm not going to say what I think!"

I could hardly wait for Mingteh to get home to tell him the great news, but when he arrived, I saw from his face that he already knew. How? Again, the greatest mystery of the Chinese information exchange. On the one hand, the most patient and exhaustive legitimate inquiry cannot elicit a single relevant fact. On the other, the most unpredictable people seem to know all about your most carefully guarded secrets better than you do yourself.

We were sitting around the dining table gloomily contemplating plates full of bones. We should have been happy, because it was Sunday, the rest day at Zhong Da, and like everyone else we had devoted all our efforts to finding, cooking, and eating some meat. Mingteh had gone off before daylight on his bicycle to the farmers' free market some miles away, and there had bought a goose. He had brought it home, honking, tied to the luggage rack. It was expensive, and it was troublesome, but it was the only way we could get a piece of meat big enough for everyone to eat his fill. Because the weather had turned rather warm, we had to finish as much as we could in one day; there was no ice. First Mingteh had to behead the bird, which he did with reluctance. Damei then took over the plucking, which, if the goose is still wearing its winter underwear of down, is done only by those who want to eat a goose very much. By the time Damei had finished, her interest in a goose dinner was almost gone. Still, after Tientung and I had cooked it, the whole family ate heartily. Yet we were feeling gloomy.

It seemed downright mad to me to have asked for permission to leave before we had decided where to go, before we had any clear plans about future work for any of us. I had to put my trust in Mingteh's assurance that until it was necessary there was no use in asking questions that could not yet be answered. But after dinner we found ourselves going over and over our problem. I wondered how many more times we would go through a similar routine with the goose in our efforts to keep alive. Then the mailman brought us the answer.

It was a copy of the Boulder, Colorado, "Welcome Wagon" magazine, intended to inform new residents of that happy city about its various facilities. It had been sent to us by a college friend, my roommate back in 1929 at the University of Chicago. I had not seen Dorrie Carter Snow for nearly half a century, but we had kept in touch when we could, and her now more frequent letters were a constant source of encouragement and merriment to us all. She had recently moved to Boulder herself and was full of delight at the amazing "life-styles" of the city.

Mingteh retired from our somewhat circular discussion of difficulties and buried himself in the illustrated pages of the newly arrived magazine. Suddenly he turned to Tientung and me and announced firmly: "This sounds like heaven on earth! Let's go to Boulder!"

Eagerly we all looked at the pictures of the glorious mountains, read the accounts of opportunities for study—free—of nursery schools where well-nourished, happy-looking toddlers grew strong in the wholesome air. We noted that medical expenses were high, but that there were facilities for all, even if incomes were low. We read about the concerts, the sports, the dancing, the incredible system of citizen initiatives in managing local affairs. But the most appealing thing of all was a certain breezy friendliness, a promise of an open sort of life, with freedom to choose among many possibilities. Here was a place where nonconformity was not a matter of guilt.

"Done!" For me Boulder had an even greater lure than for Ming-teh—the prospect of renewing the friendships of long ago with Dorrie and her sister, Alice. We should, at least, go there first and pause to consider where we had best settle permanently.

Having permission to go and having decided on a destination, the time between began to have some shape. There were to be long months of waiting for papers to be processed, but we no longer suffered from that paranoid feeling that delays were anything more than the normal behavior of bureaucracy getting over a revolution. We learned how many thousands of applications were waiting to be processed, a great backlog of cases held up during the years of the Cultural Revolution, and we no longer felt we were the only persons in the PRC mad enough to want to leave for their own varied private reasons.

I had been surprised and greatly troubled by the way both Ming-teh and Tientung took it for granted that we must keep our plans entirely secret. I could see no reason why one had to be so discreet. Their assumption that it was normal to be so was another revelation of the effect upon them of their experience of revolution. Now that we had permission, though, a subtle change in our situation began to appear. Before we had permission, even to ask how to leave seemed like a political crime; now that we had successfully applied, we were amazed to find old friends who seemed to know all about it, and to make extraordinary efforts to come to see me.

Former students, old colleagues, people I had not heard from for years began to emerge from the mists and offer the friendliest of farewells. The first intimation that there were well-wishers out there in the silence came at Christmas in 1977. And after dark. Unexpected visitors appeared. Some discreetly shoved homemade Christmas cards under the door, others paid brief calls (and at least one left hurriedly by the back door when someone else knocked at the front). Those from farthest away came first, then little by little even those from nearby, within the FLD, broke through the barriers, and I felt overwhelmed to realize that neither John nor I was entirely

forgotten. However, I found with shame that I, too, had been cor-
rupted by the political poisons of the atmosphere to such an extent
that I wondered sometimes if the restoration to a more normal
socialization was at all connected with the fact that a rumor had got
around that I was leaving under excellent auspices.

It was harder than I had expected to leave these friends behind,
but hardest of all was leaving Tientung.

We had thought it over very carefully and discussed it night after
night during 1976, and she had remained firm in her decision to stay
temporarily, for a number of reasons. She argued that her remaining
would make our departure easier—that her application to leave
would cause much inconvenience to the Department and possibly
delay us all. But the real reason for her decision lay deep below the
surface and was not easy to explain.

"Mother, I just feel that this is not the time for me to go," she
had told me the night before we sent in our petitions. "It is really
necessary for your survival to go now, and it is right for Mingteh and
his family to go with you. But I feel I have something more to do
before it is my turn. Just trust."

Now that we were about to take off, it was a comfort to know that
I was leaving Tientung surrounded by more friends that I had dared
believe remained to us.

"No, that I will not do. That is asking too much of me." I was
being very awkward at the last minute. I had just been told that I
was invited to attend a farewell meeting at the FLD, and that the
whole family was asked to an official banquet as guests of the University administration.

Some years before, I had attended a farewell meeting for two
colleagues who had been reassigned; the program consisted of a
free-for-all criticism by their fellow workers, ostensibly meant to send
them forth to new fields of endeavor in a properly chastened state
of mind. I had heard of other similar "farewell" meetings and I
rebelled at the prospect of seeing all my former colleagues at once
for such a meeting as I envisaged. And as for breaking bread with
a select company of restored monsters—even though The Great
Man had now been replaced by a less abrasive personality—I gagged
at that, too.

"You can and you will." Tientung was stern. And I recalled that I had to leave her with these colleagues.

"You can't let us down now. We've almost made it." Mingteh was pleading. I remembered his years of anxiety.

"They are doing the correct thing in asking us. You have to meet them halfway," Tientung went on. I thought of John's infinitely forgiving attitude.

"After what you've already done, this will be nothing," Mingteh urged. "Think of the effect on . . ." He glanced toward Tientung. But I was already thinking of that. I was thinking, too, of a patched and faded overcoat laid over me at the hospital; I was thinking of a mud-stained, barefooted young cadre talking comfortingly to Ho Jie in her hour of fear; I was thinking of visits to ask "Technical Questions" that went far beyond the demands of mere duty in their kindness and consideration, of someone who searched the town over for a tin of coffee when I was ill, of workers who had patiently carried the laboratory recorder to me when I was too weak to go to the lab, of the cleaning woman's warm welcome back to the library, of surreptitious shy smiles of greeting on lonely paths, of sturdy worker-peasant-soldier students ignoring the "isolation atmosphere" officially promoted to come to practice their painfully acquired English, of the foreign students and foreign teachers throughout the years, who, though baffled by the political fogs and not understanding the whole situation, had yet risked they knew not what to make heart-warming gestures of friendliness. And again I thought of John, that gentle soul, now safe from persecution, even the ashes symbolic of his physical self now secure in the very heart of great China, beyond the reach of malice. And I knew perfectly well what I was going to do.

A delegation of students and young teachers was milling around the dooryard. They had come to escort me in style to the afternoon farewell session. Those who had taken on the task of pushing my chair before, in less auspicious circumstances, were eagerly instructing the inexperienced, proudly displaying that they knew how fast I liked to go, where the worst cracks in the sidewalk made caution necessary. Solicitous hands were steadying the chair. I felt surrounded by youth and kindness.

Inside the rather dark meeting room I could see that all our former colleagues were gathered, seated at long tables, where dishes of fruit and candies signaled that this was to be a festive occasion. A blackboard at the far end was appropriately decorated with a farewell message. This was all to be expected. What struck me hard was the sight of my own name, Ruth Earnshaw, in English, written under the Chinese characters for my professional name of Xia Luteh. I had not, of course, forgotten who I was, but it had not occurred to me that "Ruth Earnshaw" existed anywhere but in my own mind and in the minds of the friends in America who knew me only in that incarnation. Seated in state in an armchair at the head of the table, I was scarcely conscious of the "high brass" grouped around me while I digested the idea that I existed. Hospitable hands heaped edibles in front of me, and then a silence fell.

At such festivities the procedure is somewhat like that of a Quaker meeting—out of a preliminary silence, someone speaks appropriately. Only the protocol of who shall speak first and what is appropriate is not left to the unpredictable movings of the Spirit, but is decided in advance and is well known to all participants. I sat still and waited to learn what the direction was to be.

Even allowing for the requirements of courtesy, I was overcome by the outpouring of appreciative words, and surprised at the common theme that ultimately emerged. If I had hoped that my scholarly efforts had been noted, I was doomed to have my vanity deflated. No one was much concerned with my years of painstaking preparation of language texts, my attempts at phonetics research, my efforts to render English poetry intelligible, if not delightful, to generations of Chinese students. It was not for my hours of meticulous phonetic transcription of unpronounceable scientific words, or for the throat-destroying tape recording that I would be remembered kindly—but for the day-in, day-out coaching of the all but hopeless.

I certainly never expected anyone to find anything praiseworthy in my resistance to political education, but I was surprised to learn that in the end, our simple life-style and, in my role as a foreign teacher, my consistent refusal to accept material advantages seemed to have made a favorable impression, particularly where I would have least expected.

The little speeches, and the not so little, went on and on, and everyone who was obliged to talk did, although I felt that in some cases some effort was necessary. I had made my polite thanks and was trundling home again when, reflecting on the whole performance, one outstanding circumstance came into focus: no one had mentioned John.

At the University banquet that night I was glad to have Mingteh at hand to answer the inevitable toasts and say the correct things. My only responsibility was to preserve an amiable expression and avoid eating what I knew I could not digest. This was not too easy as dish followed dish in an impressive display of Canton's most delicious fare. If the quality and quantity of the food offered is a mathematically calculable index to the honor done the guests, I had no reason to feel anything but extreme gratification. It was perhaps graceless on my part to recall scanty meals prepared over that enemy, the coal-cylinder stove, to remember the weeks when Mingteh and his comrades in the commune had lived on rice and green melon soup, to think of Tientung and her friends in Gansu making a feast of millet porridge.

The polite speeches were over and the table cleared; I had been presented with a farewell souvenir gift of a beaded bag and some lovely tapestry pictures and we were about to disperse. Then one of our hosts, a newcomer to Zhong Da—at least I had not seen him before—turned to me and asked if I had any suggestions to offer— the usual request, but, I felt, with a little more than the usual significance. I knew in my heart that I had something to say. But dare I say anything now, on the very brink of departure? In a way I felt I might be risking everything by raising a question that everyone had so clearly been avoiding, but I could not leave John's name unspoken, as if I accepted all that had befallen him.

"There is one question I would like to raise before I go," I said, hoping Mingteh and Tientung would approve, but determined to risk it. "When the Red Guards searched our home in 1968, they took away the manuscript of some linguistic research that my late husband, Dr. Lo Chuanfang, had just completed." I could feel tension rising. The newcomer among the officials looked inquiringly at the Department leaders. He appeared not to have heard of John before. I explained, speaking directly to him, "Dr. Lo was a professor in the FLD from 1953 until his death in 1969." I continued, "I would like to request that if and when his research papers are found, they be returned to our daughter, Lo Tientung, who is now a teacher in the Department's English Speciality."

The newly come cadre looked at me keenly and wrote something in the little notebook every cadre seems to carry in his breast pocket.

"Thank you," he said. "I'll look into the matter of your husband's papers." And the conversation disintegrated into farewells.

1978

ON D DAY I was surprised to find that the Clock Tower was sending the University bus to the station to accommodate representatives of students and teachers to see us off. In China, the personnel meeting and seeing people off is an important item in protocol. It is more likely to represent policy than impulse. That is why the repetitious pictures in the newspapers showing arriving and departing diplomats are studied so eagerly by the politically alert masses. They provide clues about the development of the continuing power struggles in the capital.

John and the children and I had arrived at Zhong Da as passengers in the University bus in 1953; that was better than a truck, much better than a pedicab, not so good as a town car, far from a limousine. Today I was driving out the big South Gate in a town car, followed by the bus filled with friends and well-wishers. I noted with an inward smile that only one of the restored monsters was on the bus, the other had sent regrets—academic duties. The smile was outward, though, as I saw the two Li's, some of the Clock Tower personages, young teachers, and worker-peasant-soldier students.

I took a last look at the tree-lined roads and paths, the gardens and grassy lawns as we drove to the gate. I tried to peer down the lane that led from the FLD to Number 48, but rain, perhaps, obscured the view, and we were waiting for the big gates to open. I remembered when they had been guarded by students with guns. I glanced back at the Biology Building and thought of the lad who had been killed there by a stray bullet. I caught the eye of the "Old Aunt" who opened the gates, the mother of one of Mingteh's schoolmates, and waved good-bye. That good-bye was not only for her; it was for Ah Bi's mother, for the man in green, for the FLD message-delivering janitor, for Hing Jie in her library cellar, for my neighbor on the other side of the common kitchen wall, for Ah Po with her bangles and procession of nurslings, for dear Ho Jie and all her clan. It was good-bye to twenty-five years of young people, it was good-bye to twenty-five years of my life.

Out on the main road to Canton, we passed the security office where Mingteh had so often waited for news of his *hukou,* where he and Damei had got their pink certificate of marriage, and wove through the bicycle traffic of early morning, dodging the litter of huge pipes and the barricades about the diggings that had been going on in that road ever since I first saw it in 1953. Now we were passing the "overseas Chinese" village, stucco-fronted apartment buildings with balconies all aflutter with washing—I wished them a good day for drying. Now the big market with its lines of shoppers with their nets and baskets queuing up for the day's vegetable, trucks from the communes discharging loads of lettuce at the curb. A whiff of salt fish, orange peel, Chinese medicine, and coal smoke. Now the first and last glimpse of White Cloud Mountain in the distance beyond the Pearl River, now the river itself with its strange bridge, humped in the middle to allow boats to pass under even at high tide. Now the Trade Fair Building with its rows of red flags, then the last look at Canton's crowded inner city streets, the white-coated policeman waving our convoy on; the parade of nursery schoolers, welded to each others' shirt-tails, herded through the crowds by two teachers with tambourines; a couple of khaki-clad PLA men looking like country boys seeing the big city for the first time; gray coats, blue coats, old-fashioned shiny black cotton tunics, superficially so uniform, but every face an index to a unique life story. I silently wished them all farewell—and a future happier than their past.

The wheelchair had been folded up and stowed in the bus. Now it was brought forth, and I was enthroned in the plaza before the station. The worst part of being seen off is the waiting around, and this was tough, but Manman proved a tremendous help. The strained smiles relaxed and the repeated words became more natural as everyone competed to entertain the baby. She and I had rehearsed the drill of "going on a journey with 'Nainai.'" Manman knew that her job was to sit on my lap and hold on to her string bag full of teddy bears. And Nainai's job was to hang onto Manman and her emotions and deal out judicious rations when indicated.

To some of the students in attendance it was a rare treat to come to the station and see all the weird types assembling to go back into the bourgeois world. To others, who had had practice lessons as Travel Service Guides, this was old stuff. But to all of us, there was a certain amount of entertainment in people-watching: the clusters of Japanese tourists, all tagged and labeled, with cameras hung round their necks, anxiously keeping in touch with each other and with their guides; the long-legged, hairy Europeans, likewise tagged, but tending to scatter and lose each other; the gathering throng of Hong Kong Chinese, returning from visits with their relatives in Canton, each exotically clad visitor laden with bundles and baskets, parcels and bags, surrounded by sober blue- and gray-coated kin also laden down with odd-shaped parcels. Everyone seemed to be giving every-one else something to take home to eat. Time passed quickly. Now we were part of the surging crowd moving toward the entrance to the train shed.

Somehow Mingteh was pushing my chair, assisted by many hands, and we were in a long tunnel leading into the station. It was packed from wall to wall with people, all carrying inconvenient things, moving steadily under the dim light of overhead bulbs toward a brighter patch ahead. It was like dream fantasies of being born, the tunnel, the pressure, the light. Suddenly the light ahead was revealed as being at the foot of a long, long flight of steps leading to the track level. I had a moment of utter panic. How could I ever get up them? The top was out of sight. Then I felt myself lifted and, chair and all, I rose smoothly with the mounting throng, held up by the hands of everyone within reach. Now we were on the platform. There was Damei up ahead with her mother and sisters and uncle, who had all come down from Wuhan to help us take off. They had found the right car, Mingteh's division of labor and careful organization of his forces working to perfection.

Ticket holders were promptly pushed into the quiet of the car and accompanying friends lined up along the platform to wait for the train to pull out. I located Tientung and then avoided meeting her eyes as she avoided mine, but I was acutely conscious of her standing next to John's brother, her beloved Uncle Jamie. We had said our good-byes and had no intention of treating the general public to a display of suitable emotion. There were other eyes that avoided mine for other reasons, and some that sought me out with wordless messages. For ten thousand years we looked back and forth and then the train hooted and rolled away.

The suburbs of Canton slipped by and the great moment we all anticipated was coming. We would soon pass through Chang Ping village.

How many times Mingteh had taken that same train and alighted at the little station in the rice fields, returning to his peasant's life in the commune. How many times he had ridden that train into Canton, moved by some premonition of disaster threatening us, arriving just in time to avert it. How many times he had stood in the mud of the paddy field, watching that train roll on to Hong Kong, seeing the first-class passengers sitting at table in the dining car, his heart filled with very mixed feelings. He was hungry, hungry for the food he saw on the tables, and hungry for the world of experience from which he was shut out. And yet at the same time, he felt a stiff-necked pride in the hard manual labor he was doing, and a proud identification with the indomitable peasants who had accepted him as one of themselves. And now he was rolling past Chang Ping on his way to a new world. No looking back now.

Shum Chun. Passport inspection. Baggage inspection; some slight difficulty with Manman at having her bag full of bears disturbed. Train travel was no novelty to that veteran of the Changsha-Canton run, but inspection of her bears was taken as an affront. Fortunately, the inspectors and the Travel Service Guides were all either Tientung's students or old friends, so no serious problem.

I could see that Mingteh was expecting the sky to fall, the wooden bridge to collapse, or a posse of monsters and Red Guards to rise out of the ground and carry us all off before the well-orchestrated climax of crossing the border. None of these things happened.

With Damei trundling the luggage cart with our two suitcases, Manman on my knee, the bears clutched in her arms, Mingteh pushed the creaking chair over the bridge, and we were in Lo Wu, in the Other World.

1978

Mingteh emerged from the immigration office at Lo Wu, where he had been waiting for our papers to be processed, with a look on his face combining bewilderment, amusement, and disbelief. Damei and Manman and I had been courteously parked outside in the station waiting room, where we could watch the endless stream of returning Hong Kong residents going through routine procedures. Our affairs were more complex and took longer. Mingteh had entered the office, I was sure, ready for any kind of disaster. Now his tight smile broadened into a grin as he approached, saying, "Everything's okay! It's a new experience to be called 'sir'! "

I realized that it was. Although the peasants in the commune where he had lived had always treated him and his schoolmates with tolerance, even kindness, every official with whom he had ever had contact had treated him as politically suspect. Like a Jew in Nazi Germany, he was labeled for life. The son of a Rightist, there was always a shadow hanging over him. Now, over the border, he was "Mr." and "sir." It began to sink in that he would no longer be haunted by his father's political "crime."

Encouraged by the civility of Her Majesty's civil servants, our little party now ventured into the station restaurant to get some lunch, while we waited for the late train to Kowloon, Hong Kong. We had talked about this first meal a good deal, and made what mental preparation for it we could in advance for the behavioral traps that might lie ahead. Except for their wedding feast in Wuhan, arranged by the relatives at a big restaurant, Mingteh and Damei had seldom had occasion to dine in public and they anticipated all manner of difficulties. Mingteh could read and understand English exposition of electronics mysteries that conveyed no meaning at all to me, but he had never seen a menu in English. Damei could gracefully serve a fish with chopsticks but was dubious about knives and forks. And none of us felt too sure about paying bills and tipping waiters. I tried to reassure them that no matter what they did, no one would laugh at them—after all, some pretty strange characters passed through Lo Wu—but they were apprehensive.

Happily, the tact of a China Travel Service Guide, who drifted up at this point and showed us where to go, plus common sense, got us through this difficult situation without disaster. The dazzling choice of ham or cheese sandwiches, coffee, and ice cream cheered us all, especially Manman. She entirely approved a meal that began and ended—for her—with ice cream. The tense moment of tipping the waiter rather spoiled Mingteh's enjoyment, I fear, but even that passed off all right. In the PRC tipping is looked upon with official abhorrence as the quintessence of bourgeois patronage of the working class, and the idea of offering cold, raw money to the lad who waited on our table was painfully embarrassing to someone who identified himself with the worker. Embarrassing to Mingteh, but not in the least to our waiter.

On the train to Kowloon, I began to feel for the first time that it was all real. Like Mingteh, I had half expected the skies to fall before we got through all the formalities, and now, here we all were, trundling through the green hills of the New Territories, now and again glimpsing villages and roads, now the blue waters of the bay, washing plastic bags up on the rock-strewn beach, wild and beautiful and polluted, just as the books had all foretold. It was reassuring to us all to find something we had been expecting to see. What no one had prepared me for was the breathtaking visual beauty of Hong Kong by day and by night, its skyscrapers, its lights, and its endlessly fascinating streams of people. Compared with the drab, dimly lit arcades of Canton, it was a glittering fairyland.

Kowloon Station was huge, echoing, and at this end of the afternoon, perfectly empty. We came down the ramp and looked about like lost children. Like lost children, with one accord we turned in at the office labeled with the familiar "China Travel Service" sign, to find out where and how to telephone. As we had been delayed, there was no one in sight to meet us, and we had to call our friends.

Again the shadow of the past loomed over Mingteh as I picked up the phone and dialed the Bishop's office. (One of my first friends in Hankow in 1937 had been Patty Sherman, the late wife of the Bishop of Hong Kong. Although I dared not write to a public personage like the Bishop while I was still in the PRC, I had been in touch with Patty.) I felt a load rolling off my shoulders as it came through to me that now I could ring up anyone I wanted to, and it was nobody's business. It was especially delicious to be calling up the Bishop, as I recalled how outrageous such an action could be made to appear by some officials now left behind.

It was the first time I had used a telephone in thirty-one years.

While waiting for the Bishop to appear, Manman's inevitable needs caused Damei and me to seek out the ladies' room. It was here, I think, that the realities of the New World first began to impinge upon Damei, as she saw the sparkling cleanliness, the to our eyes dazzling luxury of the washroom, and realized incredulously that the scented soap, the white paper towels, the marvelous soft toilet paper were all there free for the public to use. Manman danced about happily and could hardly be dissuaded from taking along a week's supply.

Hong Kong served us very well as a decompression chamber. We were especially fortunate in being lodged at the Holy Carpenter Guest House, a Church institution combining some of the features of a university settlement house and of a way station for people in transit between two worlds. The warmhearted staff members were well accustomed to the bewilderment experienced by those coming out of China into the dazzle of Hong Kong. They were used to helping people who, like us, found air conditioning almost a painful luxury; who were at a loss when faced with the choices to be made in their excellent dining room among offerings of Chinese food such as we had not seen in Mingteh's lifetime. They were patient and helpful in explaining about taxis and tips and how to write checks and where to shop for suitable transitional clothing. For years they had provided shelter and all manner of assistance to youths who had made the desperate swim across the shark-infested bay, some of whom were fleeing from justice, no doubt, but most of whom were just youngsters convinced that they were hopeless misfits in the countryside to which they had been sent, and were willing to risk their lives for a new life. At Holy Carpenter's they found job training, recreation, medical care, shelter, and friendly counsel.

We were amused that everyone asked us whether or not we were experiencing "cultural shock," a phrase we had never heard before, and our friends were amused in turn by Mingteh's reply that it was "remarkably easy to get used to being comfortable and having enough to eat." It was not so much a shock as a deep satisfaction to me to find that my hopes were realized. In a situation where telephones, taxis, moderate comfort, and suitable food made my physical life possible, I felt like a new person, eager for experience and able to cope with it.

When I found that now I could pick up the telephone book, find the number of an old friend, call her up, take a taxi, meet her at a restaurant, and order a meal, I knew I could look ahead to a physical liberation from the personal dependence on my children that had seemed to be my inescapable role for the rest of my life.

But the sudden material improvement of our life was not an unmixed pleasure. A guest at a magnificent tiffin at the luxurious Peninsula Hotel, I was prey to confused emotion. The sight of the British lions guarding the doors, the Union Jack scarlet against the once Chinese sky, the well-fed European diners gorging on the delicacies of the Sunday buffet revolted me. An item on the menu caught my eye and I had no appetite for the tempting dishes: "hami melon flown in from Gansu." I thought of Tientung's friends, still living in that distant wilderness; to them a few extra potatoes made a feast. They would never have a taste of that delicious melon—it was raised and reserved for export to titillate the palates of those who had money to burn. Pictures flashed through my mind: Tientung's peasant boys and girls in their village in the loess hills of Gansu, gathered on the *kang* in their cave dwelling, making a holiday over a bowl of wheat flour noodles; Mingteh and his schoolmates rejoicing over the gift of a crock of pickles from a kindly peasant neighbor; ourselves sitting in our dark smoky kitchen under the dripping laundry, carefully dividing up the shreds of pork in the Sunday soup. At our first meal in the Holy Carpenter's dining hall, we had not been able to finish the mountain of rice set before us and were aghast at the necessity of leaving some meat and vegetables on the serving dish. And here in this fabulous hotel, the eager diners were refilling their plates at the buffet.

The most overwhelming personal experience in Hong Kong for me, however, was to find myself suddenly surrounded by old friends, former students of John's and mine, who had known and loved him and were eager to hear all about him, old fellow students from our University of Chicago days, old friends and connections of the Lo family in Wuhan. I was transported from a world where his name was not to be mentioned publicly to a circle of warm, appreciative friends. At first it was almost too painful to endure, hearing them speak of him, but little by little I could feel a frozen place thawing in my heart. It was an infinite comfort to see how his former students had grown up to be such a credit to their beloved teacher, to realize that his work was not forgotten, but lived in them.

Suspended between two worlds in the Pan Am plane between Hong Kong and San Francisco, I hoped that my heart would be strong enough for the flight, but I didn't care much if it weren't. I had seen Mingteh and Damei transformed before my eyes. I knew they could make their way in the New World. I had enjoyed myself more in the three weeks in Hong Kong than I had in the preceding ten years. I knew now that John still lived in the hearts of friends on both sides of that bamboo curtain.

But the curtain was still firmly in place on that day in April 1978. On the inside of it were Tientung, waiting for "something"—she didn't know what—and many others of our family, and students, so many good people still living under the shadow of anxiety, fear, poverty, illness, despair.

I thought back over the long, weary struggle we had had to get away, and I allowed myself a little feeling of encouragement for those left behind. After all, we had succeeded. We had begun our effort to leave at a time of nearly total confusion, and we had nearly despaired of making it, but just when it seemed hopeless, the tide had turned. I hoped, and tried to believe, that things would be better now for all.

At San Francisco John's relatives welcomed us. We filled in the events of the years between and promised ourselves more leisurely visiting over the blessed telephone that could link us all. Then, on to our target, Boulder!

Stapleton Airport, Denver. So many Americans! To be invisible in a crowd, and yet to be treated with such consideration by total strangers! The breathtaking spectacle of marvelous machines coming and going out of the sky, and no one apparently at all impressed. A woman—a black one—competently and cheerfully driving a miraculous little electric cart through the crowd—something I couldn't have seen in 1936! Being addressed as "sir" or "ma'am" by friendly Western voices; then the man-made miracle of the beautiful colorful cars, weaving, so orderly, so cooperatively, through the mazes of the highway, approaching the natural miracle of the rampart of the Rockies. The twinkling lights of the little city. Then welcome to Dorrie's house, where there were books on the shelves that we had shared at college fifty years before. I was really home.

From the moment we arrived in America, a new chapter in our family history began, another story, which must be left for another time. Suffice it to say, homecoming was a success.

1978–1979

BUT NONE OF us could feel entirely satisfied, of course, as long as Tientung was on the other side of the seas, waiting for "something."

Late that summer of 1978 we had the first inkling of what it was. Tientung wrote us the astounding news. John, who, along with seventeen other Zhong Da teachers and staff, had died during the chaotic years of the Cultural Revolution, was to be honored at a ceremonial memorial meeting at the University. It would be Tientung's duty to attend to represent the family and to hear his name read out with the honorable prefix of "comrade" restored. What could all this mean? Certainly it signified that he was now counted among those "liberated," not cast out of the "class ranks," the stigma obliterated, his family and friends no longer under the shadow of his alleged political offenses.

Soon came further word. The meeting had taken place on July 29, 1978, in the auditorium of the University. On the stage were enlarged photographs of the eighteen to be honored, with the usual wreaths of pine and paper flowers, with the names of those individuals and organizations wishing to express publicly their respect and love for the dead. At last John's life, his work, and his death were an acknowledged reality in his community.

The vice-secretary of the Communist Party Committee of Zhongshan University, Comrade Huang Huan-qiu, gave the principal funeral oration, saying in part:

> Today, with deepest grief, we are holding a ceremonial memorial meeting for eighteen comrades who unfortunately [sic] passed away [twelve were suicides] during the Great Proletarian Cultural Revolution, and who, because of the interference and destruction caused by the counter-revolutionary revisionist line of Lin Biao and the Gang of Four had no memorial ceremony held for them. These

WU JI BI FAN

物极必反

comrades are: [the names of the eighteen, including Lo Chuanfang, were read off].

First, let me on behalf of the University Party Committee and University Revolutionary Committee, express deep mourning for the above eighteen comrades, and warm sympathy to their families. [Then followed a brief summing up of the history and work of each.]

Comrade Lo Chuanfang, male, . . . formerly professor in the Foreign Languages Department at Zhongshan University, died of illness June 11, 1969, at the age of sixty-five. Comrade Lo Chuanfang had been teacher and professor after Liberation, was Dean of the College of Arts, Dean of General Affairs, and Head of the Foreign Languages Department of Huazhong University. . . . Working for a long time in the field of education, he took a serious, responsible attitude toward his work, and maintained a high professional standard. He did a great deal of scientific research in modern Western linguistics. Comrade Lo always fulfilled his tasks. His teaching got good results and was praised by students and teachers alike. Comrade Lo made definite contributions for the training of personnel. . . .

I could imagine our daughter standing among the assembled teachers and students, seeing her father's pictured face on the platform, hearing these words, and thinking what thoughts?

The next letter gave further details. She had been handed a form, filled out by those investigating John's "case" during the Clearing of the Class Ranks movement, stating specifically what the "problems" were. They included:

the period of Dr. Lo Chuanfang's history before and after 1948 in Huazhong University. At that time he was Dean of General Affairs and Dean of the College of Arts; took part in academic activities of the Harvard Yenching Institute; took part in the then "World Government Movement" and propaganda for the Wuhan District Chinese Gallup Polls and in religious propaganda. After Liberation, he had admitted to the above activities many times. During this investigation no new problems have been discovered. The above are in the category of ordinary historical problems.

So these were the political crimes that John was guilty of, that the investigators had labored so diligently to establish, and that had been considered so heinous that even on his deathbed, he could only be "provisionally" liberated.

At last I knew.

True to Party policy, every accusation had been traced down and verified and weighed. His actions all fell within the bounds of "internal people's conflict." In other words, it was now decided that he had belonged within the ranks of the people all the time.

But the end was not yet.

On April 10, 1979, Tientung received, at the FLD General Party Branch Office, one more official document about her father. It concerned his being hatted as a Rightist in 1958, and it stated that the University Party Committee had reinvestigated his case. It had been decided that the action taken was "a case of incorrect designation."

This announcement had been issued on March 21, 1979, and included an order that it be communicated to John's primary unit and to his family. Tientung only learned of its existence when another "wrongfully designated Rightist" made inquiries about his own case at the "Office for Carrying Out Policy at the University."

So John was not only "within the class ranks," but had never really done anything to merit the punishment he had endured. The "hat" that had shadowed all our lives for twenty years was all a "mistake." Henceforward, members of our family would no longer have a note in their personal dossiers that they were related to a Rightist.

There were no answers immediately available for the questions in my mind: how could such a mistake be made? By whom? And where was the announcement of rehabilitation between March 21 and April 10? Without the intervention of the "Office for Carrying Out Policy at the University" would Tientung ever have seen it at all?

Tientung joined us in America late in the summer of 1979. She brought with her the picture of her father that had appeared on the stage of the Assembly Hall on that memorable day when his good name was restored. It is before me now as I write, and as I look upon that face I know what he would say: "It is more important to try to understand than to blame or to regret."

So as I think over the crowded events of the past forty-odd years, and especially of the last decade, I wonder how to make sense out of it all: the idealism of the early days of Liberation; the rise to power of the opportunists within the rigid structure of an unchallengeable authority; the harassment of the politically vulnerable by local leaders; the overthrow with violence and vengeance of those "persons in authority taking the capitalist road"; the spectacular public punishment of those "monsters"; the restoration of the same "monsters" to their original seats of power; and now the rehabilitation of their victims by a higher power again. Only one thing is immediately clear to me: there is no end to struggle in the People's Republic.

The causes of this unending, frustrating, destructive struggle must be sought in the peculiar circumstances of life in China and in the Chinese view of that life.

There are three things about China that all Americans seeking to understand that country and its people have to try to comprehend: there are a billion or more Chinese occupying a limited living space; there is never quite enough food for everyone; there is no traditionally sanctioned, generally accepted way for the masses of the people to express dissatisfaction and initiate change.

During my lifetime in China, the population has increased fantastically. Our own family's history from 1949 to 1978 was a series of moves from better housing to worse, except when we were "kicked upstairs" in conformity with the bureaucratic principle of preserving the order of rank. The upheaval of the Cultural Revolution was the signal for everyone to scramble for more space to live in. Joe Doakes was no isolated villain; he was typical, in motivation, viewpoint, and methods.

When Mingteh was denied the scientific higher education he longed for, and was sent to work as a commune peasant, he was not alone in this experience. There were not enough places in China's colleges for all who aspired, and Chinese society's only way for disposing of the surplus aspirants was to weed out those who were politically vulnerable and send them into the rural areas. What happened to Mingteh happened subsequently to tens of thousands. The more crowded the cities became, the more pressure there was on the urban authorities in the late sixties and the early seventies to send youths into the countryside, where their discontent would make less trouble, and their own labor could supply them with the day's rice. When Tientung went to Gansu, her "exile" was strictly in line with ancient Chinese tradition. For a thousand years and more, potential dissidents of the scholar class have been sent to the far Northwest, beyond the Great Wall.

For centuries, most people in China have had to adjust themselves to living in groups in the crowded quarters of the extended family, in the crowded streets of growing towns and cities. Nowadays, crowding is more acute than ever before. Americans do not always immediately grasp that the social patterns of behavior that they see as "typically Chinese" have been developed in response to this group life: the ceremoniousness and formality of manners; the observance of strict protocol and a rigid hierarchy of rank and seniority; the patience; the conventional smiling good humor; the emphasis on "face" and the preservation of "gray areas," rather than insistence upon clear-cut lines. I see in Ho Jie the personification of Chinese ways of survival based upon being one in a million, one in a billion.

People who don't have quite enough to eat become irritable, partly because of the physical discomfort that hunger entails, partly because of the insecurity involved. During all my years in China I was aware that everyone, including myself, thought about food more or less consciously all the time. The nicest thing a guest could do was to bring along a present of something to eat. It is no accident that the common greeting all over China is a version of *"Chih liao fan meiyu?"* ("Have you eaten?") and the only acceptable answer is *"Chih liao"* ("Yes, I have" whether true or not). During our last year in China, I learned from experience to watch what the neighbors brought home in their market baskets as they came back from work, tensely observing that this one had found green beans, or that one had a nice head of cabbage, wondering anxiously if Damei would find something similar on her way back for lunch. Planning how to use the meat-ration tickets to best advantage would be the main topic of family conversation for hours. Exasperation at the limitations conflicted with real thankfulness for the degree of security that the rationing provided. People will endure many shortcomings in any organization of society that ensures a fair share of what food there is. And people who have suppressed their irritation and endured the intolerable by exercising miracles of self-restraint for long periods of time will react with violent emotion to anything they see as a threat to that all-important basic security.

The ideological conflict in which John was one victim was a reflection of the conflict of people in authority with differing ideas as to how to solve China's great problem of too many people and too little food. The very bitterness of the conflict, the extremes of opinion, I see as evidence of the vitality of Chinese society, a society determined to survive against fearful odds. Even the local "monsters" who engineered John's being "wrongfully designated" along with so many others as Rightists were acting in defense of their rice bowls, against what they saw as a threat to their privileged positions in the hierarchy.

One great weakness in Chinese society today is the lack of an effective way for dealing with dissident opinion. The difficulties of life are so overwhelming, the contenders for political power so committed to their varying programs that the ruthless disposal of dissidents, and those even suspected of being potential dissidents or rivals for position, is tolerated as a political necessity. At intervals, for brief periods, there is a relaxation in the struggle. But while the basic problems of living space and food are unsolved, no nonconformist, no social critic can feel safe.

Like the typhoon that blows in from the sea, destroying all that stands in its way, and then, in an instant, reversing its direction, the political power groups surge through Chinese society, sweeping everyone first in one direction, then in the opposite. The political forces themselves move in response to the pressures implicit in the struggle of too many people for too little food.

Wu ji bi fan. This ancient Chinese saying is translated in various ways into English: "Extremes turn into their opposites." It certainly expresses the essence of the Chinese experience of the last decade. But there is another, possibly less accurate, translation that I like better, having heard John say it so often. It gives a clue to one source of the indestructability of the wonderful Chinese people, in expressing their dauntless optimism: "When things can get no worse, they must get better."

Black Material: Written material prejudicial to student activists and thought to be inserted into their personal dossiers at the beginning of the Cultural Revolution.

Bourgeois: In modern Chinese the term is used broadly to connote any life-style or ideology that is considered to be non-working class.

Canteen: Dining hall set up by any work unit for the members of its group. Service is similar to that in a Western-style cafeteria.

Cadre: The usual English translation for the Chinese word *ganbu;* meaning an official. In American usage "cadre" is plural, but in China it is used in the singular.

Capitalist Roaders: Historically those Party leaders who advocated a more conservative line for the development of the socialist state than Chairman Mao's. The purpose of the Cultural Revolution was to remove them from power.

Chinese Opera: Traditionally a very popular form of entertainment. After Liberation and especially during the Cultural Revolution it was used to propagate the Communist Party line.

Clearing the Class Ranks: Political movement beginning in 1968, the aim of which was to identify and investigate and possibly purge anyone accused of being non-working class. At the beginning of the Cultural Revolution there were seven classes of persons who were politically disgraced: landlords, rich peasants, counter-revolutionaries, bad (i.e., criminal) elements, Rightists, traitors, spies. Soon "unreformed capitalist roaders" became the eighth group, and before the end of the Cultural Revolution there was a ninth category, the bourgeois intelligentsia. China's traditionally respected scholar class was ranked lower than spies, traitors, and thieves. Anybody could accuse anybody, and every accusation had to be followed up. It was a confusing and vicious political movement.

Commune: An administrative, economic, social, cultural, political unit in the countryside started in 1958. Beginning in the mid-1960s, educated youth from the cities have been sent by the government to the communes to do agricultural work. Once transferred from the city to the commune, it is very difficult to return to the city. For five years Mingteh lived at Chang Ping Commune, located southeast of Canton on the Canton to Kowloon (Hong Kong) railroad line.

Comrade: A title, the use of which implies that the person addressed is within "the ranks of the people" and therefore politically acceptable.

Da Zi Bao: Handwritten political poster in large Chinese characters, which since 1957 has been used widely as a form of political expression.

Days of Yan'an: Yan'an was the center of the Liberation armies and headquarters of the Chinese Communist Party in the latter part of the War of Resistance to Japan in the early 1940s.

Distribution: Upon graduation from institutions of higher education, all students are "distributed" to jobs according to current needs as assessed by the government. Pay is the same for all graduates, regardless of the work assigned, but some minor adjustments are made related to living costs in different areas.

Education Revolution of 1958:   The first major movement to organize China's education according to the Party's educational policy as formulated by Chairman Mao.

FLD: Foreign Languages Department.

Ganbu: A term used loosely to mean either an administrative official paid by the government, a professional such as a teacher, or any minor bureaucrat.

Guan Bo: Public-address system.

Hatted: Traditionally, in China, criminals have been punished by having to wear some badge of shame; in ancient times, a wooden collar, or a placard hung round the neck. During the Land Reform, landlords were paraded wearing pointed dunce caps, and this made the "hatting" a common synonym for political punishment. In the Anti-Rightist Campaign of 1957–58, Rightists were said to be "hatted," although no actual hats were used.

Hukou: The small paperbound book in which the members of each household are registered, as living at a designated address. It is essential for all but commune peasants to be registered in a *hukou* in order to get their rationed commodities.

Hung Wei Ping: Red Guards.

Inconvenient: The Chinese word for "inconvenient" covers a wide range of meanings and is an excuse that cannot be overridden or investigated without embarrassment.

Interpreting: Official protocol requires that official statements be made in the national language *(Putong hua)* and interpreted as necessary into the local dialect or language of the person addressed, even when the speaker is perfectly fluent in the language or dialect in question.

Jia-shu: The Chinese word for "family members"; the *Jia-shu* organization includes all nonemployed members of a community, and provides opportunity for political study and volunteer social service activities. Both men and women are included. At Zhong Da, retired workers, staff members, teachers took part in the *Jia-shu* activities, and domestic servants, although employed privately, were considered as members of the household for which they worked.

Kang: The heated platform common in the loess caves of Gansu, on which the family sleeps at night and where they sit during the day. It is the only source of warmth for these cave houses.

Liberation: Name of the political period that began in 1949 with the establishment of the new government under the leadership of Chairman Mao and the Communist Party.

The Little Red Book: A collection of quotations from the writings of Chairman Mao under such subject headings as: classes and class struggle, the mass line, "serving the people," criticism and self-criticism, etc. During the Cultural Revolution practically all persons in China had a copy and carried it with them. One might be criticized severely for neglecting to study it constantly.

Mao Uniforms: They were introduced after the Revolution of 1911 and were called Zhongshan suits (presumably because Sun Yat-sen [Zhongshan] wore them). They are persistently called Mao suits by Westerners.

May 7 Cadre School: A political training center, usually in the country, where cadres partook in strenuous manual labor, studied Marxist classics and Mao's works, and took part in self-criticism. The groups lived collectively in dormitories, and often families were separated.

Middle School: Equivalent to American secondary education—junior and senior high school.

Model Opera: During the height of the Cultural Revolution no Western music was played. Instead eight *model* operas were authorized to be performed all over China. They were models in ideology primarily, but also established the acceptable forms for music, singing, dancing, costuming, etc.

National Level University: A university that is directly under the Ministry of Higher Education in Peking. It is considered academically higher than provincial universities or teachers' colleges. There are no private educational institutions in China.

Newspapers: All newspapers (like radio and TV) are government publications. There is no private press in China.

"On the Wall":   When a person is being politically criticized in *da zi bao*'s posted in public, he is said to be "on the wall."

Overseas Chinese: In 1966, "overseas Chinese" was used to mean ethnic Chinese living in another country, or such Chinese who had returned to China.

Peking Review: Official Chinese political journal published weekly in Peking. The journal is printed in the major languages of all five continents and has a worldwide readership.

PLA: People's Liberation Army. The army led by the Communist Party that liberated the country in 1949 and has enjoyed great prestige among the people.

PRC: People's Republic of China.

Putong Hua: Means common speech; it is the standard national language based on the dialect of Peking.

Ration Tickets: Coupons that entitle the holder to purchase a determined amount of such essentials as: rice, flour, sugar, meat, oil, coal, cotton cloth. Issued by the government to individuals.

Revisionist: Broadly speaking a non-Marxist.

Seal: A stamp carved with the Chinese characters of the owner's name used by virtually all adults for official and financial transactions, taking the place of a signature.

Self-criticism: A kind of self-psychoanalysis from a political point of view which was carried on in all political studies by the masses as well as by Party cadres. It has always been a basic element in Chinese Communist Party discipline.

"**Serve the People**": Universally quoted slogan, the title of one of the three most famous essays by Chairman Mao.

Shanghai Communiqué: Document establishing the basis for Sino-American relations following the Nixon visit to the PRC in 1972.

Speciality: Specialty.

Student Stipends: Very nearly all students in universities before and during the Cultural Revolution received government financial aid—primarily for food and some pocket money. There was no charge for tuition and rent.

Yuan: Basic monetary unit of China. One U.S. dollar equaled about one and a half yuan in the mid-sixties.

OUR PURPOSE IN writing this account of a family's experience in the People's Republic of China during the Cultural Revolution is to share with American friends, as far as possible, something of the quality of life at that time in that place. This life experience inevitably influences many of America's Chinese friends. To understand it, even a little, may help in cementing the alliance of two peoples with many common goals and values—and many bewildering differences.

This book has not been written primarily for Chinese readers. In deference to the convenience of any Chinese friends who may see it, however, let me explain one or two points. The incidents recounted are essentially factual, but the words spoken ten or twelve years ago must be reconstructed from memory, and the speakers, I hope, will tolerate it if their recollection of some detail varies from my own. Sometimes I have used fictitious names to avoid embarrassment to living persons.

It would be impossible to recount, and boring to read, all the events of such an eventful decade as that of 1966–77, and I have had to select those incidents that seem most illuminating to American readers. In this selection process I have been assisted both by my partner, Katharine Kinderman, who made tape recordings of many hours of reminiscence, and by many friends of China who have listened to my lectures in the course of this past year. I am aware that Chinese readers will not find much to interest them in descriptions of daily life in China, but I assure them that to many Americans such concrete information can be enlightening.

Finally, as to spelling: we have retained a few traditional spellings of place names, such as Canton and Peking, but for the most part have used the new official *pinyin* system.